# Marketing to Boomers and Beyond

## Strategies for Reaching America's Wealthiest Market

### David B. Wolfe

D0067827

McGraw-Hill, Inc.

New York  St. Louis  San Francisco  Auckland  Bogotá
Caracas  Lisbon  London  Madrid  Mexico  Milan
Montreal  New Delhi  Paris  San Juan  São Paulo
Singapore  Sydney  Tokyo  Toronto

Library of Congress Cataloging-in-Publication Data

Wolfe, David B.
    Marketing to boomers and beyond  :  strategies for reaching
    America's wealthiest market  /  David B. Wolfe.
        p.      cm.
    Includes bibliographical references and index.
    ISBN 0-07-071431-2
        1. Marketing—United States—Management. 2. Aged as consumers—
    United States. 3. Consumer behavior—United States. I. Title.
HF5415.13.W648   1993
658.8'348—dc20                                                    92–28252
                                                                        CIP

1 2 3 4 5 6 7 8 9 0   DOC/DOC   9 8 7 6 5 4 3 2

ISBN   0-07-071431-2

*The sponsoring editor for this book was Karen Hansen, the editing supervisor
was Kimberly A. Goff, and the production supervisor was Pamela A. Pelton.
This book was set in Baskerville by McGraw-Hill's Professional Book Group
composition unit.*

*Printed and bound by R. R. Donnelley & Sons Company.*

*Previously printed as a hardcover under* Serving the Ageless Market:
Strategies for Selling to the Fifty-plus Market.

This book is printed on recycled, acid-free paper containing a minimum of 50% recycled de-
inked fiber.

*With love and my fervent wishes for their deeply fulfilling later years to my beautiful children, Sabrina, Laura, Karen, Brian, Michelle, and Stephanie; they have been, are, and will continue to be my ultimate inspiration in life.*

# About the Author

David B. Wolfe is president of Wolfe Resources Group, a resource network serving producers of products and services for mature markets. He is the founder and past president of the National Association for Senior Living Industries (NASLI), based in Annapolis, Maryland.

Mr. Wolfe publishes the newsletter *D. B. Wolfe's Maturity Market Perspectives: The Marketer's Guide to understanding Older Consumers*. His numerous articles on marketing to seniors have appeared in *American Demographics, Marketing Communication, Journal of Healthcare Marketing, Provider,* and *Marketing Insights.*

Mr. Wolfe's consumer-sensitive, business-practical approaches to serving mature markets have earned him an international reputation that has carried him to Europe, Asia, and Africa to lecture and consult. He is widely regarded today as one of the foremost experts on mature markets.

# Contents

# Part 3. Perceptions

# Part 4. Implentation

# Foreword

Winston Churchill, describing the Soviet Union, said, "It is a riddle wrapped in a mystery inside an enigma."[1] Such a description might well describe most attempts to understand senior citizens and, more specifically, their economic and social behavior.

Both ends of the age spectrum have historically been misinterpreted and misunderstood. Children until quite recently were considered to be merely smaller and simpler versions of their adult relatives. They were dressed as miniature adults and were expected to understand and comply with adult logic and behavior. Researchers such as Piaget confirmed that the child's brain is truly immature and underdeveloped in many areas. Until age 12, children have problems with abstraction and difficulties in comprehending size and volume. (For example, many children believe it is impossible for a short fat goblet to hold as much liquid as a tall thin one even when it is demonstrated before their very eyes.)

With our dismal history in trying to understand children (Why is it that we get good at parenting when we have finished raising our own children?), it is not surprising that we have so much difficulty in understanding our parents and their peers. Too many students of geriatrics have tried to assess the needs and wants of "seniors" by extrapolating from the concerns of those in their young and middle years (people like the researchers themselves), only to find their conclusions unworkable and unresponsive to the population they seek to serve.

Projective analyses for "seniors," like retrograde analyses for children,

---

[1]Sir Winston Spencer Churchill, in "The First Month of War," radio broadcast, Oct. 1, 1939.

will always fail The reason for these failures is both disturbing and simple: *Seniors do not think the way the rest of us do.* Mature thinking is the result not merely of chronological age but of the healthy development of capacities that exist in all people throughout life.

Abraham Maslow, Ph.D., although he did not realize it, understood the mature thinking of "seniors" better than anyone else ever has. Maslow studied the successful and self-actualized people of our society in order to gain clues about "what makes healthy people healthy." In his quest Maslow studied many mature adults. Initially he was baffled by the idiosyncratic nature of their thinking and behavior. Eventually he came to recognize that individuals who fully develop their capacities as human beings (self-actualizers) use a qualitatively different cognitive pattern (Being-Cognitive) than that used by most adults under 50. Such cognitive patterns are generated in response to a focus on growth and maturity, and are contrasted to the patterns displayed in Deficiency-Cognition, which arises from the need to fill deficits or make up for losses. B-Cognizers use intuition, perceive reality in a holistic manner, and are more capable of spontaneity and openness of mind than D-Cognizers, whose thinking is "in pieces," is firmly grounded in logic, and tends to be more conservative.

Healthy people, as seen and studied by Maslow, have an ability to focus intently on issues at hand without being distracted by time concerns, egocentric positions, the need to acquire material possessions, or the need to control others. They have reprioritized their values, emphasizing such attributes as increased acceptance of self, greater demand for autonomy, and expanded identification with the human species.

Self-actualizers also exhibit superior perception of reality and greater richness of emotional reaction (see Chapter 6 for details). These attributes of self-actualizers are important to understand because they describe many characteristics of great numbers of older people. While most "seniors" would not entirely fit Maslow's definition of self-actualization, as a group they reflect many of the values, exhibit the thought patterns, and are motivated by the principles he described as operative in the behavior of self-actualizing adults. Therefore, Maslow's studies of self-actualization And B-Cognition offer insights to the behavior of a population which has previously resisted description, at least in terms of consumer behavior.

Marketing researchers have failed to understand the "senior" market in part because they have not recognized that many "seniors" think in the special way that Maslow described. Their failure manifests itself in a most obvious fashion: Seniors frequently have not bought what marketers have tried to sell them even when it appeared obvious that the goods or services were vital for the seniors' benefit and welfare.

David Wolfe has now provided marketers with the tools to speak to seniors in their own language with an understanding of what is important to them. To relate effectively to seniors we must first accept their reality, and then try to understand the differences in values and behavior that a more mature thought process produces. For a society with a rapidly maturing population, this book makes relevant and comprehensible the concepts of unique thought and motivation that characterize seniors and mature thinkers.

To understand these concepts one must understand Maslow: to understand Maslow is to understand the *ageless market* and its members.

*Louis E. Kopolow, M.D.*[2]

---

[2]Dr. Kopolow is a practising psychiatrist who studied under Maslow in the late sixties at Brandeis University prior to earning his medical degree. Dr. Kopolow served as adviser to the author of *Marketing to Boomers and Beyond* in the interpretation of Maslovian theory in its application to marketing to older consumers.

# Introduction to the
# Third Printing

Though it has been just under three years since I completed the manuscript for the original printing of this book, originally entitled, *Serving the Ageless Market*, a number of events have tested some of its key propositions. For example, Chapter 1 carried predictions that a sustained period of economic difficulty lay ahead, led by what was referred to as the Great Real Estate Depression. Those predictions have begun materializing. In most regions of the country, real estate values have fallen (in real dollars) by 6 to 12 percent and in some areas by as much as 20 percent. In 1991, new home starts fell to their lowest levels since the end of World War II, putting further downward pressures on residential real estate values.

Serious troubles were also predicted for the commercial real estate industry. Many suburban malls are now in trouble, activity in the commercial real estate sector has been at record lows and the world's largest real estate investor/developer—Canada's Olympia and York—has filed for bankruptcy.

I take no satisfaction that those and other predictions made in Chapter 1 are already being fulfilled. I would sooner have seen a strong response to the proposition that "creative action taken today in penetrating older markets will allow a smoother transition" to a slow-growth economy. But to date, few if any economists, and certainly few business planners and marketers have moved significantly in that direction. The paucity of press coverage on the effects of the unprecedented rise in the median age of consumers indicates a dearth of awareness of just how serious the great demographic shifts taking place are.

In Chapter 10, I predicted troubles ahead for the number one retailer in America, Sears, Roebuck and Company. As of this date, Sears has fallen to number three ranking. Again, there is no satisfaction in having foreseen coming troubles for so large an organization because when such venerable organizations experience difficulty they add to the unsettled economy which affects us all.

Also in Chapter 10, difficulties were projected for the senior housing industry unless it members made major changes in product design, marketing, and community operations. Little change has taken place and, in general, the industry is a deeply troubled one. In 1992, the U.S. Department of Housing and Urban Development terminated its so-called "retirement housing" programs after experiencing financial difficulties in more than 50 percent of its projects. The senior housing industry has yet to define itself or to widely reflect a deep understanding of older consumers, their most compelling needs and desires and how their minds work in the marketplace.

On a more positive note, new research is validating some of the more significant propositions made in *Serving the Ageless Market* regarding older consumers and their behavior. The proposition that the cognitive operations of older people undergo significant shifts in later life has received strong support in the work of Cynthia Adams of the University of Oregon and other researchers.[1]

New knowledge of the workings of the brain has buttressed the hypothesis made in Chapter 6 that there is a shifting of some degree of cognitive operations from the left to the right hemisphere of the brain which results in marked changes in how older people perceive the world. This includes how older people perceive marketing communications. With a better understanding of the brain, we are learning that older people's general dispositions toward advertising and other forms of marketing communications are shaped by more than just experience.

I also proposed that certain kinds of memory loss experienced by older people may be the sign of a more efficient method of processing information. There is new evidence that this may very well be the case. This being so, a corollary proposition that conventional research techniques and methodologies used in studying older consumers may be inadequate seems even more likely.

One study testing for differences in cognitive abilities of male executives of varying ages found "The older executives'...performance

---

[1]Cynthia Adams, "Qualitative Age Differences in Memory for Text: A Life-Span Developmental Perspective," *Psychology and Aging*, The American Psychological Association, Arlington, VA, Sept. 1991

level...was close to that of brain-damaged patients." However, they were observed as functioning "very adequately in high managerial positions," strongly suggesting that the means used for testing mental acuities of younger people are inappropriate for measuring the mental acuities of older people.[2] There is no evidence, however, that market researchers have begun changing their research techniques and methodologies to deal with the much changed mind of the older consumer.

It is becoming increasingly clear that the past is not prologue and that we are at a place no one has ever been before: a developed society dominated by people who think, function, and behave differently than the youth and young adults who have numerically dominated our society since the founding of the nation. In 1989, for the first time in U.S. history, the majority of adults were over the age of 40. By around the year 2002, the majority of adults will be over the age of 50.

We do not understand much about older consumers because their smaller numbers and lower levels of affluence in previous decades made knowledge about them relatively unimportant. Now, understanding the unique behavior characteristics of older people is a matter of survival for many American businesses. Simply stated, businesses must change because the behavior of the demographic core of consumers in the marketplace has changed.

Businesses that are able to change in step with the changes driven by the Great Demographic Shift of the 1990s will be those most likely to survive into the next century. Thus far however, the forces of status quo seem to be more compelling than the forces of change throughout much of American business. As a result, corporate bankruptcies are at the highest levels since the Great Depression.

Many companies yet to fail are expecting the economy to return to full vigor during the 1990s. But the decline of more than 8 million consumers in the 18 to 34-year-old age group is working against that. Growth for companies who continue to rely heavily on youth and young adult markets can only come from stealing market share from competitors during the 1990s. Nearly two decades of negative growth birth rates are finally adversely bearing down on the consumer economy in full force. The prospects for growth are not good for industries catering primarily to the under-50 population even beyond this decade. Between 1990 and the year 2020, the under-50-population is projected to grow by only one percent. But the 50-plus population is projected to grow by 74 percent!

Also working against a return to a fully vigorous economy is the al-

[2]Timothy A. Salthouse, "Cognitive Competence and Experience in Aging," *Handbook of the Psychology of Aging*, edited by James E. Birren and K. Warner Schaie, Academic Press, Inc., San Diego, 1990, page 311.

tered behavior of older consumers. In a society that is not noted for deep study of issues on a long-term basis and that is obsessively oriented to quick results, few have devoted serious attention to learning about the altered behavior patterns of older consumers.

I should reiterate a point made in *Serving the Ageless Market* that the altered behavior of consumers is not something that takes place in *much* later life, but something that begins around the onset of middle-age. The retitling of this book was inspired by the recognition that when one speaks of "older consumers" most people infer that the discussion involves people over 60 or so. The title was changed to make it clearer that "older consumers" refers to people middle-age and older. The point of the original title is still valid: As people move into middleage and beyond, age per se, becomes decreasingly significant in defining their values, lifestyles, and motivations.

During this decade, middle-aged populations are the only ones with any significant growth other than the 85-plus population, which outside of health care, is not a statistically important economic group. The fastest growing five-year segment of the economically active consumer population is the 50 to 54-year-old age group, followed by the 45 to 59 and the 55 to 59-year-old age groups. All told, the 1990s will see more than an 18 million increase in the 40-plus population as compared with the 8 million loss in population in the young adult group.

The famous Swiss psychologist Carl Jung was the first to propose that significant changes take place in the psyche around the onset of middle-age. He said that forces build within the individual that begin to shift the individual away from materialistic values. One might quickly thrust forth with the rejoinder, "But middle-age is when people spend the most money." That is true. Those 45 to 54 do have the highest *per household* expenditures and those 55 to 64 do have the highest *per capita* expenditures. However, they spend without the impetuousness and passion of younger adults, and they are much more discretionary in their product and service choices.

Marketers need to better understand the behavior of the less passionate consumer. Different cues are required to stimulate their interest in a product or service and they have different ways of appraising a product's or service's value. Moreover, they tend to perceive fewer differences between competing products, but greater differences between competing companies. They are quicker to register initial emotional responses that lead to a go-no-go decision to further consider a purchase, yet commonly take longer to get to the final purchase decision. And unlike younger consumers who often buy a product to reflect membership in a peer group, older consumers often buy a product that shows they are not a member of a particular peer group.

There is another change, a change which is strongly related to the decline of materialistic influences beginning in middle-age: people begin to become more *subjective* in their world views. They begin to take fewer cues from the external world and more from inside their own psyches. It is common in early middle-age for people to become more introspective and begin asking themselves questions about their purpose, the meaning of life, and wonder, "Is this all there is?" This shift to a more subjective mode of thinking has enormous implications for market research, product design, market strategies and techniques, and in the servicing of consumers.

The rise in age of the "average" adult consumer is subjecting marketing professionals to marketplace behaviors they have never before experienced. As a result of their unfamiliarity with changes in how the mind works in later life, marketing professionals are having increasing difficulty in predicting consumer behavior. This has led marketers to see consumers as increasingly patternless in their buying behavior. Many explain this behavior by saying, "Consumers have so many options today, they don't lock into one style or category of product." But that fails to adequately explain the behavior of middle-aged and older consumers, for they are not whimsical consumers. Rather they tend to be highly thoughtful and deliberate consumers.

Declining brand loyalty, which has increasingly concerned marketers as the median age has risen, is also related to mid-life changes in mental processing. Marketing professionals claim that consumers are increasingly independent and more given to "I can take it or leave it" attitudes. But anyone who closely studies Abraham Maslow's ideas should not be surprised at these and other consumer behavior changes in today's marketplace.

Specifically, if one studies the contents of Chapter 20, "Further Notes on Cognition," in Maslow's *The Farther Reaches of Human Nature*, clarifying insights into the perplexing behaviors that are showing up in today's marketplace begin to emerge. Chapter 6 in this book is entirely devoted to Maslow's thinking on the behavior and motivations of older people.

All marketers are of course aware that there are unconscious influences on consumer behavior. But it is much more difficult to discover and identify those influences in older consumers than in younger consumers. Among younger adults, identifying unconscious influences on their consumer behavior is not very difficult. Their motivations are relatively transparent because they are objective in their perceptions. They take a substantial portion of their behavior cues from the outside world. They are heavily peer group influenced, a commanding fact that has long guided market research and marketing strategies and techniques.

Signs of young adult consumers' motivations appear in easy-to-recognize symbols: Styles of cars, clothes, magazines read, food, restaurants, etc. tell a lot about younger consumers' inner psyche workings. This is because younger people spend a good deal of energy and thought on "fitting in." They draw on easily observable visual and audible cues to indicate that they belong to this group or that group or relate to this set or that set of values.

Older consumers are considerably more difficult to fathom because of their more subjective natures. They tend to spend more energy and thought on gaining comfort with themselves than on gaining comfort with others, thus peer group influences decline. Their motivations are not so readily seen in the metaphorical social status meanings of the products they buy and services they use. They take their cues from values residing in their inner selves more than from values set by society and represented in visual or audible symbols.

Because the motivations of older consumers are more invisible and more subjective, marketers cannot depend as much on what older consumers say in surveys because they must use the language of an objective world in order to describe a subjective world. That results in imprecise characterizations of what is being described when an older person attempts to say how he or she feels about something in answering a researcher's question.

Many a consumer survey or round of focus groups involving older consumers has sent marketers off in directions that have proven disastrous because objective-minded researchers were unable to read between the lines of subjective-minded respondents. Ultimately, says Cynthia Adams, one cannot understand older people of a given age until one has become that age. My own research and experience support Adams' opinion. Still, companies continue to give young researchers a larger role in determining research results than is generally appropriate because younger researchers command smaller salaries.

One key finding of Adams makes the point. She has found that the younger a person is the more he or she is likely to perceive the world in black and white. They interpret communications in a much more literal way than older people. On the other hand, older people interpret communications by integrating deeper psychological and metaphorical meanings. They are more inclined than younger consumers to see multiple aspects in a matter, thus they tend to construct perceptions in shades of grays.

The net effect of these differences is that literal-minded interpretations of what older consumers purport to be their views and feelings are likely to miss important aspects of their values, motivations, and behavior. Ultimately, subjective minds can produce only approximations of what they really believe and feel because the subjective side of the brain—the right side—does not have the facility of language. It deals in the subjectiveness of feelings while the left side deals in objectiveness of language. The challenge facing marketers in dealing with minds that move progressively deeper into subjective perceptions of the world should not be underestimated.

Only by learning more about how subjective thinking works can marketers gain a better understanding of how the older psyche works in the marketplace. This book, now in its third printing, is intended to offer marketers important insights into the psyche of middle-aged and older consumers. Other writings by me and others will continue to explore the relatively uncharted pathways of older consumers' decision-making processes. In the meantime, this book hopefully serves as a solid foundation for the beginnings of an ever-expanding storehouse of knowledge for those who are willing to take the time to learn about the consumer behavior of older consumers.

*David B. Wolfe*

# PART 1
# Challenges

# 1
# Statistics Don't Buy

## A Bounty of Confusion

The Seniors are coming! The Seniors are coming! The hottest demographic topic of the times is the "graying of America." Articles appear regularly in newspapers, news magazines, and business and professional journals about the vast economic power of America's senior population. The number of titles in bookstores on topics related to aging is on the rise, giving added testimony to the new economic regard for older people. All across the country, seminars are being conducted that purport to teach anyone in almost any field how to understand, market to, and service the rapidly expanding older population.

All over, business is saying, in effect, "We're just wild about seniors," as the perennial love affair between business and youth markets begins to lose some of its glitter. If a week goes by when I don't receive at least one promotional brochure for a senior markets seminar, I think I'm not getting all of my mail.

Countless organizations and institutions are attempting to improve bottom lines and otherwise meet organizational objectives by promoting special products and services to seniors or by providing products and services to others who deal directly with the senior population. Reflecting the changing agendas of every sector of our society, these organizations include business firms, universities, government agencies, and trade and professional organizations.

The shrinkage of youth markets, which began with the advent of the "birth dearth" in 1964 when the birthrate plummeted from "baby boom" highs, has contributed much to this feverish interest in older markets.[1] Were the ratio of youth to older people the same as it was 10 years ago, we probably would not be seeing this phenomenon—even if the senior population were twice as large as current figures indicate.

### Older Adults: More and Wealthier; Young Adults: Fewer and Poorer

By 1995, there will be 20 percent fewer 18- to 24-year-olds—nearly 5 million fewer consumers—than there were in 1988. At the same time, the 65-plus population will be increasing at the rate of 1.7 percent *per year*.[2] Should current trends continue, the 1.8 fertility rate (births per 1000 women between the ages of 18 and 44) would be less than the 2.1 required just to maintain a zero population growth. Thus we should recognize that this sudden interest in older people is largely born of self-interest, even though, on the positive side, it is beginning to result in a more respectful, accurate view of older people than traditionally has been the case.

There are other compelling reasons, besides the shrinkage of numbers in younger markets, for business to devote more attention to older markets. Older people in general are faring better in terms of income improvement than young people. Until recently, earnings in real dollars of the 35-and-under group had been on a decline since 1970, while social security income for the 65-plus group increased about 40 percent in real dollars. In 1988, the staff of the House Civil Service Committee issued a report claiming that the value of federal retirement benefits has increased nearly 10 percent above inflation since 1969, while federal pay has decreased nearly 18 percent during the same period.[3]

The hope is that growth in senior markets, often described as the "$800 billion market," will compensate for lost business in youth markets. For the first time in history, seniors are being looked to for their contributions to a society's economic picture. Business isn't alone in seeing the possibilities in a burgeoning affluent senior population. Colleges are targeting retirees to boost enrollments. Public human services budgets reflect the growth in senior populations. And significant reductions in those budgets are unlikely, for citizens 65 and older vote at higher

[1]Throughout this book *older markets* and *older people*, unless the context indicates otherwise, refer to the 50-plus population. Similarly, the term *maturity markets* generally refers to the same age group. However, as discussed in Chapter 2, not all older people are members of the maturity markets because not all older people are fully matured personalities, a condition that is highly significant in sizing and targeting older markets.

[2]B. Townsend, "What's at Stake?" *American Demographics*, August 1988, p. 10.

[3]J. Havemann, "Uncle Sam's Dual Standards," *Washington Post*, Jan. 23, 1988, p. A-1.

rates than young adults, a fact that does not go unnoticed by politicians—as evidenced by Congress's embarrassed reversal of the 1988 catastrophic insurance program in 1989 when hundreds of thousands of older people said, in effect, "We don't like the 1988 bill!"

## Distorted Views of Older People Are Pervasive

Under the excited conditions that currently surround the subject of older consumers, the self-oriented perspectives of business and public policymakers and administrators have led to a plethora of quasi-facts, quasi-experts, and quasi-good intentions. More cynically stated, there is much ignorance about older people, their situations, conditions, aspirations, and behavior. There are also many business opportunists who, attracted by statistics like mice to a cheese-baited trap, fail to perceive the jeopardy of being mindlessly driven by financial goals without regard for the complexity of older markets.

Much misguided activity is encouraged by marketers' willy-nilly dispensing of statistics that equate economic opportunities with raw demographic data on seniors. A decade ago John Cobbs wrote, "The U.S. obsession with statistics is so deeply rooted that it takes an occasional error to remind users that some figures might as well be pulled out of a hat."[4]

There is a veritable bumper crop of distortions and inaccuracies about the behavior, needs, desires, health, and money of older people. This is not to say that people are widely using "bad statistics," but rather that many statistics *become* "bad" when removed from their natural context, thus leading to faulty conclusions. Statistical products and analyses cannot, of course, be totally disregarded, but one can err on the side of overly regarding them. That, I believe, has been generally true in attempts to understand the aging-of-America phenomenon.

## The $800 Billion Seniors Market Is Misleading

This may come as a surprise to seminar sponsors who tout the $800 billion seniors market ("Come to our seminar and learn how to get your share"), but the oft-referenced $800 billion market (which grew in 1989 into a $900 billion market in some seminar promotional brochures) is *not* an $800 billion market. (Incidentally, the $800 billion figure refers to the 50-plus market, not to the 65-plus market, as widely and incorrectly believed.)

[4]John Cobbs, "A Misplaced Faith in Numbers," *Business Week*, Nov. 19, 1979, p. 17.

Some of the money in that famous $800 billion is paid in taxes, and thus not all is available for marketplace transactions. Most of the rest of it is not available on an open-season basis to anyone who has some kind of product or service to sell to seniors. Older people tend to be good savers; a good amount of their income goes into passive investments, not into the marketplace. Other dollars go for necessities, such as prescribed medicines, health care services, gasoline for automobiles, and utilities, which involve little occasion for discretionary consumer behavior. The advertising firm of Olgilvy and Mather estimates that a "paltry" $150 billion remains after all taxes and necessary bills have been paid.[5]

### Older Consumers Still Represent a Huge Market

Now that we have injected some reality and accuracy into the income picture of the 50-plus population, which leaves "only" about $150 billion for U.S. business to fight over, we can introduce another perspective to rebrighten the picture. Somewhere between the $150 billion in discretionary income and the monies left over after taxes and necessities lie several hundred billion dollars for necessities that can be met through a variety of competing products and services. These range from housing, food, clothing, and transportation to financial services, insurance, sundry household items, and nonprescribed medicines.

While the size of older markets, in dollar terms, has been overinflated, they still are of such a dimension that few consumer product and service businesses can afford to ignore them. Some recent studies have shown that older consumers are much more prone to change brands of products than they were formerly believed to be. This is good news for marketers who want to compensate for dwindling youth markets in meeting business growth goals. It means that if the market for their products is not expanding through population growth, they can improve their market share through advertising and promotional programs aimed at older people who need or want their products.

## The Boom That Won't Be

There is a notion in many quarters that the consumer economy is on the edge of a great boom as a result of the graying of America. That phenom-

---

[5]"Planning for a Retirement Residence," *Washington Post*, Apr. 18, 1989.

enon means just the opposite, however. As the percentage of the older population increases, and especially as young adults decline in absolute numbers, *fewer, not more*, dollars will flow into the consumer economy.

There are several reasons for this. For one thing, older people spend less money on hard goods. Once their families have been raised and their careers have peaked or ended, people buy fewer homes, household furnishings, clothes, and cars. Moreover, while older people generally spend more on services than they did in their younger years, there is no evidence that they spend more in postretirement than they spent when fully involved in their careers, health care services excepted. The evidence, in fact, is to the contrary, as can be seen in Table 1-1.

Those on the cusp of "seniordom" or in the early years of that status are the most affluent and biggest spenders of all groups in Table 1-1. But while the income of the 55-to-64 age group is the second highest, that group's spending per household drops dramatically, followed by a huge drop-off in the 65-plus group. However, note that Table 1-1 is presented in terms of *household income* and expenditures, not *per capita* income and expenditures. Therefore, both income and expenditures on a per capita basis will compare somewhat more favorably with younger households because there are fewer people in older households.

## U.S. Real Estate Headed for Prolonged Major Decline in Values

Another factor which common sense tells me is going to have a dramatic adverse effect on the consumer economy, and in fact on the entire national economy, is that for the first time since the end of World War II, residential real estate will begin to depreciate on a national basis—a phenomenon which might come to be called the *Great Real Estate Recession* of the 1990s. This seems hard to believe: "Real estate has always increased in value over the long haul. Nothing is going to change that." That is what some people have told me, arguing against predictions of a national recession in residential real estate values. But the arithmetic is simple: Fewer young people means fewer new household formations; fewer household formations mean fewer sales and rentals of homes and apartments. Gluts will occur because supply will exceed demand, and existing homeowners will begin selling their homes for less when they need to move. By the way, that prediction should be amended to include *all* real estate, because the commercial economy is ultimately tied to the consumer economy.

A study released in 1989 by the National Bureau of Economic Research supports these predictions. The study projects that over the 18-

**Table 1-1.** 1985 Index of Consumer Spending by Consumer Age

| | Under 25 | 25–34 | 35–44 | 45–54 | 55–64 | 65 and over |
|---|---|---|---|---|---|---|
| Households (in 000s) | 5,438 | 20,014 | 17,481 | 12,628 | 13,073 | 18,155 |
| Average household size | 2.3 | 2.9 | 3.4 | 3.2 | 2.4 | 1.8 |
| Average household income | $16,643 | $26,177 | $33,389 | $36,002 | $30,516 | $18,279 |
| Relative expenditures (average = 100.0) | | | | | | |
| Total expenditures | 63.4 | 102.8 | 126.1 | 130.9 | 99.6 | 61.6 |
| Food | 60.2 | 94.4 | 127.9 | 132.5 | 102.0 | 67.1 |
| Food at home | 56.3 | 91.8 | 129.2 | 131.1 | 102.5 | 70.6 |
| Food away from home | 72.2 | 102.4 | 124.0 | 136.4 | 100.8 | 56.8 |
| Alcoholic beverages | 114.0 | 125.7 | 115.7 | 117.2 | 97.2 | 42.6 |
| Tobacco and smoking supplies | 68.8 | 96.3 | 124.4 | 139.1 | 114.6 | 52.3 |
| Housing | 62.3 | 112.3 | 125.3 | 115.9 | 90.4 | 69.3 |
| Shelter | 69.5 | 122.9 | 127.6 | 111.9 | 82.6 | 61.6 |
| Utilities, fuels, public services | 46.8 | 87.7 | 119.4 | 130.6 | 108.9 | 83.2 |
| Telephone | 75.0 | 103.6 | 120.1 | 125.7 | 98.2 | 67.6 |
| Fuel oil | 18.2 | 53.7 | 91.8 | 129.1 | 128.1 | 142.6 |
| House furnishings and equipment | 70.1 | 115.8 | 130.2 | 119.7 | 96.4 | 51.5 |
| Furniture | 87.6 | 133.4 | 139.7 | 100.1 | 83.2 | 40.8 |
| Major appliances | 63.7 | 113.8 | 115.0 | 133.6 | 89.2 | 65.7 |
| Apparel | 71.1 | 104.0 | 143.1 | 133.8 | 93.2 | 44.2 |
| Men's and boys' | 65.0 | 106.4 | 152.1 | 140.4 | 86.0 | 35.4 |
| Women's and girls' | 64.4 | 87.6 | 145.8 | 140.9 | 100.1 | 51.8 |
| Footwear | 69.1 | 103.8 | 152.3 | 125.8 | 89.8 | 44.2 |

| | | | | | | |
|---|---|---|---|---|---|---|
| Transportation | 74.0 | 105.4 | 124.1 | 141.2 | 102.2 | 48.6 |
| Vehicles | 83.2 | 112.6 | 127.4 | 146.6 | 94.4 | 36.6 |
| New cars | 60.0 | 103.0 | 119.6 | 149.9 | 109.8 | 48.1 |
| Gasoline | 70.5 | 104.6 | 124.8 | 137.4 | 103.2 | 51.6 |
| Vehicle insurance | 61.1 | 96.2 | 112.1 | 152.5 | 109.5 | 60.8 |
| Airline fares | 49.2 | 82.6 | 115.4 | 131.5 | 133.9 | 73.1 |
| Health care | 33.8 | 67.9 | 99.2 | 116.4 | 112.6 | 135.3 |
| Health insurance | 32.4 | 65.5 | 83.8 | 106.8 | 124.4 | 151.4 |
| Prescription drugs | 26.5 | 48.1 | 78.5 | 112.2 | 130.4 | 169.1 |
| Personal care | 48.0 | 73.9 | 114.8 | 135.3 | 123.1 | 88.8 |
| Recreation | 75.2 | 115.8 | 143.4 | 118.8 | 93.4 | 40.0 |
| Fees and admissions | 72.8 | 95.1 | 148.3 | 133.8 | 98.8 | 44.5 |
| TVs, radios, sound equipment | 95.8 | 117.8 | 125.2 | 123.3 | 91.2 | 47.6 |
| Life and personal insurance | 26.7 | 87.6 | 129.9 | 151.1 | 127.5 | 51.4 |

SOURCE: Fabian Linden, Consumer Research Center, The Conference Board; reported in *American Demographics*, Oct. 1986.

year period from 1989 to 2007, there will be an average annual depreciation in residential real estate of 3 percent, cumulatively totaling an astounding 47 percent in *real dollars.*[6]

The study, conducted by Harvard economics professor N. Gregory Manikiw and Harvard graduate student David N. Weil, has been said to oversimplify the effects of certain key demographic statistics. Some critics, for example, have called attention to the prediction that the total population will steadily increase over the 18-year period. However, those critics have failed to note that the number of new household formations will decrease during that same period, due to the effects of the birth dearth that followed the baby boom. New household formations serve as the basic foundation of the housing industry; they create new need for housing. They also serve as a major source of buyers for people moving up to larger homes.

This country has never had a *prolonged period* in its history when it did not experience significant population growth through its birthrate. The post-World War II economic boom, which has existed for more than 40 years, was fired and sustained by the baby boom. That boom is now coming to an end because boomers are approaching the lower consumer-activity years of later life and because they have had far fewer babies than their parents.

### The Post-World War II Boom Days Are Over

The prudent will relinquish the idea that economic growth is inevitable. The idea of perennial and unabated growth so permeates our collective national psyche that we cannot easily deal with contrary ideas. But the demographic statistics of today predict a different picture. So little has been written on this subject that there seems little readiness for what must inevitably come to pass. Even the spending patterns of today's older population, through perhaps the next decade, will not be a reliable indicator of their spending patterns two decades from now, when their numbers will be even greater. For example, if the projected great recession in real estate values comes upon us in full force, clearly older people will spend less, regardless of their individual levels of affluence. Because they will have less equity in their homes as a result of the Great Real Estate Recession, and because of deep concern over their future economic well-being in an unsettled and weakening economy, older

[6]K. Downey, "Home Prices to Fall, Study Says," *Washington Post*, July 29, 1989, p. E.1.

consumers will spend less than if the economy of the future were more like the economy of today.

## Housing Value Decline Poses Big Risks for Financial Institutions

Mortgage finance institutions should be particularly concerned about the projected Great Real Estate Recession. If real estate values do begin to fall on a fairly consistent annual basis, loan-to-value ratios will obviously fall, weakening the entire mortgage finance industry as loan defaults inevitably increase.

The trend during the 1970s and 1980s was to liberalize borrower qualifications. In my opinion, unless those patterns are reversed now, the housing finance industry, already beset by the savings and loan scandals of recent years, will become even more troubled and could plunge the entire U.S. economy into a massive, lengthy financial crisis. Many people in the housing industry may not like hearing such predictions. Nevertheless, it seems wiser to maintain a smaller but healthier home finance industry through tighter buyer qualifications than to experience a massive housing-induced national recession that could last for years.

Builders of communities for seniors have a great deal at stake in the outcome of these predictions. Today's seniors are generally home-equity-rich, with better than 80 percent of homeowners aged 65 and older owning their homes debt-free. For the majority of older people, financial planning and big consumer decisions ultimately center on their home equity. Most people who move into a seniors community depend on the equity in their homes to make such a move possible. If they perceive that declining real estate values will reduce their equity, many will become reluctant to move into new shelter arrangements which offer no guaranteed limits to annual cost increases. Shelter costs cannot be any better fixed than when the shelter is owned debt-free.

## Older Markets Are Not Big Enough to Replace Declines in Youth Markets

Older markets are not so much *additional markets* in the total scheme of things as they are *replacement markets*. The value of older markets to business lies in their serving as alternative markets to the traditional youth and family markets as those latter two markets decline in numbers and total buying power. If U.S. businesspeople realize this and take creative action to make up for revenues lost in younger markets by capturing older markets, then the economy will ease more slowly into its new, lower consumer-spending configuration.

It is important to take into account that wider areas than the U.S. economy are involved. Today's world is truly an international economy; what happens in this country affects what happens in other nations to a degree never before true. Also the great demographic shifts in this country mirror similar demographic shifts in every developed nation of the world. Therefore, these predictions about the future of the U.S. economy apply to the economies of all developed nations.

Creative action taken today in penetrating older markets will allow for a smoother transition after the heady growth we have enjoyed for nearly a half-century. I firmly believe that older people, within the limits of financial prudence dictated by their individual circumstances, can generally be induced to spend more than past history indicates. To the degree that increased spending occurs, however, it will be brought about by a much better understanding of the psyches of older consumers than currently exists. It is their behavior patterns, not their number or their affluence, that will influence their future contributions to the consumer economy.

## Geriatric or Lifestyle Market?

Consciousness raising about our aging society began in the early 1980s when the first reports of the 1980 census began surfacing in the media. At first, the focus was on the 65-and-older population. Now, however, statistics used in defining and quantifying "mature" consumers are for age bases starting as low as 40. This creates considerable confusion, for we no longer know what such terms as *senior, retiree, maturity market*, and *elderly* mean in qualitative or quantitative terms. We are attempting to find our directions in older markets amid statistical and semantic babble that is largely centered on age as the main determinant in market research, planning, and program execution.

As the reader will soon discover, this book is not about a specific age group as much as it is about people with certain personality traits who generally happen to be older. To a large extent, these are consumers whose lifestyles and consumer behavior are less influenced by age than was true earlier in their lives. For all practical purposes, age does not exist as a significant reality in the lives of many older people. Those for whom this is generally true constitute the *ageless market*.

The preceding paragraph deserves a special focus in the reader's mind, for the thoughts expressed in it represent the core of the critically important distinctions between this book and other books and countless articles regularly appearing about seniors. Age per se has little meaning in this book, just as it has little meaning to many of those in older markets.

If the reader substantially concurs with the general approach and the central themes of this book, it should become apparent that a significant portion of age-related statistics have highly limited value, especially in terms of market research, market planning, and market strategies and execution. In brief, too much emphasis has been put on demographic analysis of older consumers in defining market potential and in planning and executing marketing programs.

## *Lifestyle Markets* Is a More Accurate Term Than *Senior Markets*

What people refer to as senior markets might be better called *lifestyle markets*. Some people have said as much, but there is little literature that describes the *deeper essence* of these lifestyle markets in terms that offer practical guidance in understanding older people's consumer behavior. What is needed, more specifically, is identification of key behavioral motivators behind the lifestyles and attitudes of older people *in general*—not behind the individual older person. Ultimately, adult consumer behavior is more accurately defined within categories of behavior than within categories of age.

Not all older people, regardless of their wealth, are significant factors in the general marketplace, even though they show up in statistical representations of senior markets. A consumer *of any age* is significant, in marketplace terms, only if she or he has both money to spend and the inclination to spend it. Older people, therefore, are significant to marketers of specific products and services only if they are potentially or currently interested in those specific products and services and have the capability of buying and using them.

As with all adult consumers *lifestyles* and *attitudes*, not age, drive older consumer behavior. What changes with time and maturity is the way in which lifestyles and attitudes influence consumer behavior. For example, a number of people have unthinkingly predicted that baby boomers will carry into the ranks of the senior population the heavily self-oriented lifestyles and values often attributed to them. Since the oldest of the boomers are fast approaching their half-century birthdays, anyone interested in older markets would be well advised to pay attention to this unique generation—*now*!

## Predictions about Boomers Being
## Aging Children Deny the Facts

It is often predicted that boomers will fight aging "tooth and nail," because of their supposedly narcissistic, self-oriented natures, and that, as they enter the ranks of senior citizens, they will be more strongly ego-centered and self-indulgent than today's older population. It is being widely inferred from such predictions that boomers will represent major markets for self-oriented products and services not characteristic of earlier generations of older people. I think such predictions will be proved wrong. There will be those who, like some people in previous generations, remain immature; but others—many others—will psychologically grow well beyond their youthful natures.

Already there are strong signs that many of the oldest boomers may be taking on the psychological characteristics of mature older people, as such characteristics have been identified and defined by adulthood development researchers and scholars. Many boomers may actually be doing this as much as 8 to 10 years earlier than expected. Essentially, in my opinion—the basis for which I will develop more fully later—the boomers will be pretty much the same as today's older people in most significant respects. While their style of expressing themselves in how they live will be unique (as it is with any age cohort), their behavioral motivations are not particularly unique.

Boomers may live a little longer than previous generations, but not much longer, despite widespread predictions that people will soon be regularly passing the century mark. And it is an open question whether, on average, they will be appreciably more affluent than today's older people. Already predictions signal that the younger boomers will not be as financially well off in old age as the older boomers. And I doubt that younger boomers will live significantly longer than older boomers, or even the earlier older generations of this century.

## Fool's Gold in Statistics

Notwithstanding claims to the contrary, medical science has done little to extend human longevity. People today are not living much longer than they did in 1900. Probably no statistical references better reflect the mindless sensationalism with which the supposed facts of an aging population are being presented than those that relate to longevity. Errors in this regard are symbolic of a much wider spectrum of misleading representations, implications, and inferences.

To repeat, adults *are not* living significantly longer today than they did in 1900. An extra month or even a year may be significant to the individual, but from an economic point of view there is little significance to the mere year that has been added to the life of an 85-year-old person between 1900 and now, nearly a century later. Even a 65-year-old person today can expect to live only five years longer than a 65-year-old in the year 1900.[7]

Despite common perceptions to the contrary, modern medical science has not yet extended the traditional human life-span barrier and has only marginally affected the traditional life-expectancy barrier of the ordinary individual. (*Life span* is the capacity for longevity; *life expectancy* is a statistical projection of the average time that people of given demographic characteristics will live.)

So myopically riveted on out-of-context statistics are we, that I find audiences easily bewildered by the subject of current life-expectancy patterns. Some people look at me quizzically when I report that adult life expectancy has not increased very much in a century. They are positive that they have heard all kinds of statistics and representations that people are living longer than ever before, because medical science has achieved major breakthroughs in life span or longevity potential.

### Relatively Little Progress in Adult Longevity in Two Centuries

What people widely fail to realize is that the life-expectancy projections most frequently quoted are tied to the moment of birth. In those terms, there has, indeed, been significant improvement in life expectancy—26 years since 1900. In 1900, only 41 percent of all people born in the United States lived to age 65. Today 79 percent live to be 65 years old. The difference in those percentages is overwhelmingly accounted for by those who now live to celebrate their twenty-first birthdays. What the miracles of modern science have done is to increase dramatically the percentage of people who survive childhood. What they have not done is to contribute very much to taking the average person very far past the biblical "three score years and ten" of the "allotted" *life span* of human beings.

Startling evidence of how little human longevity has increased comes

---

[7]C. Russell, "Editor's Note," *American Demographics*, March 1989, p. 2.

from research into the longevity patterns of people in eighteenth-century Scotland—more than two centuries ago. A study was made of the age at death of people described as having "significant intellectual and creative achievement." The median age of death for such people was 70, with 21 percent living beyond 80 years.[8]

Those figures contrast with the median age at death of 40 (for those who survived the first year of life) for the general population in those times. The figures for significant achievers more than 200 years ago are not dramatically different from the average life expectancy in the United States today for the entire population, a population that enjoys dramatically greater opportunities for "significant intellectual and creative achievement" than the general population in eighteenth-century Scotland. Such a comparison invites intriguing questions regarding the shorter life expectancies, in the United States, of the poor in general and of blacks specifically, whose opportunities for "significant intellectual and creative achievement" have traditionally been thwarted by growth-limiting circumstances, discrimination, and outright prejudice.

### Fool's Gold in the Statistics of Senior Markets

If only out of self-interest, it is time to put some sense into the mad rush for the gold said to lie buried in the "silver markets." Would-be miners of this gold need to learn to distinguish between the fool's gold of statistics and the real gold which is concealed by human behavior that has been glossed over by statistics. Statistics don't buy; people buy.

It is true that 70 percent of the nation's personal wealth is controlled by the 50-plus population with its $7 trillion in assets. It is true that the 10-year cohort with the highest percentage of discretionary income is the 65-to-74 cohort, followed by the 55-to-64 cohort. And it is true that the 65-to-74 cohort has the second highest per capita income of any 10-year cohort; only the 55-to-64 cohort has higher per capita income. (The 45-to-54 cohort has the highest total household income.) But again, having money and having a proclivity to spend it are two different things. And what the money will be spent for is yet another issue.

None of this discussion is intended to dampen anyone's enthusiasm for so-called senior markets. There is, indeed, considerable economic incentive to sharpen one's focus on older people, if only because there are a lot of them already and a lot more to come. While adult life expectancy has not greatly increased in a century, the actual number of

---

[8]Gene D. Cohen, *The Brain in Human Aging*, Springer Publishing Company, New York, 1988, p. 191.

adults who are past the age of 50 has increased enormously. After all, 63 million people alive today have celebrated their fiftieth birthdays— 34 percent of the entire adult population! There are even more than 30 million people who have celebrated their sixty-fifth birthdays—a number greater than the total population of most nations. Even given the need for caution when interpreting statistics concerning the older population, the potential of older markets is not insignificant by any measure. The challenge facing marketers, of course, is to learn how to access these markets more effectively. That means having the right understanding and the right kinds of tools.

## Getting the Right Directions

Most consumers have finite amounts of money to devote to maintaining their lifestyles. How they spend that money is influenced by their most basic needs and desires and by the values that reflect the order of their priorities. Also affecting consumer behavior is the manner in which marketers approach them.

Obviously, marketing approaches can facilitate, condition, or inhibit hoped-for consumer behavior. Countless articles over the last several years have alleged that older consumers present the most difficult and frustrating challenges of any consumer group encountered. Brochures advertising seminars on marketing to seniors presents evidence of this. Seminar marketers have discovered the "hot buttons" of other marketers, but are such seminars equipping the marketers attending these seminars to understand the buying "hot buttons" of older consumers? Are the hopeful marketers attending these seminars receiving the tools they really need for senior markets? I think the answer to both these questions is often no. Equally important, are attendees being given the wrong tools? Unfortunately, the answer to this question may sometimes be yes.

To use an analogy, I would become frustrated if I attempted to play golf with only a driver, instead of choosing the best club for each shot. In other words, I am inviting unnecessary difficulty and frustration if I approach a task with tools unsuited to the challenges involved. The use of the driver in golf involves many of the same principles involved in the use of the other golf clubs; but even though the driver will move the ball forward, there are situations in which it does so with considerably less effectiveness, say, than a nine iron at 50 yards from the hole or a chipper at the edge of the green.

Similarly, some basic principles of marketing are valid in all market segments, while other principles have little value in some markets, and yet still others should be applied in modified fashion, depending on the target market.

## Marketing Principles and Factors for Use in Maturity Markets

Throughout this book I will identify *principles of general marketing, principles for maturity markets*, and *key factors for maturity markets*. I do not propose to rewrite marketing theory by establishing these principles of general marketing. In fact, most of the principles of general marketing in this book have been laid out before by others. My primary reason for enumerating principles and key factors is to serve the purposes of this book. These principles and factors, taken together, are like a golf bag outfitted with a full complement of golf sticks to get you around the golf course as effectively as your knowledge and skills will permit. In marketing, as in golf, there is a main tool to be used most of the time in kicking off a new campaign. In a golf bag, that tool is the driver; in the marketing bag of tools, it might aptly be called the "image driver." The First General Principle of Marketing, or the *Self-Image Principle*, is as follows:

---

**FIRST GENERAL PRINCIPLE OF MARKETING**
The Self-Image Principle

People tend to select products and services that reflect images of what they want to be, rather than what they are or what they do not want to be.

---

This principle applies to all consumers, regardless of age, income, and a host of other factors. In older markets, the critical question that should always be addressed is: In what ways does a particular product or service convey an image consistent with the image desired by targeted consumers? That question, of course, needs to be preceded by answers to an even more basic question: With what images do those in the intended market want to be associated? Equally important is the answer to the question: With what images do those in the intended market *not* want to be associated?

Those three questions are *strategic*. Throughout this book, the principles for general markets and the principles for maturity markets are used to express major strategic considerations. The key factors for maturity markets are concerned with *tactical* considerations. These principles and factors provide general guidelines for carrying out marketing programs directed at older markets. They operate within a quite broad definition of the term *marketing*.

## Marketing Is More Than Promoting and Selling

The American Marketing Association (AMA) labored for a long time several years ago to arrive at a broad, generic definition of marketing. Its efforts yielded the following definition, which was adopted in January 1985:

### AMA Definition of Marketing

"Marketing" is the process of planning and executing the conception, pricing, promotion, and the distribution of ideas, goods, and services to create exchanges that satisfy individual and organizational objectives.

By virtue of that definition, a *marketer* is anyone involved in *any* aspect of planning and executing tasks associated with the transference of a product, service, or idea from a provider to a consumer. Accordingly, throughout this book, the term *marketers* refers to a much broader group of people than those involved in advertising, promotional programs, and sales. In this context the product designer and those involved in postsale servicing of consumers are integral members of the marketing team. Researchers are also considered marketers in this context, since researchers are essential to the planning processes that lead to product design and ultimately to the introduction of a product or service to the marketplace. Research is where all marketing programs begin—or should begin.

## Mine Fields of Research Are Especially Treacherous in Older Markets

Misleading or faulty research products can be to marketing efforts what mine fields are to battle assaults. Scores of "retirement" housing projects are in deep financial trouble in the United States because researchers led clients into mine fields strewn with faulty statistics and misleading conclusions. A January 1988 issue of *Forbes* reported that the number of bond defaults on such projects exceeded $1 billion, making retirement housing the second largest single-industry bond default victim in U.S. financial history. In the spring of 1989, the U.S. Department of Housing and Urban Development (HUD) suspended "bed-and-board" and other senior housing programs being funded under its co-insurance programs, whereby private lenders shared in risks against mortgage defaults. While faulty market research cannot be entirely blamed for the more than $1 billion of coinsured loan defaults, it played a major role in laying the foundations for many marketplace failures.

The most classic research-based mistake in the so-called *retirement community* industry lies in the tendency to size markets by counting the total population aged 65 and older, despite common industry knowledge that the average age nationally for new residents at time of entry is about 78 to 79, and that relatively few people past the age of 84 take up residence in such communities. Research projections that include those between 65 and 74 years of age create an illusion of a market size nearly triple the actual market universe, both because there are many more people in that 10-year cohort and because a significantly higher percentage of that cohort are financially able to move into a market-rate retirement community than those in the older group.

Most market research for senior housing is performed by research firms that have previously specialized in real estate market research. Real estate research is famous for being long on statistics and short on consumer behavior insights. Developers paying for it are known for ignoring market research reports in developing market strategies. This gives rise to the characterization of developers as seat-of-the-pants entrepreneurs: many rely far more on their hunches than on market research.

Developers have had to employ market researchers, even when they felt there was no need to do so, because of the requirements of money lenders. Real estate market feasibility reports are often called lenders' "CYA" reports, meaning that they serve to protect lenders in the event of project failure: "Well, this market report said this project was a good risk!" Not long ago, a real estate lender said to me, "I don't pay much attention to market feasibility reports any more. Every project that fails has a market study behind it that says it will succeed. I have learned that the market plan and marketing team are what spell the difference between success potential and failure potential."

## Limited Value of Ecodemographic Research in Older Markets

The observation that real estate market research has traditionally been much more concerned with demographics and ecodemographics, or general marketplace economics, than with consumer behavior is not made to malign its professionals. Most real estate market research has been more or less correctly positioned in presupposing that markets automatically exist when the population or a subgroup of the population is in a growth mode, in terms of both population and marketplace economics. Generally speaking, this is true—among younger markets. Increase in household formations, growth through immigration, increases in family size through births, and rises in local income and general commercial activity do result in expansion of housing markets. None of these factors affect older markets, except for immigration in retirement meccas. Among older people, new households are not being formed to any significant degree, and income levels frequently decrease upon retirement.

In other product and service lines besides senior housing, economic and demographic research in older markets has been excessively relied on to the exclusion of behavioral research. In the hospital industry, failure to take into account changes in people's health and social habits contributed to an unanticipated excess of beds in recent years. Heart disease has significantly decreased since 1970 as a result of the decrease in smoking, lowered cholesterol intake, and increase in good habits such as regular exercise. Yet hospital business planners have continued to rely primarily on demographic and traditional health needs guidelines, long after thorough consumer behavior research would have indicated a different emerging picture of need for hospital beds.

Another weakness of much of the research on older consumers results from the traditional dependency on age factors in measuring older markets. Younger markets do tend to reflect consumer behavior that correlates strongly with age, which makes it important to know the number of consumers, within the context of age segments, in various occupational income and lifestyle groups. But among older markets that information has limited value without additional in-depth information on general behavioral characteristics—not just on consumer behavior.

## Mature Adults Are Puzzling

Consumer behavior psychologist Ralph L. Day wrote: (italics mine)

> Marketing professionals have learned that the mechanical use of standard demographic variables may result in simplistic and counter-productive segmentation strategies. *As difficult as it is to do, marketers must learn to depend more heavily on the non-observable variables such as attitudes, emotions, and behavioral intentions...marketing professionals should [not] become better technicians, but better social and behavioral scientists.* [9]

[9] Ralph L. Day, "Relationships between Life Satisfaction and Consumer Satisfaction," in *Marketing and the Quality of Life Interface* (A. Coskin Samli, ed.), Quorum Books, New York, 1987, p. 308.

Buying is nothing, if not an act of behavior. While basic need restricts the latitude of behavior (choices) in many product and service lines (e.g., utilities, medical attention), it is human nature to want as much choice (evidence of self-determination and individuality) as possible in purchase activities. The wider the opportunities for choice, the more complex the behavioral factors involved in making choices.

For a variety of reasons, older people, on average, have greater latitude of choice in purchasing activities than younger people. For that reason, behavioral research is more important in older markets than in younger markets. Such concepts as "sense of urgency," "buyer contagion," and "best price" have both less influence and more complex meanings in older markets because of the vigorous operation of choice in their behavior.

### The Puzzling Consumer Behavior of Older Adults

A great deal has been said and written about the puzzling behavior of older consumers, but there has been little in-depth discussion of why the puzzles exist or how to solve them. Such questions are the subject of that form of consumer research generally referred to as *psychographic research*, a type of research that traditionally has focused on correlating consumer behavior with demographic profiles. Psychographic research in older markets still is not well developed and is not adequately drawn upon by marketers. It is easier to replay old ideas and scenarios used in other markets than to seek out and adopt new ways of doing business.

"Some people, new to older markets, assert that they have the answers, when all they have are old methods that have been repackaged with new names," says Hal Norvel, director of travel services for the American Association of Retired Persons (AARP), an organization for people 50 years and older that has more than 31 million members.

In housing, researchers and consultants who have always served developers in younger markets become instant experts in older markets when they get their first consulting contract involving a senior community. They bring with them any number of ideas based on strategies that have worked in younger markets, employing those ideas in older markets without considering their appropriateness. For example, I have seen marketing recommendations, tendered by some "experts," advising developers on ways to instill "a sense of urgency" in prospects. This is a standard tactic in younger markets, but one that is of highly limited value in markets whose consumers operate on the basis that time is *not* of the essence. In Chapter 8, you will read how mature adults literally operate cognitively with a dramatically different sense of time than young adults do—a sense of time that contradicts conventional rational concepts of time.

## Older Consumers Often Seem Contradictory

One of the greatest challenges in dealing with older people lies in dealing with their apparent contradictions. We are advised, on the one hand, not to use age-based marketing strategies and to treat seniors the same as young consumers. Then we are told that older people don't want to be treated in a context that is at odds with their stage of life. "Treat them the same as others as long as you recognize and acknowledge their differences," say better-informed experts. That sounds like a paradox. But it reflects a significant characteristic of the attitudes and behavior of many older people; they seem at once simple but complex, easy-going but demanding, selfish but selfless, cautious but given to spontaneous action, and penurious but often spending quite freely.

These contradictions are widely observed among older consumers, but are not born of the insecurity and ambivalence as found among adolescents, whose contradictory behaviors stem from uncertainty about their identities. Older people generally know who they are and are comfortable with that. However, those contradictions and many others can work against a marketer's success unless he or she develops a behavioral understanding of older people and why they operate as they do.

## Limits of Traditional Psychographic Research

One of the most common techniques of psychographic research used in older markets is that of focus panels. Focus panels, of course, have great limitations because no focus group—typically consisting of a dozen or fewer people—can be representative of an entire class of consumers.

Mail and telephone attitudinal and lifestyle surveys also are heavily used, but serious questions have arisen about their dependability, given the fact that important nonverbal subtleties are inevitably missed. Moreover, such surveys are usually difficult to analyze for the content and meanings of *metamessages*, messages that transcend the literal meanings of the linguistics used in a response. For example, while Beth J. Soldo and Emily M. Agree report in the Population Reference Bureau's bulletin *America's Elderly* that four out of five noninstitutionalized people aged 65 or older suffer from at least one chronic condition,[10] a recent survey of 1200 respondents conducted by my firm, Wolfe Resources Group, showed that 75 percent of those *aged 75 or older* reported their health as ranging from good to excellent. Studies by others on seniors' perceptions of their health status reveal similar results.

Many people interpret such results to mean that older people suffer from a denial syndrome about the real state of their health. I believe that older people are saying something else, something like what my mother, aged 82, was saying just after open-heart surgery. Barely two weeks after the operation, she talked about all she had to be thankful for, especially "my good health." She was not denying her health problems, but simply leaving unsaid the qualifier *given my age and circumstances*. And she was saying something more: Such things don't bother me like they would have when I was younger. I pretty much take life as it comes and am thankful for all the life the good Lord gives me. And beyond that she may have been reflecting a sense of time in which the concept of future has lost much of its meaning. Again, Chapter 8 goes into this phenomenon in some detail.

A whole book could be written about the important implications of such a simple expression as my mother used in describing the status of her health, and some points are addressed later in this book. The point here is that there are limitations to conventional consumer psychographic research, regardless of the depth of the interviews or survey instruments used. In short, no single method of studying older consumer behavior can present a complete and accurate picture.

Also, how good a survey instrument can someone who is not older create for older respondents? And once such an instrument has been created, how well can such a person interpret the results? Some researchers may be put off by such a question, but I will present evidence that semantic and cognitive differences can—and often do—impede effective communication between people of different ages. That evidence supports the idea that *styles of thinking* vary according to age to such a degree that there may be major errors in how we perceive older people. I further propose that standard test instruments and interpretive techniques used in drawing psychological profiles of older people may be seriously flawed because of differing patterns in cognition between mature people and the younger people who design, administer, and interpret psychological tests given to older people.

[10]Beth J. Soldo and Emily M. Agree, *American Demographics*, March 1989, p. 2.

### Idiosyncrasies of Older People
### Plague Marketers

Many older people marvel at the sense of social detachment they seem to have acquired as they have aged, while at the same time developing a stronger sense of commitment to society's goals. Abraham Maslow indirectly addressed this apparent contradiction when he said that highly mature adults are less subject to "enculturation," that is, they are more "their own person" than when they were younger.

Dr. David Gutman, an adulthood development psychologist at Northwestern University, has observed that this phenomenon is particularly true of women who take on characteristics generally thought of as masculine in U.S. society. Commenting on the psychological changes that occur in both sexes commonly beginning in the fifties, Gutman says:

> We find that, by contrast to younger men, older men are more interested in giving and receiving love than in conquering or acquiring power. We also find, across a wide range of cultures, that women age in psychologically the reverse direction. Even in normal patriarchal societies, women become more aggressive in later life, less affiliated and more managerial or political.[11]

That men tend to be less inhibited about seeking and giving love and women less inhibited about projecting themselves is probably not so much a lowering of inhibitions as it is the emergence through personality growth of fuller, more expressive, and more highly individualized beings. At least, that is how Maslow viewed such changes. When we see these kinds of changes in someone we know, sometimes we view that person as having become a bit idiosyncratic.

The idiosyncratic nature of many older people reduces the effectiveness of the group-characteristics profiles on which market segmentation research and marketing activities traditionally depend. Older people might be described as round pegs that many market researchers and marketing professionals are trying to force into square holes.

By suggesting there is an "idiosyncratic" aspect to older people's behavior, I do not mean "odd" or "strange." I mean *individuated*. *Idiosyncratic* was a term frequently used by Maslow to describe what he believed to be one of the most significant behavioral traits of older people who are wholesomely developed and functioning individuals.

---

[11]Gail Sheehy, *The Pathfinders*, Bantam Books, New York, 1981, p. 236.

## New Tool for Maturity Markets: Experiential Segmentation

In his book *Market Segmentation*, Art Weinstein maintains that the greater the diversity of lifestyles of a given market, the more difficult it is to segment that market.[12] Some have observed that the older yuppies are becoming so individuated that, like older consumers, they are becoming increasingly difficult to segment. And greater individuation diminishes the practical or economic value of consumer segmentation: The more individuation there is, the smaller the subgroups; the smaller the subgroups, the less cost-effective it is to tailor marketing programs to such groups.

When *consumer segmentation* becomes impractical, the alternative strategy of *experiential segmentation* can make more sense. By *experiential segmentation*, I mean the positioning of products and services according to the experiences to which they can lead, rather than according to their direct performance attributes. For example, a car can be positioned in terms of its well-engineered performance attributes, or it can be positioned for its ability to offer exciting experiences of many types and intensities.

There are two major approaches to experiential segmentation. The first, and most obvious, is to tailor a product to meet certain experiential needs and desires of a given group of consumers. The second, and more challenging, is to create in consumer's minds multiple perceptions of what the product can do for them, thus stimulating consumers to define the product in terms of its experiential values to them. This is the opposite of an advertisement which explicitly defines the product's experiential value for the consumer.

### Better Strategy: Let Consumers, Not Marketers, Define the Product

Experiential segmentation is more suited to older consumers than younger consumers, because older people tend to be more resistant to being told what something is or is not. The older person has a lifetime of consumer experiences and generally feels quite able to make his or her own decision about the value and meaning of a product or service.

The experiential segmentation strategy depends on consumers' imaginative definitions of a product or service. It requires that marketers be

[12] Art Weinstein, *Market Segmentation*, Probus Publishing Company, Chicago, 1987, p. 13.

creative in the art of *conditional positioning* of the product or service. Instead of positioning a product in terms of what it is, the product is positioned in terms of what it *might be*. By contrast, *absolute positioning*, which tells consumers what a product or service is all about, significantly inhibits the consumer's imagination from generating alternative perceptions of the value of the product or service—perceptions that might be more responsive to the consumer's individual needs or desires.

Two recent approaches used in marketing two different brands of beer illustrate the often subtle differences between conditional and absolute product positioning. Miller Lite's tag line "Everything you always wanted in a beer. And less." is an example of absolute conditioning. It is saying that Miller Lite will please the palate while being kinder to the waistline. It is product-performance-oriented.

Michelob's line "The night belongs to Michelob" is an example of conditional positioning. It invites consumers to use their imagination to define the experiential possibilities of the product. The ad maker isn't saying what the product is, but is suggesting how the product might be associated with the consumer's very individual fantasies.

## Conditional Positioning Is a Kind of Psychological Judo

Psychologist Ellen Langer has conducted many studies concerning the stimulation of imagination as it relates to the defining of objects. She has found that the more precisely someone has defined an object for others, the less creatively the others will perceive it. In one study, those in a control group were told that certain objects were just what most would agree: A hair dryer *was* a hair dryer, an extension cord *was* an extension cord, a dog's chew toy *was* a dog's chew toy. Subjects in the experimental group were told, "This *could be* a hair dryer, this *could be* an extension cord, this *could be* a dog's chew toy."[13]

Subjects in both groups were given forms to fill out according to instructions that contained deliberate errors. The researchers, with mock embarrassment, admitted their "errors" and informed each group that because there were no more blank forms to use, the project had to be canceled. Those in the control group accepted the experimenters' decision without further thought or question. Those in the experimental group, however, came up with a creative solution. They proposed that since the dog's chew toy was made of rubber, it might serve also as an eraser to restore the blanks in the forms.

Langer's work in the study of the role of creative thinking holds im-

[13]Ellen Langer, *Mindfulness*, Addison Wesley, Reading, Mass., 1989, p. 120.

portant lessons for marketers. Knowing how to employ the consumer's imagination to engender positive responses to the product being offered is the psychological equivalent of how a judo master works. The judo master leverages the strength of an adversary to achieve personal objectives. Using the principle of conditional positioning, the marketer can have the consumer imagine more positive attributes about the product than can be described in any readable advertisement. Moreover, because the marketer has not absolutely defined the product, each consumer is free to define it in his or her own terms, according to individual self-image, personality characteristics, and individualized perceptions of need and desire. This approach to communicating with consumers follows the Second General Principle of Marketing, the *Principle of Conditional Positioning*:

---

**SECOND GENERAL PRINCIPLE OF MARKETING**
The Conditional-Positioning Principle

The less absolutely a product is defined, the greater the likelihood that consumers will define the product's attributes using their own processes of imagination in terms of their individual self-images, personality characteristics, and individualized perceptions of need and desire.

---

For reasons more fully explained later, the greater the maturity of a personality, the greater the resistance to absolute product positioning and definition. At the same time, the mature personality has probably developed a greater capacity for applying imagination to product definition than existed earlier in life.

## Experiential Segmentation versus Consumer Segmentation

*Consumer segmentation* is heavily dependent on demographic correlates with lifestyle patterns. It is most effectively used with younger, more predictable markets. *Experiential segmentation* is based more on behavioral motivations than on demographics. Experiential segmentation is defined along the lines of *generic consumer behavior*—behavior motivated by aspirations common to the majority of consumers.

An example of a *generic consumer behavior motivator* would be the desire for a break with one's routine. Virtually everyone seeks experiences from time to time that offer a break with the routine. Marketing strategies that promote a product or service's capacity for helping one to break out of the routine are targeting generic consumer behavior. Marketers applying this principle to promoting, say, a travel tour, would promote the breaking-the-routine potential of a trip, and would be targeting *generic consumer behavior*. If, on the other hand, marketers focused attention on the cultural aspects of the tour, they would be targeting *specific consumer behavior*.

The research processes leading to successful experiential segmentation may combine select demographic data with data on consumer behavior patterns that are shared by people within a similar *experiential* stage of life. *Experiential stages of life* are periods in one's personality development in which lifestyles and attitudes are dominated by certain types of *experiential aspirations*, as exemplified in one stage by the materialistic *possession experience aspirations* of normal young adults. Young adults' experiential aspirations, typically tied to the desire for possessions, strongly influence career paths, choices of friends and lovers, and general interests as well as product purchase behavior. Generally speaking, seniors' experiential aspirations are less connected to materialistic desires. These differences are more defined by species-specific behavioral attributes than by culture- and time-sensitive factors.

The process of experiential segmentation differs greatly methodologically from what we usually think of as the market segmentation process, which seeks to define *specific consumer behavior* for defined market segments. The term *specific consumer behavior* refers to behavior uniquely associated with a *specific* class or segment of consumers that have been defined largely in terms of demographic and lifestyle characteristics, as opposed to experiential life-stage characteristics. By positioning a product through the use of images associated with demographic profiles and lifestyles characteristics, the product is purposely vested with a more narrow marketplace appeal. That is what consumer segmentation is all about: identifying a group of consumers who have similar demographic characteristics (age, income, education, etc.) and similar lifestyle characteristics (yuppie lifestyle, blue-collar lifestyle, etc.).

Experiential segmentation, while taking demographic factors into account, focuses less on demographically defined types of consumers and more on consumer motivational factors, especially as influenced by various levels of psychological and sociological maturity. For example, the "I need to be recognized" imperative is a behavioral motivation factor more prevalent among the less mature than among those of greater maturity. On average, it is a more dominant motivation among young adults than among older adults because of differences in levels of maturity.

## Older Adults More Resistant to Peer Group Values than Younger Adults

Young and older adults share many requirements and desires (for example, transportation requirements and desires regarding cars), but how each fulfills those requirements differs widely. Those who are less mature tend to be more governed by peer group values.

A major influence in the determination of peer group values, as they relate to the popularity of given products and services, is their role in defining the identities of those composing a peer group. Young people generally have less resolved identities in a social context simply because they have not lived long enough to have the accomplishments which symbolize who they really are in terms of what they have done. Each peer group has its own discrete identifying marks by which its members define themselves. This, along with the fundamental need for certain things to transact adult life, represents powerful forces at work in the shaping of young people's consumer behavior.

However, those elements exert less influence in older markets because identity needs are generally not as pressing among older buyers. So older people tend to be less preoccupied with materialistic aspirations than younger people. For example, older people generally feel no great urge to define who they are by the newness or model of their cars.

In general, nonmaterialistically based *experiential desires* play a stronger role in older people's consumer behavior than do pure need or deficit. And few peer group values define older consumers' desires specifically enough to permit meaningful, broad-scale consumer segmentation.

## Mature Consumers Look for "Gateways to Experiences" in Purchases

In maturity markets, one must be sensitive to those areas of strategic planning that are common to all consumers, regardless of age, and those areas that are more specific to one subgroup or another. One of the most important differences between the less mature consumer and the more mature consumer is reflected in the First Principle for Maturity Markets, the Gateway-to-Experiences Principle:

---

**FIRST PRINCIPLE FOR MATURITY MARKETS**
The Gateway-to-Experiences Principle

Mature consumers tend to be motivated more by the capacity of a product or service to serve as a gateway to experiences than by the generic nature of a product or service.

---

Leon Schiffman, director of the doctoral program in marketing at Baruch College, City University, New York, succinctly summarizes his research findings concerning older consumers' experiential aspirations: "They buy experiences, not products or services."

Since experiential aspirations are highly individual, a major challenge faced by marketers to mature consumers is to identify ways to present a product or service so that each prospective consumer, using his or her own imagination, can perceive the product as being *especially* designed for him or her. The product, because it is then defined less by the marketer than by the collective imaginations of the consumers in the marketplace, essentially becomes all things to all people.

The experiential orientation of older consumers derives from their individual changed views about life satisfaction. Earlier in life, most sought happiness and overall life satisfaction largely in material things, activities providing an escape from the pressures of family and job, and accomplishments in their careers. In later life, the force of these influences wanes, with a resulting major shift in consumer desires and buying behavior. One of the most significant changes is that older consumers tend to evaluate products and services in terms of the desirable experiences they might facilitate.

## Higher Life Satisfaction Increases Experiential Aspirations

Older people are generally more satisfied with their lives than younger people. This fact has a significant effect on the shape and intensity of older consumers' experiential aspirations, because it strongly influences their self-images.

What kinds of self-images do older people tend to have? Generally speaking, they are not images sullied by regrets over lost youth, and they are not images strongly influenced by fears of a future which holds prospects—*but not certainty*—of growing disability. Financially, physiologically, and psychologically independent older people have more than an upbeat outlook on life. They reflect the presence of a *continuum of life satisfaction* that is only rarely found in young adults, as Gail Sheehy reported in *The Pathfinders*, and Maslow explained in his writings.

Within the context of their individual lives, studies indicate that most older people seem fairly satisfied with what they have accomplished in terms of both their material possessions and their lifestyles. As older people place less emphasis on material aspirations, their attention to growth-inducing experiences increases. Older people are not compensating for something missing in their lives. For mature people, experiences that fulfill the person are not viewed as an escape from some routine or difficulty, but as an excursion into an exhilarating encounter that sharpens their appreciation for life and its wonders. Noting that tendency, many human development psychologists have spoken of certain childlike characteristics often taken on by older people.

Even though it seems to be one more paradox of many in the behavior of older people, those who reach the higher levels of human personality maturity do become more childlike in many ways. Psychoanalyst E. Kris termed this phenomenon "regression in service to the ego."[14] It is a positive step in adult personality development, and a genuine understanding of it is vitally important to marketers of products and services to older people, all of whom may be seniors, but none of whom really compose a *seniors market*.

---

[14]Robert Ornstein, *The Psychology of Consciousness*, Penguin Books, New York, 1986, p. 204.

# 2

# Senior Markets Don't Exist

## Semantics: Victimizer of Seniors

When Buckminster Fuller, the great engineer, inventor of the geodesic dome, and expansive holistic philosopher, was in his late twenties, he found himself one night at the edge of a lake with the intention of ending his life. He had just lost his only child to illness, he felt his accomplishments to date had been nil, and he was suffering a total loss of faith in life. Before he could carry out his act of self-destruction, however, a wave of new thought, laden with newly defined purpose, swept over him. He would reorient his life—entirely.

It had occurred to Fuller that one of the greatest constraints on human development and accomplishment was semantics. He felt that we tend to become so rigid in defining the meanings of the symbols we use to communicate with one another, meanings that have been formed by consensus, that we sacrifice clear, independent thinking to a lesser or greater degree. After all, we do not examine anew each word, each phrase, each idea every time we hear it or speak it—even though time, circumstance, and context can impart many different colorations.

Wishing to free himself of his semantic imprisonment for a time, Bucky Fuller returned from the edge of the lake to begin life again, and he spent the first year of this new phase without speaking at all to anyone, including his wife. To totally reorient his life, he felt he had to purge all biases, prejudices, and preconceptions until nothing had escaped deep introspective scrutiny.

### The Word *Senior* Has Narrowed Our Thinking

Were he alive today, Bucky Fuller might well suggest that we abandon the use of the term *senior* as it has been applied to a class of older people in a variety of contexts including legal, social, economic, and marketing. Our thinking has become imprisoned by the word *senior* as applied to older adults. The term has acquired such narrow meanings—many of which reflect negatively on the individuality, competence, and human potential of those to whom it is applied—that it is not a very useful term and, worse, it can carry perjorative overtones. Older people frequently feel chagrined at being referred to as *senior citizens*.

Using the word *seniors* to define a market makes no more practical sense than grouping all other markets under the term *nonseniors*. If you exclude all those consumers under age 20 and all those consumers over age 80, then you have all other consumers whose ages span 60 years, from age 20 to age 80. Divide that group at age 50, and you get two groups, each of which spans 30 years of adulthood. Now no marketer would be foolish enough to lump all those between age 20 and age 50 into one target market. Likewise, would any thinking marketer place all those aged 50 to 80 in one target market group? Some have done it, however. No less mindless are marketers who have lumped all those aged 60 and older, or all those 65 and older, or all those 70 and older, etc., into the same target market group.

In the 20-to-50 cohort, there is enormous heterogeneity in needs, desires, lifestyles, and consumer behavior. But there is, by many measures, even greater heterogeneity in the 50-to-80 cohort. Failure to recognize that elementary fact about older markets has been the cause of many failed marketing programs. Bucky Fuller would not be the least bit surprised at all the marketplace failures in older-market marketing programs of the past few years. He might simply say, "You have allowed yourselves to become victims of semantics. The word has been ruined. Drop it. Use your imagination to find some other symbols to stand for those you wish to describe *accurately*."

## Successes and Failures in Older Markets

Bob Roskamp, president of The Freedom Group, headquartered in Tampa, Florida, and Sharon Harper, his partner, entered the overbuilt Phoenix market with a new full-service senior community in January 1988, and in the first five months they sold nearly 250 apartments.

Their success, in a field that generally considers six to eight sales per month good, contrasted dramatically with the struggles of a number of nearby projects (some near foreclosure).

During the same period, Avon Products, which less than three years earlier had acquired a major interest in Retirement Inns of America and had paid more than $220 million for Mediplex, owner of a number of retirement communities and long-term health care facilities, put its senior housing communities on the block because of unsatisfactory performance.

In the meantime, Sears was abandoning its four-year-long effort to build a vast membership organization of seniors in its Modern Outlook Group, while the American Association of Retired Persons (AARP) was adding members at the rate of more than 2000 per day.

Elsewhere Southwestern Bell was shutting down its *Silver Pages* program, a *Yellow Pages* type of directory of companies offering discounts to seniors, while across the country, in industry after industry, discount programs were attracting thousands of new senior consumers monthly.

What is behind such a mixed bag of successes and failures in senior markets encompassing every industry? Darrell Miller, of the Center for Gerontological Studies at the University of Florida, put it simply in his invitation to me to join 30 prominent academicians, researchers, and executives from Fortune 500 companies at a conference designed to chart new academic directions for its marketing curriculum. He said, "Companies of all sizes and in all industries are crying out for help in understanding the senior consumer. They are calling us all the time, asking for information and asking us if we know anyone who seems to really understand the senior consumer."

Why is the senior consumer market perceived as difficult to tap? What is it about this generally massive group of consumers that is filling marketers' heads with so many questions?

This chapter offers a summarized examination of my research and that of others, as well as a commonsense interpretation of my experience as it relates to the diversity of opinions and approaches to the largest and wealthiest set of adult markets in the United States. The following chapters discuss both the detailed foundations behind those observations and principles for achieving greater success.

## More about the Riddles of Senior Markets

When it comes to characterizing their consumer behavior, those whom we call seniors have been described, borrowing from Winston Churchill, as "a riddle wrapped in a mystery inside an enigma." They are said to be much more sophisticated consumers than seniors in the past. Because of great changes in health, affluence, and lifestyles, they might be aptly called the *New Seniors*. The real question is, are they really so different?

If we read the works of Erik Erikson, whose ideas are the foundation of much thinking in the field of human development psychology, and of Abraham Maslow, author of the famous hierarchy of basic human needs, or of such popular authors as Simone de Beauvoir (*Coming of Age*), clearly the seniors of 1989 have personality characteristics much like those of seniors 20, 30, and 40 years ago. Other sources confirm the similarities of older people across the centuries.

Nearly 2000 years ago, the Roman philosopher Lucius Annaeus Seneca wrote his timeless essay *On Old Age*, which is still widely quoted today for its emphasis on the many positive aspects of advanced age. Some 1500 years after that, in various sonnets and in his last three plays, William Shakespeare expressed attributes of old age that can bring a tear to the sensitive eye, or at least cause one to reflect wistfully, as Helen M. Luke did, on recalling a conversation of King Lear with his wife about old age:

> Surely in all the poetry of the world there could be no more profoundly beautiful, wise, and tender expression of the essence of old age....[1]

There is little evidence that human evolution has much altered the course of humankind's psychological passage into old age. We have seen that there has been little change in longevity for those achieving adulthood; and it is highly questionable that the life span of humans has changed at all in the 2000 years since Seneca. What is different about older people today is that there are many more of them and they have greater opportunities to express themselves than older people of one or two millennia ago.

### Age Is More Meaningful in Wines than in Older Markets

With 70 percent of the nation's wealth held by those aged 50 and older, U.S. business, in its usual fashion, has turned its attention toward the perceived new center of money in the marketplace: senior markets. Business's long and fabled love affair with youth markets is on the wane. Age is in, in industry after industry; youth is out. Gerontology,[2] a

---

[1]Helen M. Luke, *Old Age*, Parabola Books, New York, 1987, p. 25.
[2]*Gerontology* is the study of aging; *geriatrics* deals with the medical aspects of aging.

heretofore little known discipline, is entering its heyday. But something is drastically wrong with the tenor and the focus of much of what is being said and written about seniors.

*Age* has been the central but inappropriate focus in the great wave of publicity about the aging of America, especially in literature that purports to unravel the deepest secrets on how to successfully sell products and services to seniors. Age is the wrong focus because most people do not often think of themselves in terms of age. Simone de Beauvoir observed that among older people whom she interviewed for *Coming of Age*, "For many, age simply didn't exist."

A young person is inclined to view an older person's comments that age is not an important factor of life as an expression driven by regret over the loss of youth, anxieties over age-based health problems, and discomfort over thinking about death. But research by Wolfe Resources Group into seniors' attitudes and behavior suggests that older people's aversion to being perceived in terms of their age is less related to these feelings than many believe.

Numerous older people in focus group studies in which Wolfe Resources has participated have reported that age is much less of a bother to them than the ideas younger people harbor about them as aging people. "We have a lot more vitality than a lot of young people think," more than one respondent has claimed in those panels.

Age does not exist as a significant fact of life for many older people for two major reasons. First, to accept the idea that age is a significant factor in lifestyle behavior and choices means to associate oneself, when one is older, with a set of undesirable attributes that younger people tend to associate with age. Second, cognitive changes occur among more psychologically mature older adults that largely delete age from conscious awareness. Mark Twain had it right when he said, "Age is a thing of mind over matter...if you don't mind it, it don't matter." He recognized that in later life the remarkable human mind has endless capacities for transcending the limitations of a wearing-out body. Mature older people are too involved with living life to think much about the end of life. For them, age has more relevance in wines and antiques.

## Like Young People, Older People Want to Be All They Can Be

Brochures for senior housing commonly present images of what people don't want to be or don't want to think about. The following quotation from a senior housing brochure illustrates the point: "You will find a program that encourages independence, but emphasizes care and service." That contradictory statement reflects an image found in most brochures for senior housing: a lifestyle dominated by dependency upon others. No one wants to be in that position.

I once asked a man of 66 to review a stack of brochures I had picked up from various U.S. senior communities. He came back to me with this analysis: "They all say the same thing. In the opening paragraphs, they promise independence. Then the rest of the brochure tells you how they are going to keep you from having it. They tell you how they are going to feed you, clean your apartment, launder your linens, bus you to where you want to go, and, with a social director, direct your daily activities."

Bob Roskamp from Freedom Group takes a different approach. He holds meetings with residents of his communities, telling them, "We will take care of the grass, the buildings, and other basics, but it's up to you to make this place work." Roskamp's program can accommodate those who want to bask in self-indulgence; however, his focus, like that reflected in the U.S. Army slogan "Be all you can be," is on providing opportunities for residents to validate their lives by continuing meaningful activities. Residents run the shops and snack bars in the Freedom Group communities and otherwise take a major role in community operations. He is enabling people to have lifestyles reflective of what they want to be.

One of the great mistakes younger people make is assuming that declining physical abilities necessarily interfere with older people's being all they want to be. The eightyish, wheelchair-riding woman mentioned in Chapter 10, who travels around the world alone, is clear evidence of how much the spirit can transcend the body.

### Most Older People Seek Vital Involvement, Not Leisure

A great fiction promoted in the marketing world is that seniors are widely self-indulgent, especially in pursuit of a lifestyle of full-time leisure. For evidence, people point to such things as the famous bumper stickers claiming, "We are spending our children's inheritance" and "The boss is still working, I'm not." They bring attention to the tens of thousands of seniors who have chosen to live in recreation-oriented senior communities, communities that Gray Panthers' founder Maggie Kuhn has dubbed "playpens for wrinkled babies."

What is overlooked in the promotion of such images is that seniors give the greatest amount of time to volunteer causes and account for the largest amount of money given to charities. They are America's most responsible citizens. They are the most frequent attenders of church and temple; they vote at a rate better than twice that of people in their middle thirties and younger; they stay informed on issues by choosing news broadcasts and documentaries as their favorite TV shows, and by reading designed to increase their knowledge of life and the world.

Erik Erikson, Joan Erikson, and Helen Kivnic talk of the need for vital involvement in a book entitled *Vital Involvement in Old Age.*[3] The vital involvement of which they speak is not the kind of playtime involvement widely seen in advertisements for travel, housing, and other products and services. It is involvement that results in some product of effort perceived by others as having value. *Contributions of value* are *vital* to one's sense of well-being, hence the term *vital involvement.*

Seniors decidedly are *not* the full-time leisure addicts that nonseniors commonly think they are. Two out of three men aged 65 and older attempt to return to some kind of money-producing vocation; over one-third of those aged 60 and older would like to open a home-based business, according to a study by AARP.[4]

One grim statistic provides evidence that seniors favor a productive life over a nonproductive one: Gerontologist Ken Dychtwald reports that the suicide rate among adult males aged 65 and older is *four times* that of younger adult males. Gerontological psychologists attribute this largely to the devastating loss of purpose in life that can result from the absence of any means to validate one's existence. The purpose of leisure is to *refresh* life, not validate it. Images in marketing communications that overplay the lure and value of leisure will repel many older people.

## Another Myth: Older People Are Myopically Money-Minded

Ron Jennings, president of Advent Information Services, the Southwestern Bell subsidiary that sold advertising for *Silver Pages* (a *Yellow Pages* for older people), said, "Our research says we were doing all the right things, but in the end it didn't work. The people we were trying to attract in the end we failed to attract."[5] The people behind the *Silver Pages* made the mistake of thinking of senior citizens as a somewhat monolithic (by virtue of age), broadly segmentable class of consumers.

---

[3]Erik H. Erikson, Joan M. Erikson, and Helen Q. Kivnick, *Vital Involvement in Old Age*, W. W. Norton & Company, New York, 1986.
[4]*Understanding Senior Housing*, American Association of Retired Persons, Washington, 1986, p. 27.
[5]"Silver Pages Folds," *Mature Market Report*, July 1988, p. 1.

Unlike adolescents, older people recoil from symbols that relegate them to any grouping based on age or perceived attributes of age.

The *Silver Pages* was heavily promoted on a national basis. Southwestern Bell enlisted Bob Hope for both print and broadcast media advertising. The company developed an intimate relationship unprecedented for a business organization with the National Association of Area Agencies on Aging (NAAAA), the national organization that is tied into the nearly 700 Area Agencies on Aging, which cover every square foot of land in the United States under a mandate from the U.S. Congress under the Older Persons Act.

Southwestern Bell seemed to have done its homework well. Its research disclosed important behavioral attributes of older people. They *are* keenly disposed toward saving money; they respond better to endorsements of products by well-respected figures than younger people, especially figures associated with patriotism and national pride (hence, Bob Hope as an ideal spokesperson); and overall they have a greater respect for authority figures and symbols than younger people. The NAAAA, as a government-based social services organization, falls into that category; presumably, then, its endorsement and that of its hundreds of member agencies around the nation would capture the confidence of legions of senior citizens for the *Silver Pages*.

Older people are careful about money. According to Ron Holden, a Maryland attorney who specializes in estate practice, "They are the most financially literate consumers in the country. They understand personal economics and are amazingly well-versed, as a group, in the principles of money management. But anyone who thinks that makes them penny-pinchers is wrong."

An increasing number of businesses are offering senior citizen discounts, but like Southwestern Bell, many are finding that discounts are not as strong a purchase motivator in older markets as expected. A product or service has to have a great deal more going for it than its price.

AARP's travel services director, Hal Norvell, says, "The older traveler generally is not a cheap traveler. They come in to our travel agents armed with their research on travel programs, and they are looking for the best price, but they generally don't want to sacrifice value and quality for price. They would sooner take a scaled down package than take an inferior package."

## The Dreams of Older People

In 1987, AARP launched a series of ads designed to help marketing professionals better understand older people's aspirations and lifestyles.

Figures 2-2 and 2-3, seen later, are taken from that series which, among other images, projected older people as romantically minded, forward thinking, interested in productive activities, and significantly oriented to doing for others. Older people want to be givers rather than takers. And, not unlike adolescents, older folks think a great deal about what they want to be. The following quotation is excerpted from an essay by a senior, Paul Cummins, shortly after his retirement. It is a poignant statement about how many older people look at life and themselves:

> It has become clear to me that the only way I can ever have all I wish for is to live in two different worlds at the same time. I have yet to find a way to do that. It may be that I will have to give up some of my wishes.
>
> The days of my life are numbered. I know that full well. So eventually (maybe not too long from now), my name will be in the obituary column. I would like to be honored with a nice funeral, of course. But on the other hand, I think it is just awful what people pay for funerals these days.
>
> Until that day comes, I want to really "live it up." There are so many things I want to do and places I want to go. Unfortunately, doing and going require a bit more effort and energy lately than they used to, and I don't seem to have that much ambition these days. Maybe tomorrow I will do something.
>
> Since I retired, people keep on asking me annoying questions like "How are you using your time these days?" and "Do you find enough to do to keep yourself busy?" and "How does it feel to be living the life of Riley?" whoever he was. The implication is that my time should always be "used," presumably for some worthy purpose; I should always be "busy" about something or other; and there is something wrong about just taking it easy and merely enjoying the miracle of existence. I resent that. I've earned the right to spend these final "golden years" doing nothing if that's what I prefer. But stop to think about it, maybe I should be making better use of my time. Maybe I should find something to do that would be helpful to others.
>
> I think I may be experiencing adolescence again. Not the way you think, although I still get adventuresome ideas every now and then. Is it too late for a little excitement? But that's not what I mean. I am ambivalent about so many things, big things like: Should I, or dare I, change my image? How about my pattern of living? Are there other activities I might find interesting? How would other people react if I should risk making some dramatic change? What, now, are my goals and purposes in life? These are the same questions adolescents are forced to ask. It's embarrassing. There's not too much time now for opening new doors. But then again, there's not too much time to delay doing so.
>
> I wonder how many others are fighting this same civil war inside themselves.

There it is. This man had a successful career, enjoyed the status of being top salesperson in his company on a national basis a number of times, took pleasure in his family life, and was one of those community "pillars." And this man, at age 65, is asking the same kinds of questions about himself as adolescents do.

In a sense, even though Cummins acknowledges that age is ever progressive, he is demonstrating, in another sense, that adolescence is forever. He is evidencing the fact that human development continues throughout life—it does not end at some particular age.

### Sell Dreams, Not Regrets or Fears

In an interview with Dr. Robert Forbes, Director of Special Programs for AARP, for an article I was writing, Bob shared with me a favorite quote of his, attributed to John Barrymore, Sr.:

A man is never old till regrets take the place of dreams.

Forbes, a gerontologist, suggested that I advise my readers that the best way to sell products and services to older consumers is to anticipate their dreams and then intimate how a particular product or service can help them achieve their dreams. "Too much marketing," he says, "is directed at people's vulnerabilities and limitations."

John Barrymore would have understood Paul Cummins—at least the part of Paul Cummins that looked forward to being a continually evolving personality. Contrast that forward-looking attitude to what is depicted in so many ads and broadcast commercials about older people, for example, the TV commercial that ends with its pain-racked old man desperately complaining, "Is this what it's like to be old?" In a magazine-sized senior housing ad I recently saw, the word *why* was repeated four times, in 30-point type, across the top of the ad. Underneath was a picture of a dejected-looking man cupping his downcast face in his hands, and the copy began:

Why spend lonely days and nights trapped in your home unable to get out because of bad weather?
Why worry about the dangers of illness...?
Why take the chance of being alone in your home with no one to help you in case of illness or injury?

I had one response to that ad. *Why* would anyone read it?

The mind tends to shut down at any suggestion of fear and anxiety in an ad (or from any other source, for that matter). It is a matter of self-defense. The thoughts triggered by that ad involve conditions that none of the targeted readers are comfortable contemplating. The readers will defend against the ad's attempts to invade their comfort to make a sale by shutting off cognition of the ad's message. Think of how many times you have attempted to reason with someone who has become defensive over something you have said. When defenses are invoked and the mind has closed to a portion of a message that carries unwanted images, the mind tends to shut down to other parts of the message, too.

## How to Make Adult Absorbent Products Attractive

Kimberly-Clark has an undergarment product called Depend for adults with incontinence (bladder-control) problems. It has been widely promoted in a series of ads featuring June Allyson, that all-American girl-next-door personality of a few years ago, in a variety of upbeat scenes. The story told by the scenes is that an active, involved life is made possible by Depend for those who need the protection of padded undergarments. Figure 2-1 is one example of the Kimberly-Clark ads that were produced by Campbell-Mithun-Esty Advertising of Minneapolis.

Procter and Gamble has a similar product, called Attends. It has been widely promoted with a line drawing of a person and copy describing how the abdominal contents of a person's body put a lot of pressure on the bladder when the person stands up—as if a person needing such undergarments did not already know that!

Kimberly-Clark is directing its message in terms of human potential; it is selling dreams. P & G is directing its message in terms of vulnerabilities and limitations; it is selling nightmares. Kimberly-Clark enjoys more than a 50 percent market share in drugstores and grocery stores, while P & G has a retail market share of less than 15 percent.

The message is clear: People don't like to be reminded of their problems or fears. Older people often have a remarkable ability to ignore what might be very troublesome to a younger person, but they don't like having this ability challenged by advertisers.

It is a common thought that aging minds are prone to attacks of angst, regrets about ebbing life, and despair that the future will never be better. A 1975 national survey by Harris & Associates found things to be different, however, among the 65-and-older population.[6] They scored higher than those under age 65 in responses to the following statements:

I've gotten pretty much what I expected out of life.

[6]Gene D. Cohen, *The Aging Brain*, Springer Publishing Company, New York, 1989, p. 32.

**Figure 2-1.** Kimberly-Clark ad for Depend. (*Courtesy of Campbell-Mithun-Esty and Kimberly-Clark.*)

> As I look back on my life, I am fairly well satisfied.
> I would not change my past life even if I could.

The same people scored better than their juniors on the next statement:

> My life could be happier than it is now.

As to depressing thoughts of death, other studies have found that dread of death is more common in middle age than in later life. In many cases where older people seem to conform to the stereotypical images of anxiety and worry, easily correctable physiological conditions affecting brain chemistry have been found to be the cause of such depressing moods.[7]

Again, by the First General Principle of Marketing, images—suggested in graphics and implied or expressed in narrative form—emphasizing their limitations and vulnerabilities will repel most healthy-minded older people. In fact, numerous recent surveys have shown that high percentages of older people do not like the way in which they are depicted in ads and commercials.

## The Four Faces of the New Senior

Through countless experiences with various marketers, especially younger people attempting to fashion promotional materials for older markets, I sometimes feel great frustration in trying to describe what older people are like and what attracts and repels them in promotional messages. So I developed a one-page character sketch of older people entitled "The Four Faces of the New Senior."

In terms of behavior I do not believe that there is such a person as the "New Senior," in that older people today are not remarkably different from older people in years past as far as their basic human needs and desires are concerned. What is new is that they have vastly expanded opportunities to express themselves through their lifestyles and because of society's changing views of older people. Views of older people are changing largely because there are so many of them and because generally they are more affluent than seniors in the past. The New Senior character sketch below evolved as an attempt to replace unfounded preconceptions, frequently reflected in marketing programs, with four major aspects or faces that should be reflected in promotional materials.

---

### THE FOUR FACES OF THE NEW SENIOR

**Creativity and Intellectual Involvement**.  The New Senior is a member of the most information-driven segment of U.S. society (when information is not related to livelihood). New Seniors prefer news shows and documentaries to other TV viewing. They are big readers of newspapers and magazines. They travel to expand their intellectual horizons,

---

[7]Ibid. p. 34.

rather than for the escapist reasons that widely motivate young people to travel. They are signing up at colleges and universities by the tens of thousands. They are creative about shaping their lives and are *intellectually involved* in life. Their consumer behavior patterns reflect this bent, especially in their detailed reading of promotional materials.

**Experience and Wisdom and the Desire to Share Them**.   The now famous TV commercial by McDonald's showing the retired man going back to work symbolizes this face for the "common folk" in a way that has caught the fancy of the country. Reportedly, it not only produced senior employees (the original purpose of the commercial), but also increased restaurant patronage by seniors who apparently liked how the commercial pictured seniors. We often talk about the experience and wisdom of older people but generally ignore their *desire to share it*.

**Vitality and Productivity**.   We see a 75-year-old who is "active" and say, "That is remarkable." Well, more and more older people are being described as remarkable. One 82-year-old woman said she was tired of being referred to as remarkable. "I am just an 82-year-old version of my 22-year-old self. Hell, I was always remarkable!" she exclaims.[8]

Most seniors want to continue producing something of value, for that is the only route to self-esteem. Self-esteem does not derive from one's consumption activities. The overemphasis on leisure in the marketing of living environments is contrary to this image of productivity. A 1977 survey by the Roper Organization found that 95 percent of seniors did not want to move to a seniors' community. A 1986 study by SRI International, developers of the VALS system of market analysis, found that over 80 percent of seniors felt there was too much emphasis on recreation in the marketing of senior communities.

**Compassion for Others and Concern for the World about Them**.   Seniors are our best citizens. They vote at a higher rate than any other age group and are more heavily involved in "good works" than the rest of us. The explanation may be that seniors have more time, but the real reason may be that they care more. Otherwise, they would do what most nonseniors erroneously think they do—play all the time and love it.

---

The Four Faces provide a contextual framework from which marketers may draw ideas for presenting older people in images they will find appealing. The face of *Creativity and intellectual involvement* conjures images that can be demonstrated in a wide array of product and

[8]I agree. She is Mary Rose Wolfe, my mother, now 86, and still remarkable.

service promotion programs, including travel, senior living environments, and consumer products. For example, marketers could promote VCRs for viewing movie classics, and health care institutions that offer classes and lectures.

The second face, *Experience and wisdom and the desire to share them*, is an attribute that can be reflected in marketing virtually any product or service scene by the use of vignettes showing older people counseling others. Those being counseled may be individual young persons, groups of people, or organizations that, say, are drawing upon the older person for business management advice. In travel promotions, a tour guide may be an older person.

To show *Vitality and productivity*, it is not necessary to show an older person clearing hurdles in a foot race or scaling a mountain. I have known wheelchair-bound people whose vitality and productivity was astounding. Showing an older person in an intense application of energies in producing something of value conveys that image as well as a scene showing a person in a feverish sweat doing something.

An understanding of the fourth face, *Compassion for others and concern for the world about them*, is highly important to those developing marketing programs. It accurately suggests that its wearers are strongly outer-directed in their attitudes and life activities. They are considerably less self-absorbed than most younger people. Thus, marketing messages that appeal to selfish interests are more effective with younger consumers than with members of the maturity markets.

## Good-Works Images Are More Positive Than "At-Play" Images

Gerald Hotchkiss, publisher of a magazine aimed at maturity markets called *New Choices for the Best Years*, believes that marketers are missing some major effective communications opportunities by not showing older people engaged in productive activities that involve helping others. In an address before the National Association for Senior Living Industries in 1986, he said, "The one thing my staff and I have noted about older people that marketers should be mindful of is their great energy and their concern for others. Marketers should be showing older people, in their ads, that reflect this."

In 1987, McDonald's asked its advertising agency, Leo Burnett, to develop a TV commercial aimed at recruiting retirees, in order to compensate for the growing shortage of young people in the work force. The commercial that aired came to be known as the "New Kid" commercial. It was a resounding success and had the unexpected result cited above: It not only produced new employees, but also increased patronage by seniors because, contrary to their response to many other commercials and ads, older people liked the way in which they were represented.

## McDonald's Ads More Popular with Older People Than Wendy's Ads

The New Kid commercial projected images that were consistent with the Four Faces of the New Senior. The New Senior "reads" as productive, full of vitality, caring about others, and bright. That image contrasts with the image of older people reflected in the "Where's the Beef?" commercial by Wendy's. According to Elliot Glazer, a consumer research specialist with the Cadwell Davis Partners advertising agency, older people took a deep dislike to that commercial. Nonseniors laughed at the "crazy" old woman in the commercial who asked, "Where's the beef?" Older people grimaced.

Glazer, who traveled around the United States in 1986, conducting focus group research, showed that ad and a number of other commercials to seniors. Said Glazer, "They resented Claire Peller's depiction of an older person as an empty-headed, strangely idiosyncratic oddity."

## Marketers and Seniors Frequently Disagree on What Seniors Are Like

In 1986, the National Association for Senior Living Industries (NASLI), headquartered in Annapolis, Maryland, commissioned SRI International to conduct a nationwide psychographically oriented study of senior adults. Among the findings in the LAVOA (Lifestyles and Values of Older Adults) study, was that over half the respondents thought older people were not accurately depicted in advertising.

Since the object of advertising is to excite consumers about product or service, ad makers obviously do not intend to offend. But it happens. If one has a faulty view of older people and what might excite them, the production of images that offend is inevitable.

The Donnelley Marketing organization of Stamford, Connecticut, conducted a study in 1988 to test for variances between the views that marketers have of seniors and the views that seniors have of themselves. Table 2-1 reports Donnelley's findings. Those findings clearly reflect the basis of much of the difficulty involved in marketing to older people: Our views about who seniors are and what motivates them have not been very accurate.

Table 2-1 speaks volumes about what older people really are like in its demonstration of how they are less concerned about health and finances, less interested in travel and hobbies, and more interested in education and automobiles than marketers believe.

**Table 2-1.** Comparison of Marketers' and Mature Consumers' Views of Mature Consumers

What products or services are of interest to older consumers in order of degree of interest? (Responses on a scale of 1 to 5, with 5 being highest.)

| Product or service | Ratings of the 50-plus | Ratings of marketers |
|---|---|---|
| Health care | 4.1 | 4.7 |
| Financial services | 3.7 | 4.3 |
| Travel | 3.6 | 4.2 |
| Hobbies | 3.3 | 3.7 |
| Education | 3.1 | 2.9 |
| Automobiles | 3.1 | 2.9 |

What advertising media are depended upon most by older consumers?

| Media | The 50-plus views | Views of marketers |
|---|---|---|
| Word of mouth | 3.6 | 4.3 |
| TV/radio | 2.3 | 3.0 |
| Magazines | 2.3 | 3.3 |
| Direct mail | 2.3 | 3.0 |
| New-brand trial | 3.5 | 3.0 |
| New-product trial | 3.6 | 3.0 |

What name label do older people prefer?

| Label | 50-plus | Marketers |
|---|---|---|
| Mature | 28.3% | 26.9% |
| Adult | 25.4 | 12.9 |
| Senior | 23.7 | 2.2 |
| 50-plus | 16.9 | 43.8 |
| Other | 5.7 | 4.2 |

SOURCE: Donnelley Marketing, Stamford, CN, 1988. Reported in "Marketers Don't Understand Seniors," *Mature Market Report*, May 1988, p. 2.

The second question in Table 2-1 suggests that older people are more experimental in trying brands than marketers believe and that seniors rely less on outside sources in making their purchasing decisions than marketers believe.

## Semantic Gymnastics

The third question in Table 2-1 provides strong support for the thesis of this book concerning the ageless market, showing that only 16.9 percent of seniors like being referred to as 50-plus, whereas 43.8 percent of marketers thought seniors would like that label best. Seniors' preference for the terms *mature* and *adult* similarly reflects a bias against strong age-based labels.

In the challenges we have encountered in trying to square our views of older consumers with their own views of themselves, we have tripped all over ourselves in what could be aptly called "semantic gymnastics." By now most people trying to communicate directly with older people in promotional material have dropped the word *elderly*, substituting such terms as *senior citizen, senior adult*, and *mature adult*. There even have been contests to identify a descriptor with which older people might be comfortable. In 1987, one seniors magazine conducted a contest among its subscribers. The contest yielded such names as *prime lifers* and *emeritans*, but the most forthright suggestion came from a man who said simply, "Just call us 'old farts'. " He was saying something important, I think: Don't give us some contrived euphemism!

Renaming seniors has become a major international challenge, it seems. Japan conducted a contest, demonstrating that even governments are concerned about what to call older people. The term chosen from that contest was *jitsunnen*, meaning "time of fruition." A friend of mine in South Africa, where there is a booming senior housing industry, called me from Johannesburg to ask me to send information on terms used in U.S. marketing programs.

## Euphemisms for Age-Based Labels Don't Sell

The semantic challenges are not limited to finding labels for people. One resident I interviewed in a seniors' adult community said, "Why can't you marketing people come up with a different name for my community other than a *retirement community*? We may be retired from our jobs, but we are not retired from life."

In the LAVOA study, a large number of respondents disliked the terms *leisure years, golden years*, and *senior citizen*. A woman in one of our focus groups said, "All this trouble everyone seems to be having over what to call us and how to refer to our stage of life reminds me of the scene in *Who's Afraid of Virginia Woolf?* in which Elizabeth Taylor stands up at the faculty cocktail party and says, 'Please excuse me while I go to the euphemism'."

My solution to the challenges of semantic gymnastics is to avoid playing the game. Marketers do not generally refer to nonsenior adults in terms of age-based labels. If we want to target young adults, we indicate that in our ads by showing young models and reflecting lifestyles in graphics, pictures, and narratives that clearly indicate the intended market. I have not found it awkward to avoid age-based labels and symbols that reflect the adverse implications of aging. At times age-based images are appropriate, but even then they can be handled in ways that do not use awkward language and are not offensive to older people.

To draw attention to the kinds of people who live in a particular community in terms of their stage of life, a marketer might refer to the community as one for people who have concluded their family-raising years and who are looking to their next exciting and adventuresome stage of life.

One might describe a community for older seniors, all retired from careers, in promotional literature as being for "those who have wrapped up their career years and moved on to new ways to find meaning and value in life." One might argue, "Isn't it a lot easier and better to use fewer words, and to say, for instance, 'This is a retirement community'?" Older consumers don't mind a few extra words. In fact, they like the extra words, *if* those extra words say something. Unlike advertising to younger markets, in older markets you can use a lot of body copy to describe the product—as long as the extra words are not simply exaggerations. That is one thing older consumers definitely don't like: hyperbole.

Few organizations understand older consumers better than AARP. With more than 30 million members to whom it markets a wide variety of products and services, AARP has the experience to know what it is talking about in Figure 2-2, which tells what AARP has to say about how much older consumers want the facts.

## Why Age Should Be Taken Out of Marketing

This is *not* a book about *senior* markets. There are millions of seniors in this country, but one is hard-pressed to define seniors as a market or even a collection of markets in a way that makes marketing sense. Many people whom we call *seniors* represent enough commonalities that they appear to represent a market organized by age. However, age is more a *correlate* of a given seniors market than a *determinant* of that market. I submit that we all would accomplish more with older people if we generally ignored age *per se* in marketplace communications.

This book is primarily about *maturity markets*. The term *maturity markets* is more accurate than the term *senior markets* because the consumer behavior of older people, especially in terms of discretionary spending, is influenced far more by levels of maturity than by age. Indeed, some attributes of maturity tend to correlate with age, but those correlations are not absolute or inevitable. Classifying people in

# Don't make a long story short.

No. 1 in a series on how to advertise to Mature America.

Give them the ingredients. The warranties. The test results.

Mature Americans are experienced shoppers who've learned from a lifetime of buying experiences. They've bought their share of "lemons." Now they take the time to analyze. Evaluate. They won't make a buying decision based on 15 television seconds. To get the full story, they'll hear you out, reading every word of copy that gives them the straight scoop. Just completed Yankelovich research* shows that 50 and over is as brand-curious as it is brand loyal, with an intense need to know about new products. But don't expect change for the sake of change. These experienced buyers need compelling reasons, the more the better. Modern Maturity Magazine is full of in-depth information that helps Mature America begin new lifetimes. The circulation is 194 million strong and strongly attached to their magazine. For more lessons about America's largest population group and its magazine Modern Maturity, call Peter Hanson at (212) 599-1880.

## Modern Maturity

The beginning of a new lifetime.

*Mature Americans, The Daniel Yankelovich Group, Inc. 1987

A PUBLICATION OF AARP

19.4 MILLION RATE BASE EFFECTIVE FEBRUARY/MARCH 1989

**Figure 2-2.** *Modern Maturity* ad: "Don't Make a Long Story Short." (*Courtesy of Cadwell Davis Partners.*)

**Table 2-2.** Definitions of Key Terms Used in This Book to Define Consumers and Markets

*Ageless Market.* A term referring collectively to the diverse groups composing maturity markets; the aggregate of people in the population for whom perceptions of age have become relatively meaningless in self-definition, lifestyles, and attitudes.

*Mature adults.* People who have attained a level of maturity that places them in or beyond the advanced levels of psychologist Erik Erikson's seventh stage of human development, the *generativity stage,** who have enjoyed substantial fulfillment in the four levels of basic human needs that precede self-actualization in Maslow's hierarchy; and who have entered the third experiential life stage, which is characterized by low levels of materialism and self-service. In summary, mature adults have attained substantially full psychological and sociological development of their personalities.

*Maturity markets.* Diverse markets represented by mature adults.

*Older consumers (persons).* People aged 50 and older.

*Older markets.* Diverse markets whose constituents are aged 50 and older (irrespective of constituents' levels of maturity).

*Senior.* Any person aged 50 or older.

---

*Generally speaking, Erikson's term *generativity stage* refers to one of eight stages in individual personality development when a person's *primary* life activity focus is on investment of his or her capacities in the well-being of future generations. The eight stages are more fully discussed in Chapter 5.

the marketplace by age may be easier than classifying them by level of maturity, but what is easiest is not necessarily best.

Cheryl Russell, editor-in-chief of *American Demographics*, has problems with the way in which the term *mature markets* is bandied about. She accuses marketers of being guilty of "Laziness or ignorance—which is responsible for the sloppy definition of the mature market?"[9] She argues that most people aged 50 to 60 are not mature, but are in a state of upheaval, often with as much unsettlement as those in their twenties. This, she says, is due to the transitional nature of the sixth decade of contemporary American life, when children are grown and gone from the home, careers are winding down, and preparations are being made for life after a career and raising a family.

Russell says, "People in their fifties need specialized products to help them cope with the changes in their lives. They need to experiment with products and services they might use once they reach maturity. This is a threshold most won't cross until 60 or beyond, however. While most

---

[9]Editor's Note, *American Demographics*, August 1989, p. 2.

Americans aged 60 and older are in the mature market, most people in their 50s are not."[10]

While I have included in my definition of *maturity market* those aged 50 and older, Russell is on solid ground in considering most people in their fifties not fully matured. There is ample support in the psychological literature for her position. However, I have set age 50 as the threshold of entry in the maturity markets, with the idea that many people aged fifty are on the cusp of full maturity and begin to demonstrate the characteristics of fully mature people during the ensuing decade.

From this point forward, then, I will *generally* refer to what most others call senior markets as *older markets*, or *markets that include members of maturity markets*. However, whereas the term *older markets* is age-based and thus refers to *all* people past a certain age, the term *maturity markets* refers only to those who have achieved certain levels of psychological and sociological maturity, two key attributes of personality development which are defined in detail later. Nevertheless, the terms *maturity markets* and *mature adults* will generally denote people aged 50 and older who have achieved substantial psychological and sociological maturity, as measured by their position in Erik Erikson's broadly influential eight stages of personality development, and substantial fulfillment of basic human needs, as defined in Maslow's famous hierarchy of basic human needs.

## Not All the 50-Plus Are Members of Maturity Markets

Clearly, not all members of maturity markets are 50 years or older. Some members may be age 40, or even younger, for the consumer behavior of some 40-year-olds emulates that of many people who are 60, and there are some people aged 60 whose consumer behavior resembles that of many people aged 40 or younger.

The net result of defining older adult markets in terms of levels of maturity is to include in the maturity markets universe many adults who, in terms of years lived, are in the age category called *middle-aged*. The marketplace significance of that fact is that some baby boomers (the oldest of whom are now 44 years old) have already entered the maturity markets. Over the next 11 years (from 1990 to 2000), the first 10 years of the boomer cohort will experience nearly 48 percent growth in the 45-to-54 cohort, the fastest-growing 10-year cohort in the entire population.

---

[10]Ibid.

# Make mountains into molehills.

Don't dramatize life's problems, help solve them. Most people aren't problem free and they know it. What they would like to know from you is how you can help them cope with a condition, hurdle an obstacle. Over-50s have lived a lot. If it hurts, they know it. Don't enlarge their fears or trade on their insecurities. Be positive. Realistic. but optimistic. If you're showing people, show them handling the problem, rather than anguishing over it. How can your product help? Be specific. You may want to document your tests, your claims. Case histories of how a product or service has helped others can make your points positively. Developing positive communications with people age 50 and beyond is the purpose of Modern Maturity's booklet "How To Advertise To Maturity." For a copy. and for details on the new Modern Maturity "quarter-circ" plan which makes America's largest magazine affordable to more than the largest advertisers, contact Modern Maturity, 420 Lexington Avenue, New York, New York, 10170. Or telephone 212-599-1880.

## Modern Maturity

The beginning of a new lifetime.

**Figure 2-3.** *Modern Maturity* ad: "Make Mountains into Molehills." (*Courtesy of Caldwell Davis Partners.*)

## Age as an Effective Marketing Tool

In older markets, age is like the coarse adjustment on a microscope: It only gets you into the general range of what you are examining or targeting for some action; you still cannot see what you must to accomplish your purposes until you sharpen the focus with fine adjustment mechanisms. This metaphor deals with *objective* considerations of age. The marketer also needs to deal with consumers' *subjective* perceptions of age, including the subjective perceptions of those for whom age is essentially a nonexistent factor in life. Such people comprise the Ageless Market.

When I use the term *Ageless Market,* I am referring to those members of maturity markets for whom age has ceased to be a major factor in self-definition, lifestyles, and attitudes, by virtue of their having substantially achieved full maturity. While this phenomenon may occur earlier, it generally manifests itself in mature individuals sometime during their sixties, when a person begins to grow in Erikson's eighth stage, the stage of wisdom.

While the idea of agelessness may seem to a younger person to be merely a symbol of denial of age, or even symptomatic of yearnings for lost youth, subjective perceptions of agelessness are not rooted in denials and regrets. Rather, they grow out of a sense of timelessness of all things, including self, in terms of cosmic values.

## Age as a Determinant in Consumer Behavior Is a Non Sequitur

Age should function in market research, and in the marketing to and serving of older people, as a general-direction finder; age should not be viewed as a final determinant of market size, marketing strategies, or activities directed toward selling to and serving older people. If one accepts the idea of age playing this more limited role in marketing, one cannot so readily accept the kinds of generalizations about senior consumer behavior patterns on which marketers thrive. Carried to the next step, one may logically conclude that there is no such thing as a senior market. There are not even multiple senior markets, notwithstanding the descriptive claims of numerous marketing strategists to the contrary. Their use of such pejorative terms as "go-go's," "slow-go's," and "no-go's" serves to perpetuate groundless stereotypes and, incidentally, serves no useful marketing purpose.

In any final analysis, success in the marketplace is inextricably tied to consumers' expectations of the benefits to be derived from goods or services purchased. These expectations are multidimensional, but they are neither defined nor shaped by age factors. Instead, these expectations are shaped by *consumers'* perceptions of need and desire (as opposed to *marketers'* speculations about consumers' needs and desires), by the resources they can allocate to a purchase, and by the consumer's experiential history and level of maturity. Assuming that age is a determinative factor in the consumer behavior of older people leads to the formulation of a classic non sequitur—a conclusion that does not follow from the evidence.

# 3

# The Three Bases of Consumer Satisfaction

## The Root of Marketing Success: Consumer Satisfaction

A client of mine, Gary Solomonson of the Minneapolis-based Sage Company, a developer and operator of senior adult communities and health care centers, practices Tom Peters' "management by walking around" philosophy. On visits to his Sage communities, Solomonson regularly asks one question of residents he encounters: "Do you think you are getting your money's worth?" It is a simple, direct, and straightforward question that tends to elicit simple, direct, and straightforward answers.

Solomonson says that the answers he gets to his opening question and to follow-up questions have given him greater insight into what comprises the bases of satisfaction (or dissatisfaction) of his residents and that those bases are more complex than he once appreciated. He thinks that residents view his direct question as an expression of his honest desire to know their feelings. Were he to ask instead, "Are you happy here?" he believes that he would get answers designed to please him rather than tell the truth. The latter question is a lot like the question "How do I look?" Most people will hedge rather than risk offending the questioner. Solomonson's interest lies in probing for levels of satisfaction to guide his staff in improving operations; therefore he asks the most basic question possible: "Do you think you are getting your money's worth?"

A lot of people in research, advertising, and other fields of marketing who are involved in older markets have never asked themselves the very fundamental question, What *really* will give older consumers the feeling that they are getting their money's worth? I have asked a number of people involved in designing, developing, selling, or operating senior adult housing communities if they would like to live in what they are designing, building, selling, or operating. The response is often very hedged. The truth is that few people understand what *really* will satisfy the older consumer. And when the older consumer rejects a product or service or expresses dissatisfaction, the seller is often mystified.

## Older Consumers' Expectations Are Often More Subtle Than Those Of Younger Consumers

The enduring success of any product or service depends on sustained consumer satisfaction. Likewise, the success of any product or service in maturity markets is directly related to the degree to which it meets the expectations of the target market, or, restated, how accurately the marketers have identified the subtler wants and needs which must be met for members of that market to experience sustained consumer satisfaction. This sounds so obvious that some may gloss over the thoughts without seeing their real import.

Products and services are being designed and released into the marketplace everyday without a great deal of thought being given to the full range of consumer expectations. Many products come on-line simply because competitors have demonstrated that a market exists for the product. Demographics and buying trends are examined in an attempt to define market potential. Lifestyle patterns are studied to gain insights for winning product designs and marketing strategies. A great deal of thought is often given to what cues or symbols in words, pictures, and graphics will entice buyers. But little attention is generally paid to the subtler attributes of consumer expectations of the product that go beyond its functional performance. I propose that these subtleties are of greater significance in maturity markets than in other markets.

## Satisfaction of Consumers Begins with an Understanding of Satisfaction

"*Satisfaction guaranteed!*" is one of the most frequently used phrases in marketing. But how well do marketers really understand what it takes to satisfy a consumer? Obviously, every consumer expects to be satisfied by what he or she has purchased. And just as obvious is the fact that every provider of a product or service wants the consumer to be satisfied so that:

- The consumer creates no trouble.
- The consumer will continue patronizing the provider.
- The satisfied consumer will provide referrals to increase sales.

Seminars and articles on the subject of maturity markets are filled with allegations that senior adult consumers are difficult to satisfy. Recalling AARP's Hal Norvell's comments to me in an interview ("They are not so difficult; they simply know what they want"), I think perhaps the problem lies not so much with older consumers as with the thinking of marketers addressing older consumers. It seems safe to assume that few marketers have learned how consumer satisfaction evolves in the older consumer's mind. In fact, that problem has not been widely identified and solved for consumers of any age.

Surprisingly few marketing programs reflect an understanding of what makes for *fully* satisfied customers. The fact that a product line is successful indicates that consumers are being satisfied, but not that its marketers really understand why.

As long as the product continues to sell, what difference does it make why consumers are satisfied? For one thing, consider why some products that have long been successful suddenly lose popularity. A product which may still work as well as ever may have lost popularity because it is outdated or because it faces more effective competition. In either case, elements of consumer dissatisfaction are involved. When a product loses its capacity to meet a consumer's satisfaction requirements, for whatever reason, the consumer will cease to buy the product.

Better understanding of the makeup of consumer expectations and continued monitoring of changing expectations in the marketplace will equip a company with the knowledge to effectively alter product design and marketing strategies and techniques to accommodate changing markets.

### Paucity of Pragmatic Literature on Consumer Satisfaction

Surprisingly, there is a dearth of research on customer satisfaction. Phillip Cooper, a professor of marketing at Loyola College in Baltimore, claims, "There is a deplorable lack of information derived from in-depth research that shows how customer satisfaction evolves, takes shape, and is maintained. This has been a major focus of my research and of a handful of others in recent years, and we have a paucity of literature to draw from."

Of the relatively few papers available on consumer satisfaction, those coming out of academia often are so replete with strange formulas and scientific terms that it is difficult to break the information down for practical application. Everyday marketers need a few simple guidelines to help them achieve higher levels of consumer satisfaction.

The issue of consumer satisfaction can be addressed pragmatically and simply by studying the three bases from which it derives. These three bases apply uniformly to all ages of adult consumers, giving rise to the Third General Principle of Marketing, the *Consumer Satisfaction Principle*:

---

**THIRD GENERAL PRINCIPLE OF MARKETING**
The Consumer Satisfaction Principle

Consumer satisfaction rests on three fundamental bases by which consumers determine value and performance:

- Functional Expectations
- Social Reinforcement Expectations
- Consequential Experiences Expectations

---

All Three Bases for Consumer Satisfaction have special significance in discretionary purchases. Consumers making discretionary purchases are not usually driven by a sense of need or urgency that might tempt them to compromise their requirements and expectations. Therefore, older consumers, generally enjoying a wider latitude of discretionary purchasing opportunities than younger people, are less inclined to compromise their expectations on a broader basis than those in younger markets. The product may function beautifully, but unless the other two bases of consumer satisfaction are being well served, the mature consumer may become quite dissatisfied with the product.

## Mature Consumers Spell *Satisfaction* Differently

While all consumers employ all Three Bases for Consumer Satisfaction, there are important differences between the way younger and older consumers apply the principles inherent in the Three Bases for Consumer Satisfaction. That point is further elaborated in the more detailed definitions of the Three Bases for Consumer Satisfaction:

---

### SATISFACTION BASIS 1—FUNCTIONAL EXPECTATIONS

Does the product or service perform in a functional manner as represented by the seller and as expected by the consumer?

---

It is not difficult to understand what *Consumer Satisfaction Basis 1* means. If it works right, tastes good, looks wonderful, feels great, or provides the functional performance results the consumer wants, the consumer is satisfied as to performance. If the consumer is not satisfied, he or she may demand a correction of the problem, a replacement, or money back. If not satisfied after making a claim, the consumer may lodge a complaint with a consumer affairs agency or hire a lawyer to seek redress. The consumer dissatisfied with functional performance has recourse ranging from demanding that the provider make restitution ("Money back in 30 days if not fully satisfied") to a variety of legal processes.

We have all read remedies for customer dissatisfaction advertised by providers that at first blush seem unduly generous: "Double your money back," "Return product X if not completely satisfied, but keep your free gift," and so on. However, it seems logical to assume that the seller has studied the ratio of products returned to products shipped and concluded that for many people it's simply too much trouble to return a product or that many purchasers either don't notice or forget about the dissatisfaction remedies. Things are different, however, in maturity markets.

### Mature Consumers Take Warranties More Seriously

Experience shows that members of maturity markets tend to evaluate quite critically the representations of warranties and are diligent about seeking redress when they are dissatisfied. Younger people seem to be less influenced by warranties than mature adults. Moreover, those who have retired enjoy a greater flexibility in the scheduling and use of their time which makes it easier for them to pursue satisfaction of warranties. Notice that I did not say, "Retirees *have lots of free time* to pursue warranty issues." It is a gross fiction that all retirees have "lots of free time." Many report that they are as busy in their present pursuits as at any other time in their lives. What they have more of than younger people is not necessarily time, but flexibility in the scheduling and use of their time.

## Small-Print Warranty Statements Repel Mature Consumers

Because warranties are an important consideration to them in their purchase decisions, seniors tend to scrutinize warranty language more thoroughly than younger consumers. But if the warranty is in small print, the mature consumer, who wants to know what it says, may not read it—and may not buy the product.

Type size is an important factor in successful communications with older people. As the human eye ages, long-distance sight can actually get better, but short-distance sight invariably gets worse because the lens flattens. Type sizes in warranties should not be less than 10 point, and promotional copy is better at 12 point or even 14 point for marketing to people over age 60. By the seventh decade of life virtually everyone needs reading glasses, but even so, many people in their sixties and seventies cannot have their eyesight corrected to 20-20 vision.

There is another reason why warranties for products targeted for older markets should not be printed in small type. The term *small print* has pejorative connotations when associated with a contract or product information. The implication is that if a provider wants to hide something or deemphasize a piece of information, it will be presented in the small-print portion of an advertisement or contract.

An older person may associate small-print disclosures with attempted deception, even if none is intended. It is a case of "The medium is the message." In that context, a negative value is assigned to the type style before the reader has a chance to determine the values reflected in the words. What is at play is a form of communication linguists call *metamessages*, or meanings implied by a statement that transcend, add to, or subtract from the literal meanings of the words used.

## Products and Services May Function Well but Reflect Poor Images

Few consumers will buy a product or service that reflects adversely on their self-images:

---

### SATISFACTION BASIS 2—SOCIAL REINFORCEMENT EXPECTATIONS

Does purchase of the product or service earn the approval of peers and others—*and* avert criticism or loss of esteem?

---

We all know how much adolescents are influenced by *Consumer Satisfaction Basis 2*. Compelled by an unquenchable desire to be part of a group, most adolescents want and buy products and services that provide visual or other evidence that the buyers are part of the group with which they wish to associate or to be associated. Older people do not reflect this behavior so strongly. In fact, many older consumers have become quite immune to this kind of peer pressure, which explains in part why it is difficult to segment older consumers along the lines of defined group behavior. This is not to say, however, that Consumer Satisfaction Basis 2 is inconsequential in its effects on older consumers' behavior. In some product offerings, Consumer Satisfaction Basis 2 is the most important factor, other than perceived value and a sense of need or strong desire. Such products or services tend to be those designed to aid people in curing or compensating for disabilities, such as health care products and services, prosthetics, and retirement housing.

Among older consumers, it is often extremely important to *avoid* identification with a group. And the group they least want to be identified with is "old" people. This desire to avoid group identification is seen nowhere more strongly than in responses to retirement housing. A Roper Organization study in the 1970s found that 95 percent of seniors were not interested in moving to an all-seniors community.

## The Compulsion to Treat "Old" People as Old

An 80-year-old man walks into the sales center of a senior housing community. (Most commonly such a community is called a *facility* in the industry—a most uninviting term! Young people live in "communities," but because there is apparently a social utility in clustering and sequestering "old" people, it is quite a nice paternalistic and bureaucratic thing to refer to those places where we put older people as "facilities.")

Our visitor is greeted by a sales "counselor"—that is what they call salespeople who work in senior housing. Young people are quite up to dealing with salespeople; however, being "old" is commonly perceived as such a handicap of body and mind that the humane thing to do is to repackage the same salesperson as a sales "counselor" before he or she is permitted to go into the sales arena with an "old" person. "Old" people need counseling; young people, despite considerably less experience in buying, presumably don't.

The term *counselor*, in senior adult housing, has a paternalistic ring to it, reflecting a behavioral attitude to which older people are particularly sensitive. A helping hand extended to a young person may be eagerly accepted, but the same hand extended to an older person may be perceived as implying that the older person, *because he or she is old*, cannot competently manage the situation alone.

Such attitudes unwittingly contribute to the positioning of a product in a manner reflecting negative overtones to prospective purchasers. In the example at hand, the product becomes associated with a group perceived as having characteristics with which no one wants to be associated. Therefore, sales counselors often meet with prospective purchasers who, despite the interest evidenced by their showing up, seem ill at ease in identifying themselves with the product.

The 80-year-old says, "I am not here for myself, you understand. I am looking for my sister. [Sometimes it's his mother!] I'm not ready to retire yet." He actually retired from his career about 20 years previously, if he retired at the usual age for a man. "He's lying," thinks the sales counselor. He may sound like Joe Isuzu, but he is simply an older person, tempted by all the benefits he perceives to be available in a retirement community, who nevertheless is a little unnerved by what he imagines the rest of the world will think about his living there. The marketing people haven't made it any easier for him to get over the hurdles posed by the operation of Consumer Satisfaction Basis 2 in making his decision.

## Older Consumers Dislike Products That Advertise Their Limitations

Housing is not the only area in which products run into trouble because of Consumer Satisfaction Basis 2. Some years back, a major baby food producer learned that a significant amount of baby food was being bought by older people who wear dentures. It seemed a natural market. Nearly 40 percent of people aged 65 or older have full or partial dentures. They don't need to be persuaded about the merits of pureed food. Observing this, the company went to work, and a new line of pureed foods for denture wearers was rolled out. It bombed. Apparently, denture wearers felt that people in the store would assume they were buying baby food for their grandchildren, but buying pureed food clearly marked for adults would reveal that the purchaser wore dentures.

In another example, Affinity hair shampoo originally hit the market clearly marked for older women who needed to *improve* their appearance, presumably because of age. Older women did not buy. Instead of abandoning the product, however, the company repositioned the product in ads showing the quiet, mature, special kind of beauty a woman in her sixties can have, and sales rose.

Products and services obviously designated for seniors will generally run into resistance from older markets. Perhaps in the future, as the groundswell of baby boomers fills the ranks of senior America, age will become less of a consideration throughout U.S. society. However, U.S. society has long been indoctrinated with the idea that beauty, vitality, excitement, romance, and a lot of other good things lie exclusively within the province of youth, that to be older is to be branded as no longer in the mainstream. Many older people are repelled by marketing messages conveying such images.

Age is widely viewed as a handicap in U.S. society. Public legislation often couples the two words *elderly* and *handicapped*, as in "for elderly/handicapped persons." According to the First General Principle of Marketing (people do not buy images representing what they are or fear to be, but rather images of what they want to be), as long as *age* and *handicap* remain virtually synonymous, older consumers will frequently shun products and services associated with older people. The operation of Consumer Satisfaction Basis 2 in consumer decision-making processes ensures that.

## Products Older Consumers Seek Most: Experiences

Our behavior is dominated by motivations to achieve "good feelings." We try to avoid experiences that make us feel the opposite. When we buy a product or service, we expect not only that it will perform as represented and not diminish our social standing, but also that it will generate good feelings, as a result of desirable experiences that the purchased item or service may facilitate:

---

**SATISFACTION BASIS 3: CONSEQUENTIAL EXPERIENCES EXPECTATIONS**

Does the product or service have the capacity to serve as a gateway to other pleasing and enjoyable experiences?

---

*Consumer Satisfaction Basis 3* is reflected in a wide array of promotional programs targeted at young consumers. The automobile needed for transacting life's necessities also offers exciting escape opportunities and, if the right one is bought, might lead to some pretty exciting relationships.

Advertisements for beer and harder spirits play more heavily on the product's capacity for assisting social relationships than on how good the beverage tastes. This reminds me of Ogden Nash's famous two-line poem: "Candy is dandy, but liquor is quicker."

The consequential experiences promised to young consumers for buying products and services span the gamut of the romantic, adventuresome imagination. But too often older people are promised stultifying carefree living, dependency-oriented catering, empty full-time "fun," and other experiences that dull the mind or are only for the dull of mind.

## Don't Take the Romance Out of Life—for People of Any Age

Romance is not the private domain of the young. It is a need of all people—if you define *romance* according to its most universal meaning as *adventurous spirit, enthusiasm for life, and relief from the mundane*—a bit of an escape from reality. Romantic experiences are major contributors to an interesting life. Societal attitudes so effectively restrain older people from having such experiences that it is necessary for an older person to be fairly dauntless to seize a share of life's romantic offerings.

Romance, in its narrower meanings, often refers to intimate relationships between people that involve their sexual natures and desires. It is incredible that so many people genuinely believe that gender-based romance and old age are incompatible in "normal" people. Figure 3-1 reflects the views of AARP on the issue of romance and age. AARP's views reflect both its desires to promote more normal and natural views of older people, and the enormous amount of experience with older consumers that its more than 30 million membership represents.

## Sell Experiences, Not Products, in Older Markets

Figure 3-2 is an ad that represents a common principle used in marketing to young people: Sell the product's experiential potential, not the product. I use that ad in lectures to illustrate the kind of creativity found in marketing to young people, but so often lacking in marketing to older people.

First, the obvious strategy in the Hennessy ad is to sell not the product, but the prospect of an enjoyable experience to which the product

# Don't take the romance out of life.

Romance hasn't gone out of their lives, in fact, there's never been more time for it. Weekends aren't always with the kids. Dinner together is no longer a sometimes thing. Long-married couples have time to get acquainted all over again. You may visualize older age as gray, when it's often candlelight. To romance Mature America, understand their love for life. Dinner may be a frozen entrée, but show them enjoying it, and each other. Because they want to look and feel attractive, fashion and cosmetics are as important as they've always been. Travel may be to visit family, old friends, or new places, but always make it adventurous. Romance them, and remember that fantasy can be as motivating as reality. The authority on maturity, of course, is Modern Maturity Magazine, with an incredible 17.4 million circulation that makes it the second largest magazine in America and the fastest growing of the big three. For more insights into Mature America and its magazine, please call Peter Hanson at (212) 599-1880.

## Modern Maturity
The beginning of a new lifetime.

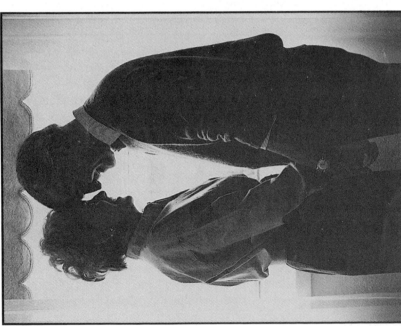

**Figure 3-1.** *Modern Maturity* ad: "Don't Take the Romance out of Life." (*Courtesy of Cadwell Davis Partners.*)

**Figure 3-2.** Ad for Hennessy cognac. (*Courtesy of Hennessy and Schieffelin & Somerset Co.*)

might lead—a romantic evening that starts out before a warming fire. The double entendre in the headline "the civilized way to unwrap" refers directly to the opened Christmas present of Hennessy, but indirectly calls attention to the bare shoulders of the couple.

Presented in full color in the original, the ad is in soft, sepia tones, and the heavy rustic stonework of the walls, suggestive of a cabin, provides the juxtaposition of "a primitive image" with the word *civilized* in the headline. The ad is for romance, not a product; buying (and consuming) the product holds a promise of real excitement.

## It's OK to Show Older People's Skin

After analyzing the ad for a lecture audience, I ask the pivotal question, "Now, can you mentally substitute for the young couple a 75-year-old couple?"

It is a real education in marketing to watch members of an audience respond, "Of course not," "Well, it depends," "Maybe," and "No!" I have seen people in an audience turn to each other and start arguing, for some can envision the substitution, while others cannot. Many object to the idea of even considering showing older people baring their skin. In one audience, a woman said, "Such an idea is demeaning to the dignity of older people." Another woman responded directly to her: "My first reaction to Mr. Wolfe's question was the same, but then I thought, 'The problem (about older people shown in "sexy" poses) is mine, not older people's.' "

I flip to the next slide—a picture of a hot tub filled with a half-dozen clearly older women and men, all bare-shouldered, having the time of their lives. Audience response is a mixture of gasps, giggles, and laughter. I then follow that slide with a picture of an ad for hot tubs that features an older couple enjoying themselves, just to show that some astute marketers have taken the plunge in marketing romance to older people. The point has been made in this interesting exchange with my audiences: A marketer's worst enemy in marketing to older people is often his or her own misconceptions about them.

## Single, Aged 60, and Looking for Romance

Marcella Bakur Weiner and Bernard D. Starr, in 1981, published one of the first major works on sexuality among older adults, *The Starr-Weiner Report on Sexuality in the Mature Years*, a report involving interviews with nearly 1000 older people. Weiner says of the interviews, "There was a flowing of feelings and attitudes expressing a desire for intimacy and romance."

Jim Moore, president of Moore Diversified Services, a market research firm in Fort Worth, Texas, tells of the time when, in a focus group panel his firm was administering, the subject of sex in later life came up. One prissy older woman said, "It's disgusting the way sex creeps into conversations. It's not everything, you know." She was countered by a pert, vivacious woman, who appeared to be in her seventies: "I don't know about that, dearie. I kind of like a tingle now and then."

In *Love and Sex After 60*, Robert N. Butler, former chief of the National Institute on Aging, and coauthor and psychotherapist Myrna I. Lewis write of the presumption that sexual desire automatically ebbs with age: "Thus an older woman who shows ... interest in sex is often assumed to be suffering from mental problems ... older men [interested in sex] become 'dirty old men'. "[1]

Recent studies have shown that it is common for people in their seventies, eighties, and even nineties to maintain an active interest in sex which they act upon. Kenneth Pellitier, in *Longevity: Fulfilling Our Potential*, reports on a number of studies of societies that have unusually high percentages of centenarians. These studies show that two factors are always present in the lifestyles of older people in those societies: *active involvement in their communities* until the end of life and an *active sex life.*

To drain romantic experiences from marketing programs for older people is to remove an important behavioral element of life from the image of older people—a behavioral element they share with all other human beings.

The experiential aspirations of older people extend, of course, beyond the field of romance, however it is defined. If one studies some of the many implications of the Four Faces of the New Senior, presented in Chapter 2, all kinds of ideas about experiential opportunities become readily apparent. Besides their functional qualities, virtually every product and service can act as a gateway through which many paths lead to desirable experiences.

To review the Three Bases of Consumer Satisfaction: The first step to success in marketing to mature consumers is to identify the nature of their satisfaction aspirations according to the generic ideas just set forth:

- The product or service must perform as expected and be backed by guarantees.
- It must not be a source of social stigma.
- It should serve as a gateway to consequential experiences that respond to the consumer's desires. Additionally, by the First General Principle of Marketing, the product or service should be positioned in a way that reflects something of what the consumer wants to be and should be lean on images of what the consumer does not want to be.

[1]As reported in D. B. Wolfe, *Maturity Markets Perspectives,* a marketing newsletter published by the author, Nov.–Dec. 1988.

## The Real Motivator: Life Satisfaction Aspirations

It is axiomatic that discretionary purchases are made by consumers in quest of increasing the satisfaction levels of their lives. Even in purchases that are nondiscretionary but which can be made in an environment of choices, the product or service chosen is selected with the expectation of making at least a piece of one's life more satisfactory for a time. In any event, mature consumers are more oriented to life satisfaction objectives in their consumer behavior than less mature adults.

When only a part of one's life is made more satisfactory over a short time by an experience, the satisfaction may be best classified as *episodic satisfaction*. "Last Friday's party was a blast, but I am now more interested in this Friday's 'episode'. " That attitude is common among younger people who look for an array of episodic experiences. Mature personalities, however, tend to savor their episodic experiences; they can get more from less.

Episodic experiences that center on the moment give us those times that make us happy, but they do not necessarily make significant contributions to our life satisfaction. An imprisoned person may have moments of happiness, but be rather devoid of life satisfaction. Episodic happiness has the transient nature of the mood reflected in the exhortation to eat, drink, and be merry. The flavor is good, but it doesn't last. And as the glee of one moment begins to fade, we soon grow hungry for another such moment. Think of episodic satisfaction as being like a Chinese meal that leaves you hungry an hour later.

When an experience yields a more enduring feeling of fulfillment than episodic satisfaction does, it might be called *ambient satisfaction* because it courses all through a person's internal environment and contributes to his or her personal growth or psychological enrichment. Episodic satisfaction runs down and requires recharging with new episodes; ambient satisfaction endures and adds fullness to a person's good feelings about self and life. A succession of ambient satisfaction experiences leads to the development of the *continuum of life satisfaction* that characterizes the truly mature adult.

### Life Satisfaction, the Missing Focus in Marketing to Mature Adults

This chapter opened with a discussion of the bases of consumer satisfaction with products and services purchased. It closes with a discussion of what I believe is the most compelling motivational influence in discretionary purchase behavior in maturity markets—the quest for an ever-enriched continuum of life satisfaction. The connection between the Three Bases of Consumer Satisfaction and life satisfaction is simple: Within the Consequential Experiences Expectations of many purchases lie an individual's strategies for enhancing his or her life satisfaction.

Phillip Cooper and George Miaoulis, professors of marketing writing in *Marketing Communications*, observed, "While all marketing situations contain a life satisfaction ingredient, that ingredient becomes more pronounced later in life. As people gain more possessions, and have more experiences with them, they come to understand that life is not only about possessions. *Life satisfaction becomes their dominant goal.*"[2]

If Cooper and Miaoulis are correct, then we must admit that life satisfaction has been a missing focus in marketing to older people. When we picture older people in situations that reflect anything but life-satisfying contexts—which prompts so many older people's complaints about senior ads—we clearly are aiming away from what Cooper and Miaoulis assert is seniors' dominant goal: life satisfaction, not "things."

For reasons that are explored in Chapter 5, members of maturity markets are not "thing-oriented," nor are they as purchased-service-oriented as commonly supposed. To the extent that mature adults are interested in things or purchased services, they are generally so for four primary reasons:

*The Primary Reasons That Mature Adults*
*Buy Things and Services*

1. To replace things they already have that are in disrepair or are obsolete

2. To maintain the lifestyles to which they have become accustomed

3. To present gifts to others

4. To gain access to desired experiences made possible by the purchase of a thing or service

Importantly, the fourth reason ties into the Third Basis of Consumer Satisfaction and the First Principle for Maturity Markets, the Gateway to Experiences Principle.

## Retirement Housing That Enhances Life Satisfaction Sells Better

With numerous surveys reporting that well over 90 percent of persons aged 65 and older are satisfied with their current homes, nearly as

[2]P. Cooper and G. Miaoulis, "The Satisfaction Syndrome," *Marketing Communications*, March 1987, p. 36. (Italics mine.)

many with their neighborhoods, and almost as many with the services to which they have access, the market for discretionary senior housing would seem small, indeed. But if a move into a senior community is seen as opening up opportunities for desirable experiences that are not easily available in a person's present living environment, then the person moving in is not buying or renting a home so much as he or she is "renting a seat in the theater." To see a play requires "renting" a seat from which you can see it. Many older people move into a senior adult community, not for the apartment they will live in, but for expanded opportunities for enhancement of their continuum of life satisfaction.

The promises of luxury living set forth in the marketing materials for most senior adult housing are not strong selling points. In most cases, prospects are already enjoying lifestyles with at least as much luxury as promised. Generally, the prospects will be moving from larger homes, with larger rooms; thus the frequent emphasis on "spacious apartments" doesn't make a lot of sense. Such promises and claims invite comparisons in which the existing home will usually come out the winner.

Despite the heavy focus on add-on services (meals, housekeeping, etc.), services *per se* are not the strong selling points commonly believed. Marketing consultant and former advertising executive Gordon French even thinks a surfeit of services may turn off many senior adults. "What you are asking people to do, when you are trying to get them to move into your luxury-services senior adult community, is to make massive changes in their lifestyles within a 24-hour period—the day they move out of the old way and into a new way. I think that has fearful prospects for a lot of people."

French, who has also served as a marketing director for several developers, believes luxury is so oversold that some people anticipate feelings of guilt over unnecessary expenditures. "A lot of today's older seniors are still influenced by the Great Depression," he says.

Older people want to have "feel-good" experiences that involve a great deal more than meals served by others—at times determined by others—and fun and games organized and *directed* by activities *directors* or social *directors*. Marketing programs should show how life-satisfaction enhancement opportunities are uniquely available in the community presented to the prospect. The Gateway to Experiences Principle needs to be more fully invoked than is customary at most projects.

## Life Satisfaction: A Life-Quality Attribute Reserved for Mature Adults

The highest quality of life a person can enjoy is one with deep inner feelings of satisfaction with life. It makes little difference to someone who enjoys the ambient satisfaction of a life that feels whole and right how he or she got there and what it takes to maintain it. The main thing, the only thing of importance, is that he or she got there. More older people get there than younger people.

In *The Pathfinders*, Gail Sheehy reports that out of 60,000 questionnaires probing the issue of life satisfaction, not a single young person attained all five conditions (Hallmarks of Well-Being) that she maintains are characteristic of those enjoying a continuum of life satisfaction.[3] None of those five conditions necessarily involves either things or purchased services. They include having a clear sense of direction in life, a sense of having achieved important goals, overall satisfaction in the way major life crises have been handled, and general pleasure with personal growth and development.

Sheehy's "Hallmarks of Well-Being" may not have been scientifically derived, but they are consistent with the work of numerous adult developmental psychologists who have addressed the subject of the continuum of life satisfaction.

## Neither Age nor Physical Condition Is a Barrier to Life Satisfaction

The clear picture that emerges of people who enjoy a continuum of life satisfaction is that they are self-sufficient, self-confident, able to get over life's rough times in one piece, and comfortable with self, others in their life, and life in general. This picture applies most frequently to people in their middle to upper forties and older, according to Sheehy, whose studies indicate there is no age at which the feeling of well-being decreases simply because of age. In fact, substantial research indicates that as the mature person grows older, he or she gains an even richer sense of well-being, despite the inevitable increase in losses due to illness and death involving friends and family.

Even adverse and activity-limiting physiological conditions are increasingly seen as no hindrance to the growth and maintenance of life satisfaction. Renowned astrophysicist Stephen Hawking, a victim of Lou Gehrig's disease, is all but totally paralyzed, cannot speak, yet is doing more to learn about the origins of the universe than any scientist alive. Many consider Hawking, a Lucasian professor of mathematics at Cambridge (the seat Newton held), to be the greatest scientist of the age, and in the twentieth century second only to Albert Einstein.

Hawking communicates through a voice synthesizer. Words roll across the screen of a computer mounted in his wheelchair, words he

[3]Gail Sheehy, *The Pathfinders*, Bantam Books, New York, 1981, p. 15.

selects with the squeeze of a finger, about the only muscle movement he can make. The computer then activates the synthesizer. Not only does Hawking's brilliance come through, despite his communications obstacles, but so do his remarkable sense of humor and strong evidence of satisfaction with his life. He once asked a reporter interviewing him to get him a cup of coffee, then apologized for the American accent: The synthesizer was made in California. Hawking is an extremely active and productive person in terms of the essence of his being. He just can't express his essence through his body any longer. It's all done with his mind.

Many who consider themselves fully fit in mind and body are too quick to measure a handicapped person's worth and abilities by their limitations as opposed to their productive capacities. Older people with physical handicaps suffer double jeopardy: They are viewed by many as handicapped by both age and physical conditions. But many of these so-called handicapped people, like Stephen Hawking, have remarkable levels of productivity.

In summary, members of maturity markets are strongly influenced in their purchase decisions by perceptions of a product's potential contribution to their continuum of life satisfaction, irrespective of age and physical condition. They expect a purchased product or service to deliver as promised, to reflect positively on them in a social context, and to function as a gateway to fulfilling experiences. However, because of their life-satisfaction aspirations, the last expectation can be more potent than the first two, thus reflecting the importance of the First Principle for Maturity Markets, the Gateway to Experiences Principle, set forth in Chapter 1. To understand that principle, and to be able to apply it creatively, is to be well equipped for success in maturity markets.

# PART 2
# Analysis

# 4

# Profile of
# an All-American
# Family

## New Ways of Looking at Old Markets

In politics, perhaps the more things change, the more they stay the same, but this is decidedly not true of individuals as they go through life. People do change as they grow older, and what it takes to market successfully to people as they change must also change.

### Difficulties in Older Markets Reflect Marketers' Resistance to Change

I firmly believe that much consternation among marketers over the alleged complexities of older markets has to do with inertia, or opposition to change. "If it ain't broke, don't fix it" goes the argument for status quo. What has been working for years in more youthful markets should work in older markets. Just change the age of the models in the ads.

The youth and young family-centered thrust of marketing strategies and techniques employed over the last 40-odd years has conditioned marketers into accepting as universal principles many strategies and techniques that really are best applied to younger markets. Most older people, for example, are not looking to impress their friends and colleagues with the latest model automobile. Most have largely finished raising children and building careers; this dramatically alters the focus

of their needs and desires. Most have satisfied countless materialistic aspirations and enjoyed a vast array of service experiences; this makes
them more temperate and deliberate in their buying. These events dis-
incline older people to repeat experiences and therefore tend to dull
their responses to traditional marketing approaches using urgency, novelty, and peer group-based reasons for buying. Such approaches may
not "be broke," but "they ain't going to work" in maturity markets.

With age, and even more so with psychological maturity, changes occur in needs and desires and in how a person thinks and makes decisions. Therefore, marketers who shift to older and more mature markets must also change perspective. They need to change the way they
think about consumers, and they need to change their ideas about strategies and techniques to succeed in maturity markets.

## Psychological and Sociological Stages Largely Define Consumer Behavior

Later in this chapter I will begin to demonstrate anecdotally how *stage
of life*, expressed in terms of personality maturity, can have far greater
influence on consumer behavior than age of life or sociocultural position in society. By *sociocultural position* I refer to a measurement indi-
cating level of personal development, according to norms established by
general social consensus, such as place in a family-life continuum or
along a career path.

While general social consensus tends to equate age with sociocultural
position, in any final analysis age does not define a person's sociocultural position. A person may be 60 years old but be undeveloped in any
or all of the above sociocultural position categories. The sociocultural
position a person is striving to achieve and maintain exerts strong influences on his or her consumer behavior. As a result, consumer behavior
can be affected much more by factors that are corollary to sociocultural
position.

A person's sociocultural position typically evolves in tandem with both
*sociological* and *psychological* stages of life, stages largely defined by societal expectations. The processes through which a person develops in
response to societally derived expectations are called *socializing processes*. In other words, a person who "fits in" is a person who has become "properly socialized."

A person's ability to become properly socialized is dependent on the
levels and qualities of achievement in various *psychological* stages of life.
Without wholesome development taking place *within* the individual,
wholesome development in a social sense becomes difficult. The central

thrust of this book is predicated on the influence of psychological development of individuals as it relates to consumer behavior.

The anecdotal pictures presented later in this chapter suggest that personality maturity is of previously unrecognized importance in understanding older consumers. By examining the individuals of a hypothetical, but typical American extended family, we will see that age, education, income, and degree of affluence do not exert as much influence on older consumer behavior as reflected in conventional market segmentation practices. I maintain that stages of psychological maturity tell more about a person's later life consumer patterns than any other single factor.

## The Limitations of Lifestyle Typologies in Maturity Markets

Contemporary market segmentation analysis has been greatly influenced by the VALS (Values and Lifestyles) program developed at SRI International (formerly associated with Stanford University) by the late Arnold Mitchell. He proposed that U.S. consumers be classified into nine basic lifestyle groups, and he gave these groups catchy names, such as *Survivors, Sustainers, Emulators, Belongers,* and *Achievers,* and thereby launched a new semantic style in describing consumer groups.[1]

One major database organization has gone further than Mitchell by identifying 49 consumer groups and giving each a catchy name. Others have developed similarly styled consumer typologies and furthered semantic inventiveness with their own catchy labels. Now, when you want ecodemographic data, you order them according to whether you need information on the "suburban blues" (blue-collar workers living in the suburbs), "privileged grays" (affluent seniors), or other consumer groups who operate in the marketplace, wholly unaware that they have been classified with such demographic nicknames.

The idea behind these catchy-name clusters of consumers is that more ponderous research types have already performed psychographic research on various groups of consumers; so the marketer only has to find out how many consumers of a given group live in an area, how old they are, how much money they make, etc. These data are matched up with what they are currently buying and a few other pieces of information from which the interpreters derive opinions that then suggest the best ways to consumer's pocketbooks.

---

[1] Arnold Mitchell, *Nine American Lifestyles*, Warner Books, New York, 1983.

There is general utility in thinking in terms of specific consumer groups according to lifestyle characteristics, but the older the consumer, the less likely lifestyle characteristics are to predict consumer behavior with respect to specific products and services, especially discretionary purchases.

### Seniors Cannot Be Effectively Segmented by Age

Leon Schiffman claims his recent research indicates that, unlike younger consumers whose purchase of one type of product can be used to predict other types of product purchases, many older consumers exhibit a highly eclectic pattern in their purchase behavior, especially in making discretionary purchases.

James Gollub, a former associate of Arnold Mitchell and project director for the LAVOA (Lifestyles and Values of Older Adults) study conducted from 1986 to 1987 for the National Association for Senior Living Industries, averred that the VALS program was of little value in maturity markets, at the time the LAVOA program was launched.[2] The chief defect of VALS in terms of attempts to segment maturity markets, according to Gollub, was its inability to take into account the influences upon older consumer behavior of the times during which they grew up. For example, he, like many others, observes that those who matured into adulthood or lived as young adults during the Great Depression are likely to be more frugal than those who grew up in the affluent boom years following World War II.

Gollub's work in the LAVOA study has led him to classify older consumers into six broad consumer groups, with members of each group having been somewhat influenced by the events and tenor of the times during which they passed from childhood to early adulthood.[3]

*Attainers.*   Youngest, most autonomous, self-indulgent, healthy, and wealthy, with the highest incomes of all the 55-plus population, Attainers are the best educated and second only to adapters in openness to change. They account for 9 percent of the 55-plus population and have a median age of 60.

*Adapters.*   Aware of their needs and seeking ways to meet them, many Adapters are single, demanding, open to change, and highly

[2]Subsequent to the LAVOA study, SRI made major revisions to the VALS program, placing less emphasis on demographic characteristics than in the original program. VALS II is briefly discussed later in this book.

[3]James Gollub, "Six Ways to Age," *American Demographics*, June 1989, p. 20.

informed; on the average, they have the second-highest incomes and the second-highest home values. They represent 11 percent of the 55-plus population and have a median age of 74.

*Explorers.* Rugged individualists, active, willing to forgo assistance from their children, of middle income, have lived 20 years or more at current address, Explorers represent 22 percent of the 55-plus population and have a median age of 65.

*Martyrs.* Turned inward, denying, closed, uninformed about the world, highly conservative, resistant to change, divorced or single, with low to moderate incomes, Martyrs represent 26 percent of the 55-plus population and have a median age of 63.

*Pragmatists.* Somewhat outgoing, middle-of-the-road, cautious but open to change, moderately demanding, likely to be 70 or older, widowed or single, living alone, with moderate or lower incomes, Pragmatists represent 21 percent of the 55-plus population and have a median age of 76.

*Preservers.* Frightened of change, frail, vulnerable people, three-quarters of whom are over 70 years old, likely to be widowed or single, with low income, possibly living in older adult housing, Preservers represent 11 percent of the 55-plus population and have a median age of 78.

## LAVOA Useful in Gross Measurements, Limited in Fine Measurements

By assuming its general accuracy, the LAVOA typology can be used by marketers for estimating gross measurements of various markets according to demographic data. But it is unwise to depend too much on the LAVOA typology or any other lifestyle typology. It would be like having only bricks to build a building; many more kinds of building materials are needed to construct the final structure.

One valuable aspect of the LAVOA study is the way in which the findings were arrayed according to four personality scales:

Independent . . . . . . . . . . . . . . . . . Dependent

Extroverted . . . . . . . . . . . . . . . . . Introverted

Self-indulgent . . . . . . . . . . . . . . . . Self-denying

Most open to change . . . . . . . . . . . Most resistant to change

The use of these scales, along with the grouping of typological types according to more conventional demographic measures, has provided solid evidence for the view that senior markets are not monolithic at any age grouping. In other words, not all "old people" are the same. Figure 4-1 shows how the various typological groups fit on the psychological scales. Note, however, that where a person fits on one scale in no way corresponds with or predicts where that person fits on any other scale. Thus no clear-cut psychological profile can be drawn by using these scales; every older person is a distinct individual who defies attempts at categorization.

Despite the acknowledged idiosyncrasies of consumers in maturity markets which make it difficult to segment older consumers meaningfully, Gollub's typology, combined with his psychographic breakouts, is moving in the right direction. For example, if he is correct in picturing Adapters, who purportedly represent 11 percent of the 55-plus population, as the most extroverted, most open to change, second most self-indulgent, and second from the bottom on the independence-dependence scale, then Adapters would seem to be the primary group to target for senior adult housing, group travel programs, and entertainment.

By similar logic, Attainers, representing 9 percent of the 55-plus population, would be the second most productive group to target for the indus-

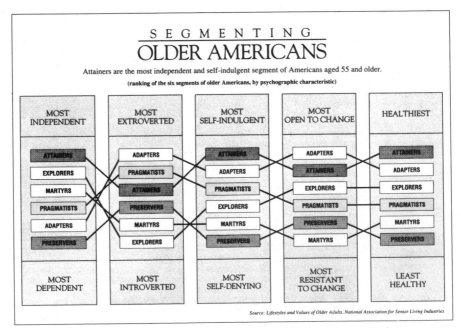

**Figure 4-1.** Selected characteristics of segments in the LAVOA typology system. (*Source: National Association for Senior Living Industries, as reported in* American Demographics, *June 1989.)*

# PSYCHOGRAPHIC
## P R O F I L E

Only two psychographic segments—Attainers and Adapters—have annual median household incomes above $20,000.

**(psychographic segments of Americans aged 55 and older by share of total 55 and older population, median age, median household income, and median education level)**

| | SHARE OF POPULATION AGED 55+ | MEDIAN AGE | MEDIAN HOUSEHOLD INCOME | MEDIAN EDUCATION LEVEL |
|---|---|---|---|---|
| **ATTAINERS** | 9% | 60 | $35,500 | 2 years college |
| **ADAPTERS** | 11 | 74 | 20,500 | 2 years college |
| **EXPLORERS** | 22 | 65 | 9,500 | high school graduate |
| **PRAGMATISTS** | 21 | 76 | 8,500 | grade 11 |
| **MARTYRS** | 26 | 63 | 6,000 | grade 9 |
| **PRESERVERS** | 11 | 78 | 4,500 | grade 8 |

*Source: Lifestyles and Values of Older Adults, National Association for Senior Living Industries*

**Figure 4-1.** (Continued)

tries mentioned. Attainers and Adapters together yield a total core market universe representing 20 percent of the 55-plus population, or about 10 million people. While there is utility in referencing the LAVOA typology, it is well to keep in mind that its psychographic breakout does not reflect level of maturity (the extent of personality development).

## Age Should Be an Index, Not a Definition, in Maturity Markets

Marketers interested in using the LAVOA typology with its psychographic scales should do so more in terms of market strategies based on *experiential segmentation* (defined in Chapter 1) than on the demographic and psychographic attributes of the LAVOA typology. I would also caution against depending on the mean-age figures used in characterizing the various LAVOA typologies for reasons that undergird the Second Principle for Maturity Markets, the *Age-Correlate Principle*:

---

**SECOND PRINCIPLE FOR MATURITY MARKETS**
The Age-Correlate Principle

Age is a correlate, not a determinant, of consumer behavior in maturity markets and hence should not be used in defining and predicting specific consumer behavior of older people.

---

Most of us have unwittingly endorsed that principle when we have described some of the older people we know as "not acting their age" or, more positively, have said, "She thinks and acts 10 years younger than she really is." A *lot* of older people don't act their ages. Better, then, that we deemphasize age in sizing markets and in developing marketing communications.

### Age-Based Thinking Led to a Weak Retirement Housing Industry

Invoking the caveat to be careful in LAVOA-type age-based segmentation constructs, Leon Schiffman says, "Using classical market segmentation techniques in a study of older consumers, one may come up with an analysis that projects a large market for a product, but one that fails to materialize when the product is rolled out."

In the early 1980s, projections were rampant about the tremendous boom in retirement housing on the horizon. Some claimed the market would demand millions of units by the year 2000. But as the 1980s came to a close, project failures proliferated, prompting the explanation that markets were overbuilt. That is true, but that is not the cause of the widespread difficulties in the senior adult housing industry. Researchers relied too heavily on age as a determinant of market demand. Market demand was measured in terms of numbers instead of behavior.

Downgrading the importance of age to the status of a correlate, rather than a determinant, does not deprive age of all meaning in marketing. Correlates are like indices: They have little meaning by themselves, but when taken together with other information, they help you to find out where you are and where you are going.

A look at a typical U.S. extended family reveals how factors other than age influence consumer behavior, especially among older people:

### Lifestyles of Older People Are Often Simple by Choice

John and Mary Erskine, each 68, drive a 4-door Chrysler New Yorker that just turned over 100,000. John figures it's good for at least another 25,000 miles or more with the same good care he has been giving the trusted old car for years. The Erskines also have a newer model car, one they use just for around-town driving, but they like the New Yorker better—it's like an old shoe.

One might think the Erskines are a little obsessed about saving money. Their main TV is a 1978 console model RCA, and Mary always saves $3 or $4 with discount coupons on each trip to the grocery store. As to TV, they don't watch it much; for the most part, news, documentaries and concerts on public television, and some sports pretty much dominate their viewing habits. Neither has a great deal of time for TV. "Other than public television, they don't have that much that is good these days," says Mary. John agrees: "I don't think much of the 'fast food' news approach on the networks—like Rather. I prefer MacNeil/Lehrer."

The Erskines do have a new VCR. One of their favorite pastimes as a couple is to watch the old movies they can't see in theaters anymore. Such evenings bring back a lot of old, pleasant memories. Besides, the old movies don't have all the sex, violence, and bad language of today's movies. "That has a lot to do with all the problems in our society today," says Mary. To her, it seems, "Today's TV shows and movies encourage self-indulgence without responsibility and make the bizarre seem normal."

The Erskines are fairly typical in their attitudes toward produced entertainment. For them, "adult themes" don't mean sex and violence. Adult themes mean information about the world, society, and their communities. This translates into media habits that favor presentations on political, human interest, and practical information such as finance, health, and do-it-yourself activities.

The choice of media for advertising should obviously take into account those media habits, but marketers would be wise to avoid the association of product and service offerings with print or broadcast media heavily oriented to themes that offend older people. Mature adults aren't prudes, but they fancy themselves as having better taste than is reflected in much of today's entertainment.

## The Mature Adult's Search for Meaning in Life

John and Mary discovered in the earlier years of their retirement that there was a limit to the time they could spend in self-indulgent leisure activities. It was not that they tired of such activities; they just had trouble feeling good about how they were spending their time:

Mary recently enrolled in a Great Books program at the local community college. She also spends a great deal of time teaching a literacy program for adults, and she paints and works with art shows.

John has a full schedule, too. He has managed to keep his golf handicap nearly where it was 10 years ago, although he now has to get out on the links at least once a week to do that. That is not always easy to do because of all the other activities in his life. He is an active member of the local chapter of Retirees in Service to Volunteer Programs (RSVP). Recently, John has been spending a lot of time with a local government housing agency, using management skills gained from his years as regional executive of a middle-sized hardware chain, to reorganize and streamline the agency.

### Retirement Is a Kind of Vocational Reorientation for Many

Retirement for the Erskines, as for millions of older people, has meant a kind of vocational reorientation more than it has meant leisure. Apart from the income derived from careers, people use jobs to validate their existence. Many people don't fully appreciate this fact until they retire. For millions of people, retirement ultimately comes to be viewed as providing new opportunities for validation of self. Career-related activities are replaced by volunteer work, personal enrichment programs, and hobbies that sometimes become serious income-producing activities. Older people are often surprised to find their new life-validating activities as time- and energy-demanding as their work was during their career years.

### Imaging Factor: Mature Adults Don't Find Life Meaning in Leisure

Many retirees have difficulty finding ways to validate their existence, and sometimes severe psychological problems ensue. Regardless of income and personal wealth, they are the "old folks" who conform closely to the stereotypical images so familiar to us. And they are the "old folks" who generally are not significant players in the marketplace, except for need items.

Several years ago, I was advising a major advertising company on how to create images that would elicit positive responses from older people. I was addressing the overemphasis on leisure and specifically the trouble some older people have in retirement years extracting a sense of meaning out of a do-nothing life. One bright young person suddenly spoke his mind with great animation: "I see. We are a society where you are what you do. When you retire, you do nothing—therefore *you are nothing*."

Advertising images of senior adult lifestyles which exalt the carefree life of leisure in a continuum of games and play are likely to miss the mark with a large number of older people. Mature adults tend to look at a leisure-dominated lifestyle as synonymous with "doing nothing." In advertising, senior adults could be depicted in purposeful poses and settings instead of in sedentary poses. The former images correspond more accurately to mature adults' self-images. Countless retirees have told me with great pride, "I've never been busier in my life." The most effective marketing of discretionary and many nondiscretionary products and services addresses the pride and self-images of mature consumers as *validated* human beings.

## Spending Patterns of Older People

Beliefs that older people are tight-fisted with money are common. But marketers have observed that the same consumers can sometimes be beguilingly extravagant. John and Mary Erskine reflect such an apparent contradiction of values.

John and Mary are amused from time to time at how their retirement years turned out to be so different from what they imagined in their youth. They had romantically imagined themselves in their retirement years as going everywhere together and being as inseparable as new high school sweethearts. They had images of ending each day together, sitting on the porch of their dream house, talking about their lives, their grandchildren, and the good luxurious life of no cares and few responsibilities.

Instead, they now live in a condominium, are deeply involved in community work, and rarely indulge in the reveries they once thought would be a big part of retirement. But, in a special kind of way, John and Mary are closer than ever. It is the kind of closeness that Kahlil Gibran spoke of in *The Prophet* when he counseled, "Let there be spaces in your togetherness."[4] Their closeness is not the clinging kind of closeness often seen in young people.

They also have noted, with occasional amusement, that despite their very comfortable level of affluence, they spend a lot less money on "things" than they might have imagined they would years before. John used to trade in their car every 3 or 4 years. Now he would keep the old New Yorker for the next 20 years if it lasted that long.

"It's not to save money," John maintains. "They made cars better a few years ago, and besides, they were bigger and more comfortable." Money is not a thing they worry much about, but both are quite frugal in managing day-to-day expenses. That interestingly

[4]Kahlil Gibran, *The Prophet*, Heineman Publishing Co., London, p. 16.

contrasts with the ease with which they will spend $100 in a fine restaurant for a dinner for two, or the more than $10,000 they spent last year on a tour of the Orient.

## Mature Consumers Reflect Declining Interest in Materialism

The Erskines are typical of millions of older people in terms of their lifestyles and values. They are not particularly materialistic. They don't spend a lot of money on themselves relative to their level of affluence, but when they do, they place a higher priority on value than on price. They do spend a lot of time on self-improvement activities and in volunteer work helping others. And they don't spend nearly the time in self-indulgent leisure activities that many younger people might suppose is typical of vocationally retired people.

Marketers of a wide array of non-health-related products and services have historically seen little potential in senior markets. The elder Erskines' lifestyle seems compatible with such a view. Yet financially independent older consumers—about 80 percent of the entire 50-plus population and about 75 percent of the 65-to-80 population—represent huge potential markets for a great variety of consumer products and services.

## The 55- to 64-Year-Olds Are Big Spenders despite Declining Materialism

The senior Erskines, by celebrating their sixty-fifth birthdays several years ago, exited the most affluent 10-year cohort, not only among older people but also among all adults. That cohort is the 55-to-64 cohort. There are over 23 million people in that group, which will grow to 39 million by 2015, a 78 percent increase. It is already a good place for marketers to put their money. Table 4-1 "tells the tale of the tape" for this heavyweight consumer group, in comparison with all older senior adults and with the population at large.

With an average household income in 1984 (the date of the data in Table 4-1) of $22,264, people in this group were ahead of all senior groups in income, with the gap increasing annually. And while this group ranks third in household income (after the 45-to-54 cohort, first, and the 35-to-44 cohort, second), the 55-to-64 cohort has the highest *per capita* income of all 10-year cohorts. One cannot help wondering, after absorbing that fact and the implications of Table 4-1, why corporate America has been so resistant to moving aggressively into maturity markets.

Table 1-1 shows how members of the 55-to-64 cohort spend their in-

**Table 4-1.** How Older People Spend Their Money
(Average Annual Expenditures of Households, in 1984 Dollars)

| | All house- holds | Households headed by older Americans | | | |
|---|---|---|---|---|---|
| | | Total | 55–64 | 65–74 | 75 + |
| Number of persons in household | 2.6 | 2.1 | 2.5 | 1.9 | 1.6 |
| Total expenditures | $20,862 | $17,144 | $22,264 | $15,038 | $10,718 |
| Food total | $3,200 | $2,900 | $3,602 | $2,714 | $1,865 |
| Food at home | 2,300 | 2,129 | 2,536 | 2,027 | 1,518 |
| Grocery stores | 2,164 | 2,029 | 2,412 | 1,929 | 1,462 |
| Convenience stores | 136 | 99 | 124 | 98 | 55 |
| Food away from home | 980 | 772 | 1,065 | 687 | 348 |
| Housing total | $6,284 | $5,079 | $6,195 | $4,562 | $3,767 |
| Shelter | 3,494 | 2,520 | 3,124 | 2,203 | 1,865 |
| Owned dwellings | 2,066 | 1,526 | 2,049 | 1,264 | 939 |
| Rented dwellings | 1,071 | 641 | 633 | 558 | 781 |
| Fuels, utilities, and public services | 1,638 | 1,645 | 1,878 | 1,588 | 1,292 |
| Household operations | 315 | 275 | 263 | 251 | 332 |
| House furnishings and equipment | 837 | 640 | 930 | 520 | 278 |
| Furniture | 270 | 178 | 283 | 119 | 69 |
| Major appliances | 141 | 123 | 166 | 115 | 56 |
| Small appliances/houseware | 62 | 53 | 73 | 49 | 20 |
| Misc. household equipment | 229 | 169 | 248 | 139 | 66 |
| Apparel total | $1,107 | $788 | $1,136 | $657 | $331 |
| Males, aged 2 and over | 285 | 177 | 265 | 140 | 66 |
| Females, aged 2 and over | 447 | 356 | 503 | 307 | 154 |
| Transportation total | $4,264 | $3,226 | $4,435 | $2,926 | $1,409 |
| Vehicle purchases | 1,813 | 1,247 | 1,814 | 1,126 | 364 |
| Vehicle finance charges | 213 | 113 | 188 | 80 | 25 |
| Gasoline and motor oil | 1,058 | 842 | 1,134 | 782 | 386 |
| Maintenance and repairs | 439 | 344 | 448 | 311 | 197 |
| Health care total | $902 | $1,256 | $1,065 | $1,360 | $1,458 |
| Health insurance | 291 | 507 | 329 | 643 | 636 |
| Medical services | 454 | 504 | 524 | 462 | 529 |
| Medicines and medical supplies | 157 | 245 | 211 | 255 | 292 |
| Personal care total | $192 | $203 | $243 | $195 | $139 |
| Personal services, females | 121 | 150 | 172 | 149 | 111 |
| Personal services, males | 66 | 49 | 66 | 42 | 27 |
| Entertainment total | $973 | $674 | $1,008 | $531 | $265 |
| Fees and admissions | 313 | 238 | 312 | 226 | 118 |
| Televisions | 219 | 154 | 204 | 131 | 93 |
| Radios and sound equipment | 91 | 50 | 92 | 24 | 10 |
| Other | 350 | 233 | 400 | 149 | 45 |

*(Continued)*

**Table 4-1.** (*Continued*)

| | All house-holds | Households headed by older Americans | | | |
|---|---|---|---|---|---|
| | | Total | 55–64 | 65–74 | 75 + |
| Number of persons in household | 2.6 | 2.1 | 2.5 | 1.9 | 1.6 |
| Reading total | $132 | $122 | $141 | $123 | $84 |
| Newspapers | 61 | 71 | 77 | 72 | 57 |
| Magazines/periodicals | 33 | 28 | 32 | 29 | 18 |
| Book clubs | 9 | 7 | 9 | 5 | 3 |
| Encyclopedias/other | 3 | 1 | 2 | 1 | — |
| Education total | $286 | $147 | $237 | $74 | $88 |
| Elementary and high schools | 46 | 15 | 33 | 3 | — |
| Colleges and universities | 175 | 105 | 153 | 60 | 83 |
| Other | 16 | 10 | 18 | 5 | 2 |
| Alcoholic beverages | $286 | $184 | $258 | $164 | $ 76 |
| Tobacco and smoking supplies | 227 | 185 | 264 | 166 | 66 |
| Miscellaneous | 295 | 232 | 324 | 174 | 145 |
| Contributions total | $706 | $791 | $874 | $681 | $800 |
| Charities | 73 | 83 | 79 | 78 | 96 |
| Religious organizations | 259 | 303 | 343 | 294 | 241 |
| Educational organizations | 13 | 10 | 15 | 7 | 5 |
| Political | 7 | 12 | 16 | 9 | 7 |
| Personal insurance total | $1,928 | $1,357 | $2,481 | $711 | $225 |
| Life insurance, endowments, annuities, etc. | 300 | 297 | 462 | 229 | 90 |
| Retirement/pensions, Social Security | 1,628 | 1,060 | 2,019 | 482 | 134 |

SOURCE: Bureau of Labor Statistics 1984 ... CEX. © *American Demographics*, September 1987, p. 39.

come in comparison with all other age groups on a *per household* basis. While they rank third and fourth (out of six age cohorts) on a per household basis, on a *per capita* basis they slip into first and second in a number of categories.

### Sociological Life Stage Has Major Influence on Consumer Behavior

Table 4-1 does not show information on the specific purchases made in most of its categories. Also, of course, there are no clues as to the reasons for purchase and the quality of goods and services purchased. Nor are there any clues as to purchases made to maintain lifestyles versus purchases made to enhance lifestyles. These are important factors to research in older markets, because they involve and reflect changes in consumer behavior brought about by changes of life stage.

The Erskines are no longer deeply involved with family and career. Those facts mean that many of their material needs, which earlier made them attractive consumers to a wide variety of providers of "things" and services, no longer exist or are in low ebb. Instead their consumer behavior is motivated much more by purchases they perceive will promote and sustain their inner growth (for example, Mary's college classes, the couple's culturally oriented Far East tour), by purchases they perceive as benefiting others (for example, community volunteer work, gifts for relatives), and by purchases associated with leisure and entertainment activities for themselves and those with whom they have social relationships.

Because the Erskines enjoy full entry into a continuum of life satisfaction, at a time when their desires for things and other self-indulgences have abated, their consumer behavior can appear enigmatic. As consumers, they largely operate on a "take-it-or-leave-it" basis. This makes them and their kind highly unpredictable consumers.

Were they suffering keen dissatisfaction with life, given their affluence, they might become spending profligates, continuously replacing possessions they already have or acquiring new possessions. Instead of an occasional haute cuisine dinner out, they might endlessly splurge in restaurant dining. But like so many of their peers, the Erskines have matured to a point in life, that is, they have entered a psychological stage of life, where the nature of their happiness and life satisfaction aspirations has dramatically altered their spending motivations.

## Inner Self, Not Outer Events, Is
## Source of Life Satisfaction

The inner peace experienced by Mary and John Erskine is a result of the level of psychological maturity they have achieved, not of what they have accumulated financially or achieved socially, or of how well their children have fared in life:

John and Mary have four grown children: John Jr., 47; Alice, 45; Jim, 42; and Peter, 40. John Jr. is a son to be proud of. He is closer to his parents in values than any of the other children.

Alice was always the stereotypical number-two child. "God knows, we tried," says Mary. "She just has to be her own person, as she used to say ... always searching for herself ... still is. She should've had kids ... that would've kept her straight ... but I guess that wasn't her fault. Still, that was a fine young man she was married to. She just didn't know when she had it good. Haven't heard from her in nearly a year. Still looking for herself, I guess."

Peter, the "baby" in the family, has had his problems, too. For a while, he was active in the peace movement and was a minor functionary in Bobby Kennedy's campaign. But he doesn't seem to have gotten much beyond that stage of life. "Bobby's assassination was probably what put him on the path to an unhappy life," Mary says.

Jim, like Peter, was heavily involved in the peace movement, but he kept his head about him and went on to get a law degree and married a fine woman. He's the one everybody talks about when they talk about yuppies. He even has a BMW. He has a good marriage, too, although several years ago he and his wife, Sara, went through some rough times. "Jim was going through his midlife crisis," says John Jr., to which Mary says, "I think they were both going through crises. But thank God they got through them in one piece!"

## The 45-to-54 Cohort Is the One!

In the Erskine family, though only a few years separate each child from the next, their differences might cause one to think they were children of different parents or even of different generations. John Jr., for example, feels little sense of connectedness with his younger siblings; he represents the "old order," typified by his mother and father, far more than the "new order" that arose with the advent of the baby boom generation.

John Jr. is regional marketing director for a large equipment leasing firm. He and his wife, Margo, live in stylish Bethesda, Maryland, on the outskirts of Washington, D.C. They have a very nice home. It was built in the 1920s and redone by John Jr. and Margo 12 years ago. They have a backyard pool, but it doesn't get used much since their youngest, Bob, left for college last fall.

John Jr. and Margo have been talking about selling the house and moving into a condo like Mom and Dad Erskine. "Remember," John Jr. said recently to Margo, "when you and I thought Mom and Dad were really going to miss the old house? Now we are talking about doing the same thing. You know, I think I wasn't happy with Mom and Dad selling the old house *because of me*. It was *I* who had trouble parting with the house with all its family memories. They didn't seem to have any trouble at all."

Margo likes the idea of getting rid of their home. "You know, with the house at the shore and the sailboat to take care of, we really ought to think seriously about simplifying our lives." John Jr. and Margo are *talking about* simplifying their lives—the senior Erskines *have already done it.*

Margo and John Jr. are following the pattern of his parents. In terms of income, Margo and John Jr. are part of the second highest per capita earning 10-year cohort in the population (aged 45 to 54), exceeded in income only by 55-to-64-year-olds. But they are members of the highest consumer products and services spending cohort. (Again, see Table 1-1.) To paraphrase the famous soft drink ad, "This is the one!" This is the cohort that spends more money than any other. And a great deal of those expenditures fall into the category of discretionary purchases. Family "need" expenses are less (except for college expenses), because children are generally grown. The major expenditures to accommodate family and career objectives are declining.

### Those in the 45-to-54 Cohort Are Unpredictable

John Jr. and Margo are becoming very much subject to the principles and factors identified in this book as important in maturity markets. While they are just beginning to think about the life they want to live as retirees, a life heavily directed toward "enjoying the rewards they have earned," the life they end up living will probably be closer in style to that of Mary and John Sr.

The junior Erskines are on the cusp of seniordom. They are still involved in family nurturing (a lot of activity with the grandchildren) and career development, but they are entering a whole new dimension of life. They *feel* as well as *know* that major changes are afoot in their lives. Once again, they are beginning to reevaluate life's meanings. They don't know yet where the inner voices that seem to be gently pressuring for a reordering of priorities will take them, but they have no doubt that things will be different in the future.

The measure of their affluence, their age, and their coming freedom from family and career responsibilities will prove to be no more a predictor of their future lifestyle as senior citizens than it was for the senior Erskines. As with their parents, it is mainly a matter of personality maturity that will determine John Jr.'s and Margo's future lifestyles. They have always planned for the future, but now they plan with an acceptance that the future will probably be somewhat different from their speculations. The idea of becoming older doesn't bother them so much anymore. They are experiencing the first stages of a relaxed attitude characteristic of many older people. They are leaving the "time is of the essence" market. Urgency does not compel their consumer behavior. They are becoming highly discretionary "I can take it or leave it" consumers. They spend a lot of money, but they do it largely outside predictable patterns, except that they are becoming much more experientially than materialistically oriented in their expenditures.

## The Boomers Are Coming;
## The Boomers Are Coming

There is increasing speculation about what the boomers will be like as they enter the ranks of the aging U.S. population. Gerontologist Ken Dychtwald, author of *Age Wave*, a book that sets out to predict where we are going with an aging population, projects that an elderly boomer population will continue to reflect basically the same behavioral characteristics as they reputedly do now.[5]

Numerous speculators on the social developments of our times have presupposed that boomers are, and will remain, at some early postadolescent level of self-absorbed, ego-centered life. In fact, many on the leading edge of the boomers, those born between 1946 and 1955 (give or take a little), in terms of psychological maturity, appear to me to be moving into the ranks of maturity markets as much as 8 to 10 years earlier than previous cohorts. This has enormous significance for not only those involved in maturity markets but also those tied to more youthful markets. Predictions about the character of aging boomers are detailed in later chapters, and there are also analyses of the importance to marketers in maturity markets of the boomers' *current* position in their shifting consumer behavior patterns. But for now, let's take a look at two boomers in the Erskine family:

Mary Erskine talks about Peter, aged 40: "Peter has never grown up. I once thought he might be headed in the right direction, even though I didn't agree with all his thinking. He used to come home, all excited, talking about how Kennedy was going to really change this country. He was really committed. He was going to change things, you know, make a difference. But he had nowhere to focus his ideals after Kennedy was shot. It's as though he decided not to grow up until he could find a substitute for Kennedy. I really feel sorry for him. He was always such a caring child, bringing home

[5]Ken Dychtwald, *Age Wave*, Jeremy P. Tarcher, Inc., Los Angeles, Calif., 1989.

stray dogs and messed-up kids. It's a pity for his two kids that his marriage didn't work out, especially the one who just ran away."

Mary Erskine says about Jim, aged 42: "Jim's the real idealist in the family. Peter thinks he is, but he's done nothing with his life, so I guess he's just an escapist, using his frustrated ideals to explain his failures and unhappiness. He thinks that if the world got better, he would be happier. But Jim, in his own little way, *is* making the world a little better. He does a lot of work for the Legal Aid Society even though he's in private practice, raking it in."

Jim is the quintessential yuppie; Peter obviously is not. Their differences symbolize the error in lumping all baby boomers together in a monolithic fashion, as is done in marketing circles—just as it is done for senior markets.

### Striving Drives Materialistic Urges, but the Mature Are beyond Striving

To understand purchase motivations of mature consumers, we need to recognize a key distinction between their consumer motivations and those of younger adults: The mature adult is beyond striving in the sense of being tied down by career and material ambitions. For example:

Margo and John Jr. have two sons besides Bob: Dan, aged 21, who is still in college, and Jason, aged 25, who is moving ahead in his career quite nicely.

Jason is a contract proposal manager for a large defense industry-oriented software systems firm. He and his 26-year-old wife, Liz, a Harvard Business School graduate, have clear-cut directions for the future. She's more anxious to start her career than to start their family. Liz and Jason agreed to that schedule before they were married. "Babies after 30," Liz had insisted. "I don't want to end up like my mother."

Liz had thought a lot about her mother who, at around age 37, with her youngest at age 12, wanted to break out of the housewife routine. She had helped her husband get through law school and somehow started a family at the same time—before she could establish herself in something. "Mom really went off the deep end. She talked about 'being herself' and wanting to be good to herself for a change. Dad couldn't stand it. I guess he had grown accustomed to the all-American, apple-pie family and didn't want to see things change. Jason, I don't want that to happen to us. I want *something* to go back to after we get our family underway. Poor Mom didn't have that. She's doing pretty well now, but I wish that she and Dad had never broken up. I had a good childhood until then. They took the rest of my childhood away from me."

Jason has gone along with Liz's plans so far. He loves her very much. Besides, they want basically the same things. Having a baby now would delay getting them. So they've decided to get their first house, to have plenty of clothes and good cars to drive, and to generally be able to do what they want, when they want, before being restricted by babies. Liz figures that they should be able to do that in five or six years. Actually, Liz even wanted to delay marriage—just to play it safe, but Jason said that their living together was bothering his parents, plus it really bothered the grandparents. "Just can't understand why young people these days can't hunker down to some old-fashioned commitments to one another," said John Sr., "and they seem to want everything yesterday. They got the idea that they have a God-given right to get what they want, just by wanting it."

### New Interest in Maturity Markets Sparked by Fewer Young Adults

Jason and Liz are familiar to us all. In their middle twenties, they and their age-range cohorts up to their middle thirties have been the primary focus of basic adult consumer products markets for more than a generation—a market that will shrink by 5 million consumers during the next decade. Among all adults under age 35 (18 to 34), the figures are even more dramatic, with a projected total of 9 million fewer consumers. Those simple demographic facts lie behind much of the attention recently being devoted to maturity markets.

The three generations of the Erskine family represent a picture of U.S. extended-family structure and life. They clearly reflect three distinct consumer faces, in terms of sociological and psychological stages. Actually, there are four extant generations involved in this family. John Sr.'s mother, Caroline, is a vigorous 89 years old, still works in her garden, and has two cats and a "divinely ugly Schnauzer," as Mary says. Mary's mother, Charlotte, is in pretty good shape at age 86, but her father, George, has been in a nursing home for the last seven months with poor prospects of surviving much longer.

So there we have it—a family that has it all: old folks, one person in a nursing home, happy new retirees, "model" middle-agers and "mixed-up" middle-aged adults, those suffering from midlife crisis, successful executives and professionals, yuppies—all with things to be proud of, things to be worried about, things to be frustrated about…successes, failures, embarrassments, family skeletons, etc., real American apple-pie stuff.

Neither the Erskine family as a whole nor any of its individual members fit neatly into any lifestyle typology. No member of the Erskine line is a clear-cut typical consumer in any segmentation profile. Each is herself or himself, with no copies. The children, all born of the same parents and reared in the same environment, differ greatly from one another.

The purpose of introducing the fictional Erskine family in this chapter was to impart some flesh and blood to the underlying statistics so excessively relied upon by many in approaching older markets. Also, through the Erskine family, the discussion of the three experiential stages of life in the next chapter may seem less abstract and more real to readers.

# 5
# Becoming a Mature Adult

## The Three Experiential Stages of Adult Life

There are, I propose, three experiential stages in adult life that largely define consumer behavior, especially in terms of discretionary-purchase behavior. They are, in order of their development, the *Possession Experience Stage*, developing generally in young adulthood; the *Catered Experience Stage*, developing generally during the middle adult years; and the *Being Experience Stage*, generally developing in the sixth decade of life.

The first stage is strongly associated with the need to establish identity as an adult, the second with enjoying the benefits of full adult identity. The third stage is a largely antimaterialistic stage in which one's fully formed adult identity metamorphoses into a broader human identity.

When complex issues are defined in simple categories, there is always a risk that oversimplified interpretations will be made. Hence, a caution against simplistic application of the hypothesis advanced in the first paragraph of this chapter seems in order. Human beings are far too complex for a chapter, much less a single book, to provide all the answers to consumer behavior of any market segment. Nevertheless, the thoughts that are developed in this chapter follow the somewhat simple idea that three experiential stages of adult life reflect the combined, highly complex sociocultural and psychological influences on an individual moving toward full personality maturation.

## Stage-of-Life Hypothesis Transcends
## Traditional Segmentation Theory

Each stage works enormous influences on consumer behavior, starting with the first stage when desires for things make consumers highly popular with consumer businesses and marketers. Those in the third stage are often viewed as enigmas by marketers, for even those who have and spend a great deal of money do so with little apparent pattern. They are "tough customers" to predict.

Since the late 1950s, when Wendell R. Smith first postulated the idea of market segmentation,[1] U.S. marketers have increasingly carved out demographically defined niches whose consumer occupants seemed to share similar aspirations and were responsive to similar styles and strategies of marketing activities. In the 1970s, the largely demography-based approach in defining segments was overlaid with psychographic factors which generally correlated consumer behavior with demographic profiles. The term *clusters* was used to describe groupings of people said to share similar lifestyles and values, and the full spectrum of clusters was arrayed in "lifestyle typologies." SRI International's VALS became the premier lifestyle typology system.

Lately, however, more and more has been written about the growing lack of effectiveness of traditional marketing segmentation concepts and strategies as they have finally evolved within the various typology systems. The stage-of-life hypothesis that is the focus of this chapter offers a new way of looking at consumers that transcends traditional ideas about market segmentation.

## The Life Stage Hypothesis Is
## Evolutionary, Not Revolutionary

The idea that consumer behavior is more heavily influenced by experiential stage of life than by age of life is more evolutionary than revolutionary. Stage of life factors are generally somewhat implicit in the lifestyle categories reflected in consumer typologies such as those used in VALS. VALS, as originally developed by SRI International's Arnold Mitchell, focused more on young to middle-aged adults than on older adults. At the time Mitchell developed VALS, there was not much point in looking very far beyond demographics and lifestyle patterns because marketers were predominantly targeting consumer segments whose be-

---

[1]Art Weinstein, *Market Segmentation*, Probus Publishing Company, Chicago, Ill., 1987, p. 3.

havior could be strongly connected to demographic profiles and lifestyle patterns.

In 1989, SRI abandoned the original VALS system and replaced it with a new VALS psychographic approach to segmentation of consumers because of major perceived changes in consumer behavior. A variety of explanations for the changes were given in an article on VALS II in the July 1989 issue of *American Demographics*, including the shifting of the average age toward more mature consumers. The author of the article, AD's national editor, Martha Farnesworth Riche, observed that with the old VALS, "Business found it difficult to use the VALS segments to predict buying behavior of target consumers."[2] Only time will tell if VALS II proves more useful. As in VALS I, there is some implicit recognition of life stages in VALS II, but because they lack clear delineation, their role and influence in the typologies are slight.

## Advertising Giant Discovers Limitations of Age-Based Segmentation

J. Walter Thompson USA recently issued the results of a study it conducted which the company feels strongly indicates that marketers should forget traditional demographics in favor of life stages. Peter Kim, U.S. director of research, says, "As Americans redefine what it means to grow old, age in many ways will become an obsolete marketing concept."[3]

The mean age has increased from around 28 in the mid-1970s to nearly 34 as the 1990s get underway. As previously observed, an older consumer population means a more difficult population from which to predict consumer behavior, especially when one is relying heavily on demographics and lifestyle patterns.

## Life Stage Is a Framework for Predictions, Not a Prediction Tool

The experiential stage of life hypothesis provides a framework for exploring *why* consumers behave as they do, as contrasted with lifestyle typologies that are more focused on *what* consumers do. In other words, the life stage hypothesis is intended to aid in ascertaining the

---

[2]Martha Farnsworth Riche, "Psychographics for the 1990s," *American Demographics*, July 1989, p. 24.

[3]Gary Levin, "JWT Researches Stages, Not Ages," *Advertising Age*, June 26, 1989, p. 30.

foundations of consumer motivation and the engagement of their motivations, rather than to merely observe the final decisions propelled by their motivations.

The experiential life stage hypothesis is not intended as a tool for predicting consumer behavior but rather as a contextual framework within which other factors can be employed to make insightful predictions. The hypothesis deals with the roots, rather than the specifics, of consumer behavior.

## Lifestyle Typologies Do Not Reflect Motivational Factors

What the stage of life hypothesis does that conventional lifestyle typologies fail to do is to define an experiential basis for the lifestyles people adopt at various times in their lives. The hypothesis deals with the origins of consumer motivation at varying points in personality development, as opposed to the typical lifestyle typology, which deals with the results of motivation, whatever its source. These are important distinctions between the hypothesis and lifestyle typologies. These distinctions go beyond the simpler meanings of demographic characteristics, correlated with purchase decisions, that commonly go into defining a given typological group. The life stage hypothesis takes into account that past experiences have a major role in defining aspirations for new experiences, irrespective of income, age, or social position.

## Lifestyle Typologies Put People into Behaviorally Illogical Categories

*Attainers* are defined in the LAVOA (Lifestyles and Values of Older Adults—also developed by SRI) typology as having the highest incomes and being the most independent, the *most self-indulgent*, and the healthiest of all mature adults aged 55 and older. On the other end of the spectrum, *Preservers* are defined as having the lowest incomes and being the most dependent, the *most self-denying*, and the least healthy of the six groups in the LAVOA typology.

According to research conducted by many adult development psychologists, Attainers should exhibit the highest amount of self-actualizing behavior because income and educational levels correlate very strongly with the achievement of self-actualization. One of the characteristics of self-actualizing (or near self-actualizing) personalities is a strong bent for altruistic behavior, the *antithesis* of self-indulgence—a behavioral characteristic attributed to Attainers in the LAVOA typology. By contrast, Preservers—

presumably less likely to become self-actualizing adults—are strong candidates for self-orientation, the antithesis of a self-denying nature, which is attributed to Preservers in the LAVOA typology. The reason is that lower incomes and lower educational levels tend to correlate with lower levels of personality development.

## Income Does Not Determine Degree of Self-Indulgence or Self-Denial

Something important is being overlooked in the broad characterization of Attainers as self-indulgers and Preservers as self-deniers. Self-deniers are found among high achievers, and self-indulgers are found among low achievers (Preservers), as measured by income. LAVOA, like other lifestyle typologies, tends to cluster people who are widely different in terms of the psychological motivations that largely define their consumer behavior.

It seems apparent that Attainers are ranked in the LAVOA typology as being the most self-indulgent in part because they spend the most money, and Preservers are ranked as the most self-denying people because they spend the least money. Well, of course! Attainers have the most to spend, while Preservers have the least to spend. But there are many wealthy people who are exceedingly selfless, even though they spend great sums maintaining the lifestyle to which they are accustomed. And there are plenty of low-income people who are anything but self-denying.[4]

The dependency of lifestyle typologies upon demographic data for consumer type definitions results in the tendency to regard psychographic characteristics as correlates of demographic profiles, rather than the other way around. In other words, if someone is of such and such an age, has $x$ income, has $y$ years of education, and lives in such and such census tract, the presumption is that his or her list of future purchases can be catalogued with sufficient accuracy to make it worthwhile to spend marketing dollars to encourage the consumer to buy certain products. In the first experiential stage of life, which predominantly involves young adults, the accuracy of predictions based on

---

[4]My critique of LAVOA should not be construed as discrediting its value. As founder and first president of the National Association for Senior Living Industries, I conceived of and initiated the LAVOA studies. I felt then that it was a worthwhile effort to undertake, and I believe there is great utility in its findings. However, it is not (and was never intended to be) the definitive word on senior adult consumer lifestyles, values, and behavior. It was my intention that LAVOA become a continuing study program, much like VALS, with each study module providing clues to the design of subsequent modules. However, to date, subsequent studies required to enrich the LAVOA body of knowledge about older consumers have not been performed.

those factors is high enough to warrant expenditure of those dollars on those predictions. But as consumers move into the next stage of life, their consumer behavior becomes more difficult to predict; and in the third stage, it is the most difficult of all.

According to Abraham Maslow's hierarchy of basic human needs, which culminates with the self-actualization level, until a person has significantly fulfilled his or her basic physiological needs, or safety and security needs, he or she will remain quite selfish. People with less income are less likely to have accomplished that and therefore less likely to have achieved a level of personality development that renders them altruistic. Sheehy's research for *The Pathfinders* bears that out. She found that lower-income people are less likely to enjoy a continuum of life satisfaction, a corollary attribute of the self-actualizing (or nearly so) personality.[5]

### Why Lifestyle Typologies Work Best in Younger Markets

Lifestyle typologies have utility in younger markets because such demographic characteristics as age, income, education, gender, and ethnic or racial attributes can be correlated with lifestyles and purchasing patterns in ways that aid in predicting the kinds of products consumers in a given typology might well buy. The younger a market's core group, the more age and other demographic data tend to correlate with *psychological* as well as *sociological* life stage; however, as we will see, an individual's psychological life stage bears less and less relationship to demographic characteristics as he or she gets older.

I am distinguishing psychological life stage, in this discussion, from a person's sociological life stage which involves chronological age, educational and vocational achievements, and family status. *Psychological life stage* refers to an individual's place on the continuum of human personality development potential, for example, according to Erik Erikson's eight stages of human personality development. The conventional lifestyle typologies are primarily more reflective of sociological life stage.

## Defining Maturity for Marketplace Strategies

Lifestyle typologies such as VALS and LAVOA would benefit from deeper psychological interpretations as to why a Survivor is a Survivor,

[5]Gail Sheehy, *The Pathfinders*, Bantam Books, New York, 1981, p. 23.

why an Emulator is an Emulator, and so on. Knowing the whys would address motivations; knowing motivations enables more accurate predictions. If that is so, this knowledge could be very useful in assessing market size for given products and in developing market strategies. Further, in Maslovian terms of how well their basic human needs have been and are being fulfilled, where people fit within a lifestyle typology provides clues about purchasing motivations and proclivities that can be of considerable value to marketers.

## Maturing Personalities Move from Self-Orientation toward Altruism

If levels of maturity influence consumer behavior as much as presumed in the experiential stage of life hypothesis, then it behooves marketers to develop an understanding of the basics of psychological and sociological maturity. Erik Erikson's eight stages of personality development, reflected in Table 5-1, provide a starting point.

The greater the number of strengths a person has developed, the less self-absorbed (or self-oriented) he or she is, a condition that can be inferred from the literal meanings of the terms Erikson uses in his list of

**Table 5-1.** Upward Path to Full Adult Maturity: Erikson's Eight Stages of Personality Development

| Strengths | Dominant period of development |
|---|---|
| Self-oriented development (self-serving): | |
| Hope | Foundations for which are established in infancy |
| Will | Foundations for which are established in early childhood |
| Purpose | Foundations for which are established in the "play stage" |
| Competence | Foundations for which are established in early/middle-school age |
| Outward-oriented development (altruism): | |
| Fidelity | For which the capacity is solidified in adolescence |
| Love | For which the capacity is solidified in young adulthood (ages 17 to 23) |
| Care | Emerges with full force in middle adulthood |
| Wisdom | Emerges full force in late adulthood (sixties or later) |

basic personality strengths.[6] For example, the focus of the first four strengths primarily involves equipping a person for defense and enhancement of self. The latter four strengths have a greater focus on others, the basis of altruism.

Think back to the fourth face of the New Senior, described in Chapter 2: Compassion for others and concern for the world about them. This face reaches fullest expression as the person concludes Erikson's seventh stage, the stage when the strength of Care fully develops, and moves on into the eighth stage when the strength of Wisdom begins to bloom. This is the time when human maturity, reaching its zenith, produces the truly altruistic human being. It is far more a matter of psychological development than a matter of unique conscience.

One of the most significant aspects of Erikson's eight stages is the movement *away* from self-orientation as one matures. This aspect gives rise to the Fourth General Principle of Marketing:

---

**FOURTH GENERAL PRINCIPLE OF MARKETING**
The Altruistic Principle

The younger (less mature) a market, the more appropriate are appeals to self-gratifying interests, while the older (more mature) a market, the more appropriate are appeals to altruism.

---

The Fourth General Principle of Marketing, perhaps more than any other general principle, spells out the reasons why marketing messages that are appropriate for younger markets often do not work well in older markets. It is a matter that involves far more than using older models in ads targeted to older consumers. I can easily conceive of effective ads for a wide range of products directed at older people which use only young people as models. However, in the context of the meanings of the Altruistic Principle, such ads, when directed at older people, should avoid self-oriented images.

The age of the people in the ad does not matter as much as the content and tone of the ad. Think of the several television commercials in recent years that have positioned a grandmotherly type next to a macho sports vehicle in a creative juxtaposition of seasoned tameness and youthful wildness. The marketers clearly could not have been targeting

---

[6]For an easy introduction to Erik Erikson's theories, I suggest a book by Erik's wife, Joan Erikson: *Wisdom and the Senses*, Penguin Books, Baltimore, Md., 1988. Apart from its wonderful readability, in comparison with more scholarly treatments of Erikson's theories, I recommend it because the best way to understand mature adults is to learn about the path they traveled in becoming mature.

the female septuagenarian market. The same principle, applied in reverse, can be effectively used in targeting older markets, where, say, the engaging dependency of an infant is sweetly juxtaposed with the comforting strength of care delivered with selfless wisdom.

Since the next chapter goes into considerable detail on Maslow's theories and their relevance to maturity markets, there is no need to discuss them here. Note, however, that there is no duplication between Erikson's eight stages of human development and Maslow's hierarchy of basic human needs, nor are there any fundamental contradictions between them. The two systems of defining and charting personality development and the motivations involved represent two different views of the same subject. The two systems are, in fact, quite complementary. And I propose that the three experiential stages of adult life simply represent another way of looking at personalities, in this case personalities as consumers or, put another way, consumers as *personalities*, not merely statistics.

## The Possession Experience Stage: The Acquisitive Stage of Life

Given the shrinkage of the younger markets and the knowledge that some 70 percent of the nation's wealth lies with the 50-plus crowd, business is taking increasing notice of older consumers and is now dealing with the answers to the question: How can we take economic advantage of the graying of America?

The answer to this question entails an examination of consumers' motivations as defined by their aspirations. By looking at the motivations and aspirations that operate in younger markets, we can develop questions on whether these same motivations and aspirations prevail in older markets. If they do not, then it is a good bet that (1) certain products will never enjoy heavy success in older markets or (2) certain products have to be marketed differently in older markets.

In seeking how best to approach older markets, a good place to start is to take a longer look at various members of the Erskine family in terms of what they represent as consumers. The consumer activity of the members of each generation is largely predisposed by their respective psychological and sociological stages of adult life and how well they have negotiated, and continue to negotiate, within those stages.

Jason, 25, and Liz, 26, are in their *Possession Experience* years. Having left their parents' nests and begun a home of their own, they want and need a lot of possessions. They need possessions not only to meet the necessities, such as a roof over their heads, cars for getting to work, and clothes, but also to provide visible evidence of who they are and what they have accomplished. They are in the *building and acquisition* experiential stage of life. That stage largely defines their consumer behavior; their consumer behavior defines that stage.

Possession Experience aspirations range from the most mundane (a stylish writing pen, a nice watch, a good-looking shirt) to the quite consequential (a new car, jewelry, or home). They involve the inanimate (things) and the animate (*my* husband, *my* daughter, *my* dog). They involve simple necessities (clothes, furnishings) and embellished "necessities" (fur coats, silk ties). Taken all together, the Possession Experience aspirations of many a younger person would fill the largest of catalogs.

## Possessions Are Signs of Accomplishment and Identity

The Possession Experience years reflect the stage of life when the acquisition of possessions, both inanimate and animate, is the root of consumer behavior. Possession Experience aspirations are strongly linked to the establishment and maintenance of the image (identity) one wishes to project to others.

Some Possession Experiences barely cause a blip in brain waves to register a sense of pleasure and fulfillment, while others cause euphoria to wash over a person. The latter I call *peak Possession Experiences* (examples appear in Table 5-2). Less gratifying Possession Experiences are

**Table 5-2.** Candidates for Peak Possession Experiences

Inanimate objects:
  First car, first new car

  First high-quality sound system

  First diamond ring; a double-the-carat-size new one

  First boat; an upgrade replacement for overnight cruises

  First home (perhaps a rented apartment)

  First house; first move-up house

  First "really first-class" furnishings

Also animate objects:

  First girl friend or boy friend

  First spouse

  First baby (and those that follow)

  First dog; dog's first litter

called *mundane Possession Experiences.* These are most common, and when linked to occasional peak Possession Experiences, they contribute much to an overall satisfaction with the progression of one's life.

Peak Possession Experiences tend to be most potent when they are first-time experiences. Although people in the midst of their Possession Experience years want to repeat such feelings, for most, repeated Possession Experiences inevitably bring decreasing emotional peaks.

People in their Possession Experience years are easier to analyze and sell to than consumers in later experiential stages of adult life. These adults are the most easily quantifiable and classifiable, in large part because most significant possessions desired by young people strongly reflect their aspirations for image projection as well. Since acceptance is an essential ingredient of social success and is vital to vocational success in most instances, possessions reflect consensus-derived values about what is and is not acceptable.

## Possessions Are Metaphors for Who We Are in Our Youth

The time that people spend in the Possession Experience years varies considerably. Some never get beyond them, while others skip over them lightly and quickly, like flat stones tossed across the surface of a pond. A few never experience any significant Possession Experience aspirations. But the vast majority of adults pass through a stage in which their lifestyles are dominantly influenced by Possession Experience aspirations and then move on to another stage.

My speculation is that most people run the course of their Possession Experience years, enjoying significant fulfillment of their Possession Experience aspirations, from the onset of adulthood to around the middle to late thirties. That speculation makes allowances for the fact that some people never come close to fulfilling their Possession Experience aspirations.

Possessions are important symbols of the younger person's being, expressing in visible ways who the person is and what he or she has accomplished. Only in later stages of personality development does a person cease to place major importance on the ability of "things" to speak for them. That is the time in life when a person becomes socially emancipated by feeling, "I don't have to prove anything to anyone."

## Some Never Mature: They Remain in the Possession Experience Stage

With full adult identity defined and other basic material needs generally met or being met, the older mature person is less strongly motivated by aspirations for things. On the other hand, a 60-year-old who continues to have strong aspirations for things may be suffering from an inadequately defined identity and may continue to act as though the person he or she is can be best defined by buying and owning things.

People who never grow beyond the Possession Experience years have probably gotten stuck somewhere at or below Erikson's fifth stage, Fidelity, which develops as a result of achievement of balance between opposing forces: "identity versus role confusion."[7] At whatever age, such people will be self-indulgers along the lines of the I-Am-Me and Emulator lifestyle groups in the original VALS typology.[8] They will reflect many degrees of excessive selfishness and cynicism about life. They will remain *ex officio* members of youth markets despite their age; accordingly, they will never enter the ranks of maturity markets.

## People's Purchases Do Not Reflect Their Level of Maturity

Financial condition, of course, also plays a role in curbing high-potency Possession Experience aspirations, especially when it becomes obvious to a person that his or her income has peaked at a moderate or submoderate level by middle age. But the amount and type of possessions a person has and continues to buy do not determine whether the person is still dominated by Possession Experience aspirations to negotiate life and define or project identity.

As noted earlier, the replacement or upgrade of possessions does not necessarily mean that possessions are the driving consumer force in a person's life. Wealthy people continue to spend a great deal of money on possessions throughout their lives. The issue is this: Is a person more thing-oriented than non-thing-oriented in the more advanced years of adulthood? If still thing-oriented, that person is still operating with the values associated with the Possession Experience years, and his or her consumer patterns will reflect those values to the extent that money is available to support them.

---

[7]Each of the strengths represented by the eight Eriksonian stages of personality development is achieved as one learns to balance opposing, or to use Erikson's words, "dystonic forces." For example, the dystonic forces involved in one's developing the strength of Fidelity could result in too strong an identity leading to fanaticism, or too much role confusion leading to repudiation of self and others. The healthy individual enjoys a flexibly defined identity somewhere between those two polarities.

[8]I-Am-Me types are described in the original VALS typology as very young, narcissistic, and impulsive. Emulators are described as young, ambitious, flashy, and highly subject to disenchantment with life as they fail to accomplish what VALS Achievers accomplish.

### Dominance of Possession Experience Years in U.S. Economy Is Waning

With the mean age of the population rapidly rising, those in the Possession Experience stage are decreasing as a percentage of the total population. This statistic will have enormous influence on the future of consumer industries and the economy at large. Housing, automobiles, and fast foods are three major industries already beginning to feel the effects of the maturing of the population. Very few hard goods industries will ultimately be unaffected. The big question now is, How many industries are prepared for this?

## The Catered Experience Stage: Time for Full Enjoyment of Adulthood

By the time the financially self-sufficient person is well into middle age, at 40 or so, Possession Experience aspirations should be beyond their peak potency and Catered Experience aspirations should be ascending. *Catered Experiences* are those experiences involving the purchase of services rather than things. Doing it yourself is out; having others do it for you is in. Being catered to is often more exhilarating than getting and having things. This is not to say that Possession Experiences do not continue to play an important role in consumer behavior. Rather, the potency of Catered Experience aspirations is greater than that of Possession Experience aspirations in terms of drive and sense of exhilaration.

The Catered Experience years reflect the stage of life when people sharpen their focus on being catered to by others in satisfying their personal, entertainment, and convenience needs and desires. When Catered Experience aspirations become strong, possessions begin to be taken for granted. The *novelty* in acquiring new things has waned, although the desire for things generally continues.

### The Catered Experience Stage Generally Coincides with Mid-Life Crisis Years

My speculation is that most people with reasonably well-developed personalities who have attained a moderate degree of financial self-sufficiency begin to enter the Catered Experience stage around their middle to late thirties, when questions begin to be posed along the lines of "Is this all there is to life?" In other words, aspirations for Catered Experiences begin to grow larger in the "mid-life crisis" years.

The *mid-life crisis years*, a term coined by Erikson, refers to a period in adult life when general feelings of unsettlement arise over one's current psychological and sociological position in life. It is a kind of revisiting of the age-old adolescent quandary over identity, purpose, and life's meaning. It is a time when all aspects of life, including one's relationships with others, are commonly subjected to reevaluation. Marriages often fall apart and careers undergo dramatic reorientation during this period. *Things* remain important, but *life issues* become more urgent. With customarily more financial freedom than the person enjoyed in the previous 15 to 20 years of adulthood, the desire is strong to buy *experiences* that serve self. This direction away from the importance of things continues throughout the Catered Experience years.

### Catered Experience Stage Wanes in Late Forties, Early to Middle Fifties

In our fictional All-American Family, middle-aged John Jr. and Margo are well into their Catered Experience years. They have been steadily fulfilling their Possession Experience aspirations for a number of years. The potency of their aspirations for things has now considerably subsided. That process began sometime in their middle to late thirties. All the children were in school by then; they had moved into their third home, bought a summer house in Bethany Beach, Delaware, had an Irwin 32 sailboat, and all in all had done pretty well in fulfilling their Possession Experience aspirations.

Getting more, or even spending a lot of money getting "better," didn't seem to have the driving force it once had. Margo had been a full-time homemaker ever since the first baby came. Once all the children were in school, she began to feel a kind of emptiness in her life. At the same time, John Jr., who was progressing well in his career, began feeling somewhat the same way.

"All the challenges have gone away, even the personal ones," John Jr. observed on his forty-eighth birthday. A few years earlier, John Jr. and Margo had seemed to be drifting apart, and each wondered if their marriage would survive. Each had retreated from the "couple" existence into a self-oriented period of introspection. Margo, however, finally realized what was happening, did not like the possible outcome, and began to lobby John Jr. for time together. She likened it to dating again.

They began to take vacations away from the family when they were in their early forties. They began to dine out at fine restaurants, and they loved going off for long weekends at resorts. At first such excursions were infrequent because John Jr. seemed tentative about getting close to Margo again. He had very strong feelings about distance and independence, and he felt Margo "closing in on him." But in time they renewed their closeness and began moving toward their fifties with their marriage fully intact and satisfying.

The house at the shore and the sailboat now seemed to be more trouble than they were worth. Earlier in their family life, the boat and shore house had represented good meeting grounds for the whole family. But as the kids got older, the shore house and the Irwin delivered less zing to their spirits. John Jr. and Margo are thinking a lot less materialistically now, and they have long since changed their lifestyles to reflect an emphasis on Catered Experience aspirations. Recently they have been moving together toward a new experiential stage of life.

The junior Erskines have left the years when acquisitions dominated their consumer behavior and served as a major source of life satisfaction. They are in the time of their lives when they are content with variations on old themes of Possession Experiences and elaboration of their lifestyle patterns in new and enriching Catered Experiences. When they buy possessions, they buy quality, but most of what they buy is to replace what they already have, rather than to increase the number and type of possessions.

## Consumer Behavior Is More Difficult to Predict in Mid-Life Years

Apart from necessary food items, basic shelter, and basic transportation, the vast majority of consumer expenditures are for services. This fact translates into considerably more opportunities for buying services than for buying things. With the greater range of purchase opportunities available to gratify Catered Experience aspirations, a consumer has more opportunity to express his or her full individuality. This makes it more difficult to segment and target people who are in their Catered Experience years.

There has been increasing talk in marketing trade periodicals about how much more difficult it is to advertise effectively to today's markets. Reasons given include the overloading of the consumer's psyche because of the amount of advertising to which the consumer is exposed and the greater sophistication of today's consumers because of higher education levels and the fact that they have "seen it all." But much of the difficulty in effectively reaching consumers today is due to the greater maturity of those at the demographic center of the market.

## Markets Have Changed; It's Time for Marketers to Change

For nearly a half a century, marketers have done quite well by directing their marketing messages at adults up to their middle thirties, adults who were predominantly in their Possession Experience years—adults whom marketers have been able to classify, segment, and target. Now that buying power is shifting more toward those entering (and already in) the Catered Experience years, marketers are dealing with masses of consumers who are more difficult to segment, target, and communicate with.

Marketers' frustrations with today's aging adult consumers derive, in large part, from their persistence in using the same assumptions, strategies, and approaches that always served them well when the mean age of the U.S. population was considerably lower than it is now. Marketers have generally failed to take into account that the consumer has changed, less because of better education and marketing message overload than because the "average" consumer is older and more mature. The greater one's maturity, the less materialistic one's lifestyle—a condition that is reflected in the Fifth General Principle of Marketing, the *Individualistic Principle*:

---

**FIFTH GENERAL PRINCIPLE OF MARKETING**
The Individualistic Principle

The more a consumer's Possession Experience aspirations are fulfilled, the less the tendency toward a materialistic orientation and the greater the tendency toward individualistic consumer behavior.

---

The Fifth General Principle of Marketing operates *generally* on the premise that the more experience we have with something that gives us highs, the more we tend to seek highs in new ways. Once one has successfully gratified Possession Experience aspirations, repetitions of previous experiences with *things* tend to engender lower levels of emotional response. A person who is not progressing in maturity, however, tends to try endlessly to reexperience highs through repetitions of previous experiences. As with any addict, it takes ever more to gratify the appetite as the highs become more difficult to attain.

As is true for Possession Experiences, Catered Experiences have both mundane and peak manifestations (see Table 5-3). Unlike many Possession Experiences, however, most types of Catered Experiences are not ranked with similar importance by different consumers. For example, it is safe to say that owning a home (a Possession Experience) ranks uni-

**Table 5-3.** Candidates for Peak Catered Experiences

Season tickets to the theater

A weekend getaway from the kids

A fine meal in a four star restaurant

Tickets to the Super Bowl

A 10-day sojourn on a cruise ship

Someone to tend to the yard (at first!—until the service becomes routine)

The services of an interior decorator

A custom-made dress (combining Possession Experience aspirations with Catered Experience aspirations)

formly high among consumers. However, season tickets to the theater (a Catered Experience) may rank high in value for one person, moderate for another, and of no value to yet another. This diminishment of universal ranking or parity in consumer valuation of purchased experiences is a reflection of the Fifth General Principle of Marketing. This lack of parity is another major reason why those in their Catered Experience years are more difficult to segment than those in their Possession Experience years.

Like Possession Experiences, Catered Experiences can play an important role in defining a person's identity. In a sense, possessions, at least in the earlier stages of adult life, say, "We are arriving." Catered Experiences say, "We have arrived!"

## The Being Experience Stage: The Climax of Human Maturity

With significant gratification of Catered Experience aspirations, questions arise once again for many people: Where am I going? What are life's meanings? Surely, there is more to life than this? Such questions presage entry into the third experiential stage of life, the *Being Experience years*. Commonly, such questions begin to gnaw at people in their late forties to middle fifties. Psychologists report that it is at this time that most people begin to confront the issue of their mortality, not at the onset of "old age." The Being Experience years also see the beginning of the processes that build the central strength of Erikson's eighth personality development stage, Wisdom. Wisdom, he says, is a strength that emerges as a result of the resolution of the polarities—or dystonic forces—of integrity (as in integration) versus despair.

Erikson's eighth stage involves a person's coming to grips with life in a philosophic way that dissolves regrets and enables the person to accept life as a wonderful experience, made more wonderful by the yin and yang of order and chaos, good and bad, joy and sorrow.

## At the Outer Reaches of Human Maturity: The Being Experience Years

After struggling for some time to find a definition for *Being Experiences* that satisfied me, I found a good one in an article devoted to sex and love relationships among elderly people. The article related the feelings, in his own words, of an 83-year-old man who had just fallen in love with an 80-year-old woman. As well as I can remember now, he said something like this:

> I can't believe how I feel. It's like I was 18 years old again. I have the same feelings. I get clammy hands, have had loss of appetite; I get this pit in my stomach; she even makes me kind of embarrassed sometimes when she looks at me a certain way. I guess that means I'm blushing.

Then he went on to say,

> I feel more connected to life because of her. And I feel a stronger sense of reality.

Falling in love is one of the great Being Experiences. It is a powerful metaphor for birth, growth, and productiveness. Nature was most generous when she gave us the capacity to feel what we feel when we are in love. I revised my definition:

> **Being Experiences**: Experiences that tend to enhance a sense of connectedness, sharpen one's sense of reality, and increase one's sense of appreciation for life. In their most emotionally rewarding occurrences, these experiences involve actions benefiting others or actions that contribute to inner personal growth.

Being Experiences may involve the acquisition or employment of possessions, but they are essentially of nonmaterialistic origin. In Maslow's terms, the means tend to be more important than the end, and becoming is more important than being. Being Experiences may involve or be coupled with Catered Experiences, but they do not focus so much on the taking or receiving aspects of Catered Experiences as on the aesthetic aspects (the charming and giving manner of the waiter, the presentation of food as an art form).

## Being Experiences Are Inner Growth Experiences

Being Experiences do not have a self-serving orientation, although they serve the self, especially in the form of enhanced satisfaction with self and life. Let's peek into the thoughts of the junior Erskines:

Of late, John Jr. and Margo have been having some restless stirrings about their lifestyles. They really don't know what these feelings are about, but since the stirrings are not so strong, they haven't bothered to try and figure them out. These feelings are, however, slightly reminiscent of the kinds of stirrings they experienced in their middle and late thirties. "Maybe," John Jr. has thought, "there is another mid-life crisis coming up. Maybe I'm going to go back to what I always thought was an adolescent question, 'What am I going to do with my life?' "

John Sr. and Mary know what those stirrings mean. While they never articulated the meanings as such, those stirrings meant that the Catered Experience years had peaked, and just as with their Possession Experience aspirations three decades earlier, their Catered Experience aspirations had lost much of their potency as the couple moved into their fifties and into their Being Experience years.

John Sr., at the peak of his career as he was entering his fifties, had wondered, "What I am going to do next?" The answers he had come up with were, for the most part, not what you would call career-oriented. But they were not retirement-oriented either. For a while he toyed with the idea of setting up his own business. He even bought some books, took a couple of courses, and talked with a couple of friends about possibly joining forces. Nothing clicked. These stirrings went on for quite a number of years. In the meantime, he began to take an increased interest in working at his church, and for a time he really threw himself into fishing. But still nothing clicked.

## Entry into the Being Experience Years Involves Much Soul Searching

Passages in life are characteristically accompanied by a great deal of introspective thinking about one's relationships with others, with life itself, and with oneself. While the essential values that are a part of a person's unique nature may not change, there can be a substantial reordering of priorities among those values. John Sr. and Mary Erskine reflected the kind of thinking shared by many people at the time of their retirement:

John Sr. took early retirement, at age 61, about the average age in the United States today. Mary and he spent the next year planning an extensive travel program. They sold the old house and moved into their condominium to free themselves. They thought for a while about buying a recreational vehicle, but somehow or other, while there was a bit of romance about it, it just didn't seem to fit the image they had of themselves.

During the year that Mary and John were preparing their extended travel program, John got involved with RSVP, a volunteer corps of retired people. It really energized him. He wasn't making any money doing what, for years, he had been well paid for—using his management skills—but he had never had so strong a sense of fulfillment. In his early RSVP experiences John helped start-up minority firms draw up business plans and develop market strategies.

Mary started taking some writing courses. She had thoughts about combining her knowledge of art and her newly refined writing skills into a book on the effect of the Vietnam war on contemporary art. But the more she thought about that, the more the whole idea of focusing on that period really bothered her. A trip to the Vietnam War Memorial in Washington, D.C., clinched it. Seeing etched in that long, black granite wall the names of the nearly 50,000 dead of a war reviled at home was a deeply moving experience for Mary. She and John Sr. had supported the U.S. involvement for most of the war, and the only artwork she could find of merit was in contradiction with the way they felt about this country and the "poor boys we sent over there without the support of the American people." She sought other ways to indulge her creative energies.

## Leisure Lifestyles Wear Thin for Many Retirees

Older people are so diverse that it makes less sense to attempt to describe *typical seniors* than those from any other adult age group. Still, a common trait seems to exist among financially self-sufficient older people: Most find a life of full-time leisure unsettling.

As John Sr. and Mary moved toward their middle sixties, they found themselves thinking less about playing and leisure as a major lifestyle focus and more about what they might contribute to life about them. "Some retirement!" John Sr. said to Mary on his sixty-fifth birthday. "I am busier than I have been in years." John Jr. thought to himself, "Dad just got into a habit of working so hard all his life, he doesn't know how to break it now that he doesn't have to work." But odds are strong—though John Jr. would probably protest to the contrary—that the day will come when he will follow the same pattern.

It is not all work for John Sr. and Mary. In fact, although their lives are still highly productive, they don't think of what they do as work. John Sr. once said, "If being retired is doing what you want, when you want, then I'm retired. But if being retired means doing nothing but playing, then I am definitely not retired, and never want to be."

## Mature Adults Know How to "Go with the Flow"

With full maturity, a person tends to adopt a more philosophical approach to life. Bob Forbes of the American Association of Retired Persons (AARP) describes the outlook on life of older mature adults as "painted in grays. They don't see things in absolutes. Few things are either all bad or all good. This gives them a capacity for greater tolerance and results in a less stressful existence." Maslow made the same observations and termed mature adults "less judgmental."

The senior Erskines both feel that they are living the best years of their lives in terms of satisfaction with life. They have a good family to be proud of, even though there were some tough times with the boys, and even though two of their children still seem to be struggling with who they are and where they are going. But John's and Mary's focuses in life are not now family-oriented. They are more tied to their current involvements and the plans they have for themselves, both as individuals and as a couple. They are living out their latter years with full and unabashed addiction to a lifestyle oriented toward Being Experiences. "Don't fight life," John says. "'Go with the flow,' as the kids say." John and Mary have learned how to do that—better than any of their kids yet have.

When I tell seminar audiences that mature older people are frequently not family-oriented, I am sometimes confronted with disbelief. But Mom and Dad were family-oriented when Mom was changing diapers and acting as family taxi driver and Dad was taking Junior to Little League! Mature older people regard family as extremely important, but usually do not plan their day-to-day schedules and lifestyles around family matters. The growing hunger for Being Experiences takes the mature adult in many diverse directions, of which family is only one, as important as family may be.

## Everyone Craves and Needs Being Experiences Throughout Adult Life

Being Experiences are something all normal adults desire, regardless of age (see Table 5-4). In fact, each category of experiential aspirations manifests itself throughout life, as indicated in Table 5-5. But older

**Table 5-4.** Candidates for Peak Being Experiences

Heading up a charity ball

Watching a fantastic sunset

Observing a precocious child

Helping a young person master a problem

Completing a carefully planned and executed task

Painting a splendid picture

Getting goose bumps from a piece of music

Having an inspiring religious experience

Learning an exciting new thing (or fact)

Taking joy in someone else's good fortune

Taking great pleasure in the beauty of a restaurant and the presentation of the food (combining Catered Experiences with Being Experiences)

Falling in love

Feeling love for a spouse, child, friend, spiritual leader, etc.

Having a patriotic experience (such as hearing "America the Beautiful" at the opening of the Olympics)

people have a corner on the Being Experience market. Younger people sometimes try very hard to get into Being Experiences and often seek artificial ways to get there. Mind-altering chemicals are one device people use to get Being-Experience-type highs. However, those are not real Being Experiences. While the feelings involved are similar, artificial Being Experiences promote disconnectedness, rather than connectedness; they provide a false reality, rather than an objective one; they promote dissatisfaction (the after-state of an artificial high). And rather than inducing a deep appreciation of all life, artificial Being Experiences are self-oriented—the person's aim is not to benefit others or to grow personally, but to indulge the self. True Being Experiences cannot be experienced through a puff of smoke or a whiff of white powder.

Being Experiences are natural experiences. They are as fresh as a dew-kissed spring morn. They are not sensual equivalents of fast-food service. They exist without regard to time; therefore, there is no motive for getting them fast. They are experiences to be savored. Unlike Possession and Catered Experiences, Being Experiences tend to get better, the more they are experienced.

There is a decidedly strong spiritual quality about Being Experiences that derives from their timeless qualities, their frequently altruistic nature, and their hypnotic command of "more, more, more," like a chant

**Table 5-5.** Distribution of Experiential Aspirations throughout Adult Life

| Possession Experience Years | Catered Experience Years | Being Experience Years |
|---|---|---|

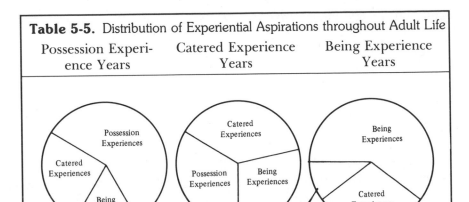

Each category of experiential aspirations plays a role in each of the three experiential stages of adult life. The name given each stage, however, is taken from the category most dominant at that time in a person's life.

The pie charts reflect general order of importance of the three categories of aspirations during each experiential stage, rather than proportionate relationships between categories of experiential aspirations. Proportionate relationships not only are unique to the individual but also vary for each individual from day to day and year to year during an experiential stage.

whose repetition raises one's level of inspiration rather than induces loss of interest and the onset of boredom. Once a person has discovered the world of Being Experiences with his or her whole being, there is no going back to dominance by the more mundane kinds of aspirations. That would be regression, not growth.

Do these descriptions of Being Experiences suggest that they are more sought after and more prevalent among the more mature than among the less mature? Yes, indeed, and their determinative effects on consumer behavior are enormous and complex.

### Big Things Become Small, Small Things Become Big for Mature Adults

After thinking about "big-ticket" Possession Experiences and the self-indulgent excesses possible in Catered Experiences, Being Experiences often seem small in scale. And that is an important idea to keep in mind when marketing to people whose consumer behavior is heavily influenced by Being Experience aspirations, an idea expressed in the Third Principle for Maturity Markets, the Big-to-Small/Small-to-Big Principle:

---

**THIRD PRINCIPLE FOR MATURITY MARKETS**
The Big-to-Small/Small-to-Big Principle

The more Possession and Catered Experiences a consumer has had, the more *things* that once were important decline in importance, and the more *experiences* that once were unimportant become important.

---

The Big-to-Small/Small-to-Big Principle suggests that marketing the same product or service to those in their Possession or Catered Experience years and those in their Being Experience years by using the same messages and images isn't likely to work well, especially if the product or service falls into the category of discretionary purchases. In cars, for example, power is a big thing among those in their Possession Experience years, but a small thing to those in their Being Experience years. Ease of entrance into a car and interior comfort are big things for those in their Being Experience years but small things for those in their Possession Experience years.

The Big-to-Small/Small-to-Big Principle affects the way in which mature consumers ascertain value. Rena Bartos, vice president for communications at J. Walter Thompson, the advertising giant, says her studies disclosed an important difference in vacation travel motivations between younger people and seniors. "Younger people," she says, "tend to travel for escape and romance, while older people tend to travel for mind expansion." Escape travel used to be "big," educational travel was "small." For the mature adult, the values have become reversed in ranking.

According to AARP's Hal Norvell, travel brochures that dominantly emphasize luxury and catered services often are less effective in attracting older people than those that emphasize history, culture, and beauty. Moreover, he notes, "Two brochures—one stressing luxury and services, the other stressing history, culture and beauty—drawn for the same destination at the same time of year when presented to our members produces an interesting difference in the marital status of those signing up. The brochure stressing history, culture and beauty will produce more single people." Also, the older the age group, the higher the ratio of women to men—an important principle for travel industry people to take into account.

The Big-to-Small/Small-to-Big Principle presents a challenge to marketers who are not there yet themselves. People tend to express themselves in terms of their own values, meaning in terms of what is important to them personally. Younger marketers, therefore, must continually evaluate whether what seems to be an important attribute of a product to them would be equally important to a person who is in the Being Experience years.

## Effects of Maturity on Price Sensitivity and Value Assessment

Remember Alice Erskine and her thoughts about "mind-expanding" travel? She's going for the Being Experience aspects of travel even though she probably will never be able to achieve the fullest potential in life-satisfaction enhancement that derives from a lifestyle dominated by Being Experiences. There are too many feelings of regret about life and what it has not delivered. Nevertheless, what really good moments Alice does have often have a strong Being Experience aspect.

To some extent, years lived do predispose people toward certain types of discretionary purchases, regardless of their levels of psychological maturity. People like Alice (in terms of psychological and sociological maturity) tend to be disposed toward products and services that support *inner-directed* and introspective Being Experiences. They are good customers for books, magazines, records, movies, and certain kinds of travel. They generally are poor customers for luxury items, household furnishings, new cars, and upscale service establishments, and they tend to be price-sensitive in almost anything they buy.

### Mature Adults Are Not Heavily Price-Sensitive

People like Alice's mother and father are not nearly so exclusive in their Being Experience aspirations. They have introspective Being Experiences, as Alice does, but they are also strongly motivated by *outer-directed* Being Experience aspirations. That is because sharing and giving have become such an important part of their lifestyle patterns. Mary's and John's community volunteer work evidences their outer-directedness, while their educational and creative activities evidence their inner-directedness.

People such as the senior Erskines are good customers for quality service establishments, better-quality grocery items, occasional fine home furnishings, good-quality clothes, and upscale things they may want to buy. Their outer-directed natures incline them more toward expenditures that involve active sociability. They go to parties, and they give parties. Alice may have one or two people over; her parents will have 10 or 12 or more over. Alice's "fixins'" are usually simple; Mary often serves a tasteful feast. When Alice goes to a social gathering, she is usually in pedestrian attire; when Mary goes to a gathering, she dresses appropriately for the occasion, with a bit of a flair.

John and Mary Erskine are sharp and bright in going through each day, trying to get the most out of each experience. Alice reflects a kind of dullness, with only occasional sparkling days and episodes. Mary and John feel to the core of their souls that they are living life to the fullest. Alice has no such sense of fullness. Her experiences are more flat than laced with enriching emotional relief.

The senior Erskines, with their strong experiential inclinations, reflect a vitally important principle for pricing strategies in any discretionary product or service market, the Sixth General Principle of Marketing, the *Perceived-Value Principle*:

---

**SIXTH GENERAL PRINCIPLE OF MARKETING**
The Perceived-Value Principle

Pricing strategies in discretionary purchases may be based on consumers' tendencies to perceive differences between generic value and perceived value of an offering in proportion to the strength of the desire for experiences made possible by the product or service purchased.

---

Goods and services have a generally easy-to-determine *generic value*, which can be broadly defined as the cost of production, distribution, and marketing plus a profit factor within the range of industry norms. Generic value is supply-side-determined.

Perceived value is demand-side-determined. *Perceived value* represents the margin of difference between generic value and what a consumer feels the offering is worth because of some quality the consumer feels adds value. Because Alice's experiential expectations have become dulled, she is not willing to pay very much for most experiences. But John and Mary Erskine will sometimes come close to being outrageous in what they pay for something. They will pay much more for a marginal difference between *generic* value and *perceived* value than will Alice.

Thus, determination of worth beyond the generic portion of the asking price is highly subjective, depending on each consumer's individual evaluation. Factors that may be taken into account by the consumer in assessing perceived value include:

- *Positive image projection potential.* How well will it project my image as I want to be perceived by others?

- *Operational dependability.* Is it worth the margin of price difference in comparison with competing products in terms of hassle-free ownership?

- *Limited-edition factor.* Since limited editions inflate value, is the offering meaningful enough to me to pay the inflated value?

- *Added quality.* Example: "I can spend half the money at another restaurant, enjoy the meal and get just as satisfyingly filled up; are the service, the ambience, and the food worth the extra cost?"

- *Consequential experiences.* Will my purchase of this offering lead to desirable experiences in any unique way that justifies the price differential between the offering and its generic cousins?

### Mature Adults Are Least Price-Sensitive for Being Experience Purchases

An important corollary to the Sixth General Principle of Marketing is the Fourth Principle for Maturity Markets, the *Being Experience Value Principle*:

---

**FOURTH PRINCIPLE FOR MATURITY MARKETS**
The Being Experience Value Principle

Mature consumers perceive a proportionally greater difference between generic and perceived value when the anticipated direct or indirect results are Being Experiences.

---

AARP's Hal Norvell speaks again: "No group of consumers are any more astute than members of maturity markets when it comes to ascertaining value. They are the Ph.D.s of consumers. Any idea that 'seniors' as a group are tightwads deprives them of their rightful reputation as just plain good money managers. More often than many believe, they choose value over price."

In preparation for an article I was writing, I asked Bob Forbes at AARP for his general opinions on how best to market to senior adults.

He answered me by giving me the quote from John Barrymore, Sr., that I cited earlier:

A man is never old till regrets take the place of dreams.

He went on, "If you show older people how your offering can aid in fulfilling their dreams, you get ready reception; deliver to them what you promise, and you have a loyal friend for life who will pay a good price for what you offer."

Maturity market consumers are generally more liberal in valuing *consequential experience* potential than in valuing any other perceived-value factor. Their *dreams* are more tied into experiential aspirations—more particularly those of a Being Experience nature—than into image projection potential, operational dependability, or other factors of perceived value.

Mary Erskine takes her wad of discount coupons to the grocery store to save $3 or $4 a trip, but she and John Sr. will spend $100 in a very fine restaurant for dinner for two. Recall that Mary and John Sr. have a nine-year-old Chrysler New Yorker with over 100,000 miles that they would like to keep a lot longer, yet they spent $12,000 on a trip to the Orient last year.

The senior Erskines reflect, in their consumer behavior, what Maslow called the beguiling "polarities and oppositions" observed in people whose lifestyles are dominated by self-actualizing experiences—experiences that are synonymous with Being Experiences. Many members of maturity markets seem penurious and profligate at the same time. It is the Fifth Principle for Maturity Markets at work:

---

**FIFTH PRINCIPLE FOR MATURITY MARKETS**
The Price/Value Principle

Consistent with the quality desired, mature consumers tend to place a higher value on price in purchasing basics, but in more discretionary-type purchases, they tend to place a higher value on the potential experience resulting from the purchase. Accordingly, with respect to discretionary purchases, mature consumers generally are:

- Not deeply price-sensitive
- Very aware of affordability
- Highly value-discriminate

---

By *basics* I mean those products and services necessary to maintain the fundamental lifestyle to which the mature consumer is accustomed

Mature consumers reflect a strong proclivity to spending "tightly" on goods and services necessary to maintaining lifestyles and more "loosely" on products and services that *enhance* lifestyle.

Thus, when desire for a discretionary product or service arises, it is more the value, in experiential terms, than price, that makes the mature consumer a prospect, and the consumer's capability of affording the purchase that makes him or her a *serious* prospect.

## Declining Interest in Possession and Catered Experiences Is "Programmed"

The decline in the potency of Possession and Catered Experiences with repetition may have a great deal to do with a tiny unit of the brain called the hippocampus. To introduce a little neuroscience into this discussion, the hippocampus imbues us with an insatiable appetite for novelty and stimulation. Its rather energetic neurons (brain cells) have a habit, however, of falling asleep when they tire of responding to the same old thing.[9] Frequency of experiences (there are exceptions—primarily Being Experiences) tends to breed boredom; boredom breeds appetites for new experiences. Newly defined non-Being-Experience aspirations, like a moth drawn to the flame, tend to seek their own extinction, thus resulting in new boredom. This is a never-ending pattern in human life that is affected not by age, only by levels of maturity.

Recent brain research has provided evidence that there are strong biological forces at play to maintain the cycle of boredom to excitement and back to boredom again, in order to ready the system for a new round of excitement. New experiences must be produced to keep the hippocampus "satisfied"—which means always finding and playing new music to keep it dancing—until the time when Being Experiences dominate the experiential diet of the person, for then the hippocampus becomes self-starting.

The relevance of this short detour into neuroscience, for those interested in doing well in maturity markets, is the explanation it provides as to why mature adults yawn over marketing communications that excite younger adults. As the old saw goes, "You can't fight nature." Ads developed for communicating with the natures of the

---

[9]R. Restak, *The Brain: The Last Frontier*, Warner Books, New York, 1979, p. 28.

young often are out of sync with the different natures of the mature, as determined by psychobiological forces.

## Psychological Growth Continues Long after Physical Growth Concludes

When we think of human growth, we tend to think more in terms of physical growth and years lived, despite our characterizations of some people as having "never grown up." All physical development does cease in the twenties; however, psychological development (growth) for the healthy-minded person continues for a much longer time, certainly well into the sixties. Erikson's eighth and final stage of psychological development is usually entered into in the sixties, and Maslow found the sixties to be the time when self-actualizing adults first made the grade.

The biological brain plays a key role in keeping us on a path of continuing personal growth, a path laid out for us by whatever biological or spiritual powers that guide us, and a path that, if not followed, produces problems for our mental well-being.

Continued dominance by Possession Experience aspirations in later life suggests suspended growth in personality development. Apart from getting the things required for fulfilling basic needs, the purpose of possessions, as discussed earlier, is to serve as symbols of personal, professional, and social success. These symbols should be pretty much in place and doing their communications job by the time one is in middle age. That means it is time to move on to new categories of experiences.

Those who continue to be dominated by materialistic aspirations into and past middle age have problems. They don't understand or accept the limited power of "things" to define their identities, so they keep buying more things—or suffer deep disappointments when they cannot afford to fund their Possession Experience aspirations. These ideas translate to the First Key Factor that operates in maturity markets, the *Antimaterialism Factor*:

---

**FIRST KEY FACTOR FOR MATURITY MARKETS**
The Antimaterialism Factor

Members of maturity markets, by definition of their maturity, are not major prospects for things except (1) necessities, (2) replacements of things they already have, and (3) things that serve objectives other than the desire for symbols of personal, vocational, and social success.

---

The third exception in the Antimaterialism Factor is an important one for providers and marketers of things, especially of the discretionary sort, to study. Mature adults may be low in materialistic aspirations for themselves, but not necessarily for others. To the extent that their financial conditions define prudent expenditures, mature people are great gift givers—husband giving to wife, wife giving to husband, parents giving to children and grandchildren, etc. Gifts may be as small as a charm bracelet with names and birthdates of grandchildren or as large or expensive as a new car for the grandmother or a piano for the prodigy grandchild. The point is thus taken that the Antimaterialism Factor in mature adult consumer patterns does not necessarily mean that mature adults are not significant buyers of things.

To the extent that mature consumers do buy things that are necessities or replacements of things they already have, marketers who are able to position those things as gateways to Being Experiences will fare better than marketers of competing products who focus on the functional attributes of the products. A product's (or service's) perceived capacity for facilitating Being Experiences is an important factor in the mature consumer's determination of a product's value. Recall, for instance, the comparisons between the Depend and Attends ads discussed in Chapter 2. Depend promises to make possible a remaining lifetime filled with Being Experiences, while Attends promises only to handle bladder problems.

Generally the more a product is perceived as contributing either to personal growth (introspective values) or to the welfare of another (outer-directed values), the better the mature consumer's response. In either case, the consumer is being motivated by self-actualization aspirations and processes, a major focus of discussion in the next chapter.

I will close this chapter with two important key factors that reflect the increased influence on consumer behavior of Being Experiences as one becomes more mature:

---

**SECOND KEY FACTOR FOR MATURITY MARKETS**
The Antiselfishness Factor

Marketing messages that focus on the *intrinsic* attributes of a product are less effective in maturity markets, where Possession Experiences are at a low ebb, than in younger markets.

---

In senior adult housing, for example, to focus on floor plans and overall ambience draws yawns from mature consumers. Chances are that they are already living in a home that is at least as luxurious as the one they are invited to rent or buy in a senior adult community. Simple replacement of one package of luxury accommodations with another is not seen as a worthwhile effort.

---

**THIRD KEY FACTOR FOR MATURITY MARKETS**
The Antiluxury Factor
Marketing messages that stress "luxury" or self-indulgent services are generally less effective in maturity markets, where Catered Experience aspirations have declined from their previous peak interest levels, than in younger markets. In making discretionary expenditures, members of maturity markets respond more favorably to products and services that they perceive as facilitating Being Experiences.

---

Those who can afford luxury services are already enjoying them; otherwise, they likely would not have an appetite for the ones being offered, as older people tend not to increase their levels of lifestyle expenditures—they more commonly reduce them. Therefore, if discretionary services to which they are not accustomed are being offered to them, older people are quite likely to look at buying them as wasteful or at least extravagant. In a preliminary report of the LAVOA study, only 8 percent of respondents were reported as feeling that the package of services offered by a senior adult community would be a major inducement to rent or buy.

The Third Key Factor for Maturity Markets, the *Antiluxury Factor*, recalls the First Principle for Maturity Markets, which states that mature consumers place high importance on the capacity of a product or service to serve as a gateway to consequential experiences. The kinds of experiences that are most attractive to mature consumers are those that qualify as Being Experiences. The most successful marketers will be those who know how to associate the products and services they promote with symbols that convey strong Being Experience images.

The Key Factors for Maturity Markets just identified, *antimaterialism*, *antiselfishness*, and *antiluxury* attitudes, reflect the nobler images of highly mature personalities. These attitudes represent the humanistic values that characterize Being Experiences. Symbols used in marketing campaigns which reflect the opposing values—*materialism, selfishness, and luxury*—will often play poorly to mature people, regardless of level of affluence. They are also incompatible with the spirit of the Four Faces of the New Senior (Chapter 2).

In crafting marketing communications for maturity markets, the trick is first to identify the values at play, and then to identify the symbols that best reflect those values. To master this, professionals must first understand how their prospects came to be mature, the subject of this chapter, and just what it means to be mature, the subject of the next chapter.

# 6
# Maslow's Market

## The First Authority on Maturity Markets

Were Abraham Maslow alive today, his presence might be enough to make him one of the most dominant forces in efforts to understand maturity markets. In fact, he may become just that in any event. There are already signs of a strong resurgence of Maslovian theory which is steeped in the massive and intricate subject of human potential. Maslow's ultimate focus, after a lifetime of studying human personality development, was on the mature personality and the process by which one reaches maturity; however, in Maslovian theory, the state of maturity was not the end of the line. The lofty pinnacles of humanness, for those who arrive there, mean a state characterized by continuing progress in deeply satisfying ways, beyond the often painful patterns of continuing personality growth.

Since Maslow's death in 1971, extraordinary advances in neuroscience have provided an impressive amount of psychobiological support for some of his most significant theories, including the idea that mature people cognitively organize reality in different ways from less mature people. That fact leads to much of the consternation marketers feel in dealing in maturity markets: Many older people—those who are highly matured specimens of the species—simply see things differently from less mature individuals. It is almost as though they speak a different language, thus making it difficult for those who do not speak that language to communicate with these older people.

I genuinely believe that the touchstone for success in maturity markets, especially with respect to the marketing of discretionary products and services, lies embedded in Maslow's bundle of theories and hypotheses. To sell to maturity markets, marketers are going to have to learn a lot about mature personalities.

With Maslow's death, much of the life force he imparted to the field of psychology faded. Many came to deprecate his thinking as too simplified in some respects, too complicated in other respects, and overlaid with innumerable contradictions and scientifically unsubstantiated assertions. The truth is that from certain perspectives all those characterizations have validity. But in many respects, those characterizations also mirror the ambiguities, the "polarities and oppositions," to use his words, that marketers have widely attributed to members of maturity markets.

Older people have been observed as being selfish but selfless, rigid but flexible, skinflints but spendthrifts, ponderous but spontaneous, dogmatic but open-minded—along with numerous other polarities and oppositions. *All* these attributes are accurate, according to Maslow. I draw upon his thinking in this chapter to clarify the confusion resulting from such seeming contradictions.

## Understanding Mature Consumers
## Poses Challenges to Young
## Marketers

The riddles of senior markets that have befuddled so many people have a lot to do with what Maslow observed about self-actualizing people, people who have reached the highest levels of human maturity. He proposed that they think differently; that is, they see the world differently from less mature personalities. He said that this different way of thinking resulted in what appeared to less mature personalities as wide-ranging and numerous contradictions.

Maslow confessed to his own earlier inability to comprehend the contradictory behavior of highly matured personalities. By his own logic, this might well have been more related to cognition constraints imposed by his own lesser maturity than to any lack of basic knowledge and intelligence. If that is so, it portends a tremendously significant challenge to many attempting to understand and communicate with older people: Until a person has achieved a certain level of maturity that generally only evolves in middle or later adulthood, a full and balanced understanding of the mature older person is difficult.

This is not to imply that young people can never adequately understand members of the maturity markets. Rather, that it is a considerable challenge that some will master and others will not.

## The Foundation of Maslovian Theory: The Hierarchy of Basic Human Needs

A marketing professor observed to me, "To gain a full understanding of Maslow in your lifetime, you need to pull out his key works about once every 5 years and at least scan them. Only then will you be able to see your own growth in relation to Maslow's ideas in ways that make increasingly more sense of both." For the purposes at hand, it would be worthwhile to review Maslow's famous "hierarchy of human needs." Maslow charted his list of basic human needs, from top to bottom, as follows:

*Self-actualization (full maturity)*
*Self-esteem and esteem of others*
*Love and belonging*
*Safety and security*
*Physiological needs*

He characterized the first four needs levels as "deficit-driven." That is, they are needs for things and experiences the human personality requires to achieve a "fully functioning" (his words) state of being.

### Each Need Area Represents an Area of Dominant Behavioral Influence

While Maslow categorized basic human needs in five groups and established a priority for each in terms of its contribution to growth toward maturity, he never spoke of these categories as a hierarchy. Others coined the term *Maslow's Hierarchy*. The term *hierarchy* connotes a precise order of value ranking and developmental direction which Maslow did not perceive to apply to the discrete behavioral motivations represented by various needs categories. Regardless of a person's level of maturity, he or she is motivated by needs in each category throughout life. The term used in marketing to define the reach of a broadcast station's influence, *area of dominant influence* (ADI), is an apt term for putting Maslow's "hierarchy" in the proper context, one that conforms better to his views of basic human needs in terms of human behavior motivations.

Each Maslovian level of basic needs represents a set of behavioral motivations whose forces for compelling action vary with circumstance and level of maturity. If a person is progressing toward full maturity, there is a time in life when one level would be a *motivational area of dominant influence* (MADI) and a time when it no longer would be.

## Lower-Level MADI Personalities Suffer Identity Problems

Maslow referred to the bottom two needs levels of deficit-driven needs as "lower-level" deficit needs and the next two levels as "higher-level" deficit needs. The distinction drawn is important because many, if not most, adults' behavior will reflect motivations emanating from the MADI of the third and fourth levels in his category of basic human needs for at least half of their adult years. From experiences resulting from that behavior, they will ultimately derive enough satisfaction with self and life to please the spirit, even if they never come fully within the MADI of the fifth level.

Basic physiological needs involve those related to fundamental biological survival and well-being, including food, sleep, and sexual expression. These needs obviously sustain throughout life, and while their potency may subside over time, they cannot be permanently met.

Safety and security needs involve physical safety and security, but extend deeply into a basic psychological sense of safety and well-being. As long as a person feels psychologically insecure, he or she will experience difficulty in achieving a comfortably defined sense of identity. Such people tend to be highly defensive and are suspicious of others to the point that commitments to relationships are difficult. They perceive the value of others primarily in terms of what the others have to give. They either go through many friends or have no real friends at all.

## Some People Are "Frozen" at Lower-Level Deficit Needs MADI for Life

One does not grow beyond lower-level deficit needs MADI by virtue of years lived, but through substantial gratification of the needs of the lower MADI levels. Some cannot make the grade. Conditions in early childhood may have created emotional blocks to substantial gratification which a person may never be able to get around. These emotional blocks are most likely put in place during the first four of Erikson's eight stages of personality development, in which the strengths of Hope, Will, Purpose, and Competence are initially developed. Deficiencies in those strengths, all of which are self-oriented, are generally concomitant with lack of significant gratification of basic safety and security needs.

Adults suffering needs deficits in the area of basic safety and security tend to be pessimistic people (without well-developed capacity for Erikson's Hope): Fantasy often substitutes for true Hope, anxieties frequently substitute for pragmatic realistic judgments. They also tend to suffer from defective Will, unresolved Purpose, and narrowly defined Competence, in an Eriksonian sense. These are the people we call *insecure*.

## Marketing Implications of the Maturity Factor

As consumers, adults who suffer inadequate gratification of safety and security needs may be spending profligates, endlessly trying to establish their identity through images projected by things and fancy services; or they may be socially withdrawn people who spend only for the barest of necessities. Some may spend a lot of money on others, but it is done with expectations of getting something in return. Given to bitterness and resentments, in later life these people can be difficult customers to please.

The life patterns of adults who are stuck at lower-level deficit needs (or at the self-oriented levels in Erikson's stages of development) tend to be confusingly peripatetic; that is, they walk around life in continuous search for life satisfaction and inner peace which are ever-elusive. They frequently move from job to job, relationship to relationship, and idea to idea without ever fixing on clearly defined goals. Others move in an opposite behavioral direction. They fiercely resist changing jobs, no matter how bad the work conditions; they do not enter into intimate relationships; and they become fixed on ideas, compulsively clinging to the status quo, rather than setting and pursuing goals.

In their later life consumer patterns, lower-level deficit needs people become the most difficult consumers to sell to, for they are rarely sure of what they really want or they are totally resistant to anything they perceive as less than perfect according to their close-minded perceptions. To use the labels of the LAVOA and VALS II typologies, these people will not be found in great numbers among Attainers or Achievers. Although many may be reasonably affluent—some even rich—their numbers will generally be greater as one descends the socioeconomic ladder. Marketers can estimate lower-level MADI consumers' physical location and numbers through probability estimates that are, in part, based upon conventional demographic data, sales management data, and lifestyle reports.

## Lower-Level MADI People Tend to Seek Out Like Types

During the 1970s and early 1980s, I owned a company that managed communities with condominium and homeowner associations. In the 12 years that I owned the company, we set up or managed more than 400 communities in more than 30 states. This experience with communities representing more than 600,000 homes provided unique opportunities to learn about people and their behavior in their primary living environments.

Over time I learned that communities reflect personalities, much as individuals do. There are wholesome, stable, and mature community personalities, on one hand, and there are disturbed, immature, and neurotic community personalities on the other hand. Levels of income and social position reflected in communities were not necessarily indicative of the nature of the psychological profile of a community's personality.

In one middle-class community containing over 900 homes, there were a fair number of retired lower-grade military officers along with a large number of middle-aged supervisory white-collar workers. There were few people who had achieved relatively high positions within their respective fields. You could easily imagine a lot of the community's residents having strong feelings that life was passing, or had passed, them by. This was a community of people who had inched upward in their careers, but never made it to the decision-making level, and many felt cheated in life.

The attitudes of individual personalities in that community contributed to the nature of the community personality. We found that community extremely difficult to manage. The board of directors seemingly could not be satisfied, no matter how much time and attention were devoted to the community's management requirements. Complaints from homeowners were more frequent than normal. Discontent seemed to be the preferred mood of the community's inhabitants.

I could discuss in great detail the individual personalities of many of the communities that my company managed, but they appeared to have one thing in common: Considerable support for the idea that among humans, "Birds of a feather flock together." I found that architectural design, the land plan layout of the community, a community's location in the region, and the marketing program all were factors in pre-selecting an aggregation of people who widely shared certain major personality traits.

## It Costs More to Market to Lower-Level MADI Consumers

I have concluded from my experiences in community management that researchers can locate target markets somewhat according to the prevailing levels of maturity, especially when targeting a local market, because people tend to aggregate with others similar to themselves. The ability to identify and characterize target markets on this basis can be of great value both in saving marketing dollars and in getting the optimum return from marketing dollars spent.

In targeting older consumers at lower MADI levels, marketers should be aware that greater costs of penetration are likely and effective strategies will be different from those that work in other markets whose constituents operate at a higher level of basic needs. For example, for older people frozen at lower MADI levels, Being Experiences will probably not significantly influence their consumer behavior. However, lower MADI consumers are more subject to appeals to their fantasies. They respond to the loud, the weirdly unusual, and claims of extraordinariness. Many prefer *National Enquirer* to *National Geographic*, although there are a number of more scholarly low MADI consumers as well.

It is perhaps no coincidence, in this context, that there are higher sales of state lottery tickets to the demographic groups who have the highest percentage of lower MADI consumers who can least afford highly speculative outlays of money. Unfortunately, these people are also most subject to being taken advantage of by those who seek unconscionable exploitation of others. Fantasyland is the domain where con artists do their work.

## Older Adults at Higher MADI Levels Represent Richer Markets

A person who has had substantial fulfillment at the next Maslovian level—love and belonging needs—tends to be on a more even keel in life and tends to follow more consistent behavioral patterns without being obsessively compulsive. Such people have true romance in their souls rather than escapist fantasy. They are less tempted by the outlandish, although they can be outlandish on occasion. They are more realistic, in a pragmatic way, than those who operate at a lower MADI level; therefore, it is more difficult to dupe them. In advertising and in sales conversations, they prefer facts to hyperbole.

The need for self-esteem and the esteem of others, the fourth Maslovian level, involves introspective evaluations of self and the evaluations of others about one's worth. People with a healthy self-esteem, who both understand and like themselves, understand and like other people in general. They have a positive outlook on life and make allowances for weaknesses in themselves and others—including providers of products and services.

Markets that comprise more highly matured older people are generally easier markets in which to work; their higher levels of education and greater affluence tend to correlate with high levels of a sense of overall well-being. While their expectations can be high, they know it is not a perfect world, nor they, perfect creatures within it.

## Dealing with the Mature Personality

By self-actualization, Maslow meant a level of maturity in which a person is beyond striving, beyond basic psychological fears, beyond a need to demonstrate who he or she is, beyond shaping his or her own life largely around the expectations and views of others. It is a stage of life where a person is "being all he or she can be." Fortunately for marketers, few people ever reach a full state of self-actualization, since self-actualized adults tend to be quite nonmaterialistic and have relatively low interest in luxury living. In any event, Maslow reported that he rarely found anyone younger than age 60 who qualified as a self-actualized personality.

Despite the rarity of the self-actualized individual, most older adults acquire many of the personality attributes associated with those who have reached what Maslow called "the farthest reaches of human nature." It thus behooves marketers—and all others interested in understanding older people—to learn about the characteristics of fully or nearly fully matured adults.

### Inexperience with Mature Adults Accounts for Maturity Market Problems

In thinking about all the frequently discussed challenges posed by maturity markets, it is important to remember that the vast amount of well-researched marketing experience accumulated over the last half century has overwhelmingly centered on consumers under age 50, with most of that involving adults under age 40 and their adolescent offspring. Maturity markets are perceived as more difficult than other markets largely because they are not well understood, rather than because they are inherently more problematic. In the past, buyers from that group have generally represented "gravy" to marketers of products more directly targeted to younger consumers. Accordingly, U.S. business has had little in-depth, well-studied experience with mature consumers.

Once the life-perspectives of mature adults are understood, it is easier to develop marketing strategies and communications. Those life-perspectives are heavily drawn from the behavior motivation ADI of the fifth level of basic human needs, self-actualization.

## Mature Adults Are Growth-Oriented, Not Deficit Need–Oriented

Self-actualization motivations are not directed toward compensating for deficits, as is true of the lower needs levels, but are directed toward increased richness and growth in a life that now has few deficits, relative to their number and motivational power in earlier years. Inspiration, not hunger, now motivates behavior. Action-motivating emptiness gives way to action driven by gratitude for the experience of a life with a persistent sense of fulfillment. Beauty is seen everywhere. The emotions abound in good feelings, continuously delivering life's finest ecstasies. And there is a strong desire to share this bounty with others. (Review the Four Faces of the New Senior in Chapter 2.) That desire grows out of the strengthened sense of connectedness that mature people feel toward the rest of existence.

Think of some great experience that you have had that made you almost burst with the desire to share it with others so that they, too, could have the same uplifting feelings. When you have had such an experience, it enhances your sense of connectedness with others, which is what makes you want so fervently to share the experience with others. Such feelings occur frequently for highly matured people. Simultaneous with the feelings of detachment which derive from a sense of their uniqueness, they experience the opposing feeling of strong connectedness with others and the world in which they live.

Upon entering a self-actualizing mode of being, one becomes a fully matured personality, a "fully functioning individual." But while psychological growth has concluded in terms of ascent to the highest possible levels of maturity, certain skills increase in competence, especially those involving life wisdom. Paradoxically, while psychological growth has reached its zenith, the self-actualizing person experiences urges each day to become more than he or she was yesterday. This reflects the idea that *the very essence of being is the process of ever becoming.*

## Mature Personalities Are beyond Striving

In Maslovian theory, each of us is subject to a biological encoding to grow, grow, grow—to grow in terms of our personalities from the time we are born until the time we lose possession of our cognitive selves or until growth becomes displaced by stultifying resignation, or we have reached the pinnacle of growth potential which Maslow characterized as being a point "beyond striving." Enrichment, rather than continuing growth, defines the *vive modus operandi* of the fully mature individual, and at that point a person has achieved, in Maslow's term, "full humanness." That premise is basic to understanding everything else in Maslow's theories of human development, and it is equally basic to understanding those who compose what we call *maturity markets.*

Maslow saw humanness as transcendent to what we call "our animal natures." Humanness, he said, is "godlike," meaning kindly but not indulgent, gentle but strong, compassionate but not patronizing. Our bodies make us human, but our minds give us humanness. Without our minds, our bodies can contribute nothing toward achieving humanness, but regardless of the condition of our bodies, our minds can take us the distance. That is why the physical condition of an aged body says little about the person.

Those in the maturity class of consumers are the farthest along in realizing their humanness. They are living proof that psychological growth operates in a differently defined time frame than physiological growth; that for as long as life and conscious awareness prevail, one's natural course is to become ever more human in terms of one's unique individual potential.

## The Term *Maturity Market* Refers to a Reality, Not a Euphemism

The shift, in Chapter 2, from use of the term *senior markets* to use of *maturity markets*, was not, as explained, to make *maturity* a euphemism for *senior* or *elderly*, as is usually the case. Being older doesn't necessarily instill one with more humanness, but being more mature does. Not everyone achieves the highest levels of Maslovian humanness, but many older people progress far enough in that direction that the accompanying personality changes alter their consumer behavior. Consequently, in marketing discretionary—and even many nondiscretionary—products and services, it is considerably less useful to think about consumers as seniors and nonseniors than to think about them in terms of their levels of maturity.

## Maturity Is a *Relative*, Not an *Absolute*, Concept

Extrapolating from Maslow a definition for maturity, I would set out to describe *psychological maturity* as a *relative*, rather than an *absolute*, concept describing progress toward the realization of personality potential. Some aspects of the concept of maturity largely reflect subjective values, because their meanings, as defined by social consensus, vary somewhat from culture to culture, as do experiences "permitted" a person according to cultural perceptions of maturity achieved. Further, because each person has a unique set of potentials, maturity itself varies for each person.

The term *maturity* is more aptly used to describe the development of *particular* attributes of the human personality and physiology, rather than to describe the *whole* person. That is because not only are there different categories of maturity, for example, physical maturity, intellectual maturity, emotional maturity (and subset categories of those), but also there are categories involving *physical-capabilities maturity* and *experiential maturity*.

*Physical-capabilities maturity* refers to the stages of development of psychological skills and of physical abilities, such as motor skills. Measurement of degrees of physical-capabilities maturity is generally tied to levels of competence in some skill within the context of most people's progress at similar points in their lives. A child of 10 to 15 months, for example, is mature relative to his or her then-current potential if walking skills have developed to the levels of competence of most of the child's peers.

## Experiential Maturity Is What Marketers Need to Understand

Experiential maturity involves various personality-shaping normal life events a person experiences within the context of the customs, values, and expectations of society in relation to chronological age. For example, deep sexually oriented love experiences are normally entered into during adolescence, whatever the means and limits of fulfillment. A person of 40 who has never had such experiences will necessarily be quite immature in terms of capacity for sexually oriented intimacy.

In terms of consumer decision making, a 40-year-old who has never had many consumer decision-making experiences likely has not developed a matured ability to make smart consumer decisions. Practice not only makes perfect, but also *tends* to enhance prospects for maturity, or the achievement of one's highest potential in any category. Note the qualifying word *tends*. For any number of reasons, a person may have no capacity for continuing growth toward maturity in a skill area, regardless of how often an experience is repeated.

The idea of experiential maturity has been key in the development of this book. In Chapter 5, I developed the hypothesis of the three experiential stages of adult life. In that context, a person who at age 60 is still predominantly influenced in consumer behavior by Possession Experience aspirations is immature. He or she is *experientially* immature. While Maslow never, to my knowledge, spoke of experiential immaturity, nevertheless it is an idea that is implicit in all his thinking. There simply are certain experiences that are associated with certain levels of psychological development. That is why an adult whose behavior is dominated by unfulfilled lower-level basic needs, which should have long since abated, is emotionally immature.

## Mature Adults Live for Continuing "Actualization" of Their Potentials

One of Maslow's key terms was *potential*. We live (or should live) for potential rather than for status quo. This is a critical point for understanding members of maturity markets. On the whole, they are not as oriented to a life of full-time leisure and play as many believe. Such an orientation reflects an abandonment of life's meanings and possibilities in favor of the status quo, and *an abandonment of the pursuit of one's higher potentials*.

Maslow felt that neuroses were caused primarily by anxiety-ridden underlying feelings stemming from a shortfall in the gratification of certain basic needs, especially in lower-level basic needs. As long as a person is compulsively driven by such shortfalls, neurosis will continue and block the person from achieving the life-satisfying realization of higher potentials. Realization of full human potential for each person, according to Maslow, is dependent on deficit-needs gratification to the extent that the level in which they operate ceases to be an area of dominant influence in the person's behavior. Until that happens, a person's psychic energies, however wholesomely or perversely deployed, are directed more toward needs gratification than toward life activities in reflection of his or her full human potential.

## Maslow's Basic Tenets and Their Meanings in Maturity Markets

To better grasp the relationship of Maslow's ideas to maturity markets, we need to review some of the basic tenets of his thinking in the context of a personality's progression through his hierarchy of basic needs:[1]

> **Maslovian Tenet 1**: Substantial needs gratification must take place at one level of basic needs before a person is able to achieve substantial needs gratification at a higher level.

Some people get stuck at a lower basic needs level, staying there longer than most of their chronological peers. Gradually, the gulf in maturity between them and their chronological peers increases to the point where the growth-retarded person may become painfully aware that life is not delivering what it should. Such people are more likely to regard their problems as bad luck than of their own making. Honest admission of immaturity is virtually impossible. One can never see one's own face.

Operating at more or less the same levels of immaturity for 20 or 30 years can drain a person's zest for life. Demoralized individuals have diminished interests and, consequently, reduced significance as consumers of discretionary expenditure items. Let's take another look at Alice Erskine, for it is important to understand both why she is economically insignificant to marketers of discretionary goods and services and that there are millions of Alices who should be eliminated from marketing projections for a vast array of products and services.

Alice Erskine is stuck somewhere on Maslow's ladder between "safety and security" and "love and belonging." She can never fully commit to others because she is perpetually insecure. She has not defined herself in ways that give her a comfortable sense of identity, or a sense of really belonging. She seems condemned to a Sisyphean sentence of periodically glimpsing success in her aspirations, but falling back each time in frustration and disappointment.

Alice, at age 45, should be about to join the ranks of the maturity markets, but she probably never will. She has gone beyond the years

---

[1]The tenets presented are not in Maslow's words, but are my presentation of key concepts involving his hierarchy of basic human needs.

when Possession Experience aspirations would have been likely to dominate her behavior, without ever experiencing much gratification. She is particularly unfulfilled in terms of animate possessions. To her low-simmering bitter regret, she has no family of her own making.

Alice owns a small condo, enjoys a better-than-average income as a real estate sales agent, and has a moderately priced 4-year-old car. But her worldly possessions are few, her expenditures for services increasingly less, and her dissatisfaction with life great. Alice does not define her self-image by possessions, although she once dreamed of a home in the suburbs, a husband, children, and most of the accoutrements of the traditional life that characterized her childhood.

Alice is a good book customer, however, who frequently buys "how-to" books promising solutions to personal problems: *How to Get a Man, How To Get Rid of a Man, How to Advance in Your Career, Why Happiness Is Not Tied to Career Advancement*, etc. What Alice has been unable to find in the natural course of life that might lead her into full mature adulthood, she is trying to find at Dalton's or Waldenbook's.

Alice is a nascent senior travel customer. She has taken a few trips over the years, in search of the romantic, but now she is thinking about some long trips to learn about things—culture, geography, and history "sorts of things."

Apart from some basic necessities (food, clothing, cosmetics, etc.), Alice has no particular distinction as a consumer. She doesn't fit very neatly into anyone's consumer typology. What she needs and what she buys bear little relationship to her age. She is of little importance to those targeting mature adults; she is not a mature adult, likely will not be, or in Maslow's terms, will never attain "full humanness."

Alice's brother Peter is not going to be much of a factor in the maturity markets, either. Now 42 and not much different from Alice in material possessions and quality of friendships, Peter will probably fade from significance as he grows older, not making much of a dent in what he perceives to be a wholly un-ideal world.

### Millions of Alice Types Distort
### Reports of Maturity Market Potential

How many Alices and Peters are there? How many insecure, disenchanted, frequently depressed middle-agers, who are not significant in discretionary markets, irrespective of their incomes? A 1989 study by J. Walter Thompson (JWT) USA projected this group at 8 million consumers. The study, referring to this group as *Mature Singles*, mean age 45, noted, "They tend to be divorced or separated and 81 percent have been so for 10 years or more. The group, far from the stereotyped career-climbers, are instead considered insecure, pessimistic, alienated, and indifferent to work. Marketers will face the toughest hurdles reaching this audience, but Club Med and other vacation spots could benefit from repositioning themselves toward this group," according to JWT.[2]

I would hazard a guess that as many as 25 percent of the 40-to-60 population are not significant discretionary-purchase consumers.[3] The Alice types and Peter types are not all single people either. Many married people reflect the same paralyzing attitudes toward life. In some cases only one spouse feels that way; in other cases, both feel that way.

Alice and Peter were significant consumers during the Possession Experience years of their lives, but now they have largely lost their significance as consumers, except for basic necessities. Their chronological passage, in a few years, into the ranks of seniors does not convert them into members of maturity markets. Nevertheless, they will be counted in demographic reports, even in marketing reports that purport to be psychographically oriented, maybe under a heading "Middle-Income Grays," or some similar catchy heading. Thus, to the extent that the Alices and Peters are included in those reports, the size of markets for a great range of products and services will be overstated.

## Lower-Level MADI People Respond to Self-Oriented Marketing Messages

Whatever the reasons, Alice and Peter seem stuck at a low MADI level. This is not to say that neither can access the pleasures of higher levels. People whose psychological development is retarded do taste the pleasures of higher levels, but without extended engagement of their full psychic energies because so much psychic energy is continually devoted to the frustrations of unmet lower-level needs.

Now for the next tenet:

**Maslovian Tenet 2**: The lower the needs level in which a person predominantly operates, the more self-serving (selfish) that person is.

Tenet 2 has major implications in the development of market strategies and promotional messages for maturity markets. Marketers are accus-

---

[2]G. Levin, "JWT Researches Stages, Not Ages," *Advertising Age*, June 26, 1989, p. 30.
[3]One supporting reference for this contention can be found in the descriptions of lifestyles and values of those comprising three of the nine VALS lifestyle types. Those three groups—Survivors, Sustainers, and Emulators—account for 20 percent of the U.S. population. They are, of course, of all ages; however, one can presume there are Alices and Peters among some of Arnold's other lifestyle groups, such as among Belongers who account for 35 percent of all consumers.

tomed to crafting strategies and campaigns which appeal to those with self-serving orientations. The less mature the members of a target market, the more effective that approach. Years of directing marketing philosophies and methodologies toward the less mature youth markets have predisposed marketers to employ "selfish appeal" messages across the board. That tendency has to be unlearned by anyone accustomed to youth markets who hopes to be effective in dealing with consumers in the very different maturity markets. This unique consumer requires an understanding of the Fourth Key Factor for Maturity Markets, the *Altruistic Factor*:

---

**FOURTH KEY FACTOR FOR MATURITY MARKETS**
The Altruistic Factor

Members of maturity markets tend to respond more favorably to marketing messages that emphasize introspective or altruistic values and less favorably to marketing messages that emphasize selfish interests.

---

Persons operating at lower needs levels are more selfish (less altruistic) than those operating at higher needs levels, and, according to Maslow, they are more limited in their ability to understand and relate to others in any deep sense. Self-oriented people are more narrow, less objective, and less holistic—characteristics Maslow associated with being less realistic.

### Self-Orientation Has Strong Links with Psychobiological Factors

According to neuroscientist Robert Ornstein, right brain cognition activities literally involve less brain activity than left brain cognitive activities, and thus it may be that either the right brain has more memory available to it to construct larger and more concrete pictures of the world,[4] or that the left brain simply consumes a lot more memory than the right just dealing with detail. Maslow, who did not know of the specialization of the brain's hemispheres, nevertheless accurately described the dichotomy of thinking processes and products now used to describe hemispheric specialization. This dichotomy reflects the differences between self-actualizing people and those yet to become so, and he observed that the cognitive processes used by the less mature "must be

---

[4]Robert Ornstein, *The Psychology of Consciousness*, Pelican Books, Baltimore, Md., 1986.

more fatiguing," while those used by self-actualizers probably are "fatigue-curing." (See Table 6-1, later in this chapter.)

There are limits to the brain's memory systems and thus to how much information can be processed at a given time. For that reason, regardless of the current dominant hemisphere, cognition necessarily involves an elaborate screening process designed to inhibit the admission into consciousness of information that is extraneous to one's objectives. In other words, the conscious mind tends to discount what is not relevant in order to make room for what is relevant. If the most relevant thing is oneself, then things related to other selves tend to get screened out except insofar as they have something the screener wants.

## Altruism of Mature Adults Is Different from Youthful Altruism

Maslow opined some 40 years ago that the primary purpose of behavior was to "defend against the psyche," meaning that behavior is oriented to coping with inner-felt "dissatisfactions." That is, behavior is oriented to acting on emotional responses to unsatisfied or ungratified needs.

By definition of what a young person lacks when entering the adult world, there tends to be a greater focus on self than on others. Even young people who enter a field that ostensibly involves altruistic acts, for example, the Peace Corps, can be very self-oriented people.

Many young people may embark on altruistic ventures because they feel safer (reflecting a deficiency in meeting basic safety and security needs) among disadvantaged people. Or they may be seeking appreciation and affection in places where they believe their good works will guarantee such recognition (possibly reflecting deficits in basic love and belonging needs). Or the person may have strong identity-definition needs that might be best filled in doing good works. In other words, such behavior by young people often is reflective of a *giving to get* level of motivation.

Maslow said:

> The deficit-motivated man is far more dependent upon other people than is the man who is predominantly growth-oriented. He is more "interested," more needful [of others], more attached, more desirous.
>
> This dependency colors and limits interpersonal relations. To see [other] people as need-gratifiers ... is an abstractive act. They [other people] are not seen as wholes, as complicated, unique individuals, but rather from the point of view of usefulness.[5]

[5] A. Maslow, *Toward a Psychology of Being*, Van Nostrand Reinhold Company, New York, 1968, p. 36.

What Maslow is saying, as paradoxical as it sounds, is that until one comfortably develops a sense of detachment from others, one cannot *altruistically* do for others. Altruism, thus, is not defined by the act, but by the attitude behind the act.

The fact that many older people do not give in order to receive, yet give substantially, means that selflessness is a strong part of the self-image of many older people. Therefore, consistent with the First General Principle of Marketing, images reflected of older people in marketing programs should be weak on self-oriented values and strong on outer-directed or altruistic values. Older consumers generally will be more responsive to marketing materials that depict them as generous rather than selfish.

### But What about the Reputed Selfishness of Older People?

Of all the "polarities and oppositions" of self-actualizing personalities that beguiled Maslow for years, the seeming coexistence of selfishness and selflessness was among the most perplexing. Mature adults can, indeed, be highly selfish, but it is neither the mean selfishness of ruthlessly ambitious people nor the blind and generally benign selfishness of young children. It is a highly conscious selfishness, a selfishness that is kind, a selfishness that avoids indulgence at the expense of others.

The selfishness of mature adults tends to be expressed in activities that enlarge the person by enriching his or her connectedness with life. Their selfish activities are not self-directed so much as inner-directed, or introspective, and are engaged in with a view to their impact upon others. Thus, mature adult selfishness is not so much "self-serving" as it is "serving of self" in the best sense of the idea.

### Mature People Seem Contradictory Because We Categorize Them

The many polarities and oppositions found in the personalities of older people are, in reality, not mutually contradictory. They only seem that way when one fixes absolute meanings on certain concepts. Much of the confusion about the so-called contradictory behavior exhibited by older people may be explained by a basic thinking strategy upon which people draw to help organize their realities and understand the world.

The left brain seeks cognitive simplicity by arranging things into categories. But once something has been placed in a category, it has lost something of its full nature because it has been removed from its natural environment or context. Categories are ultimately artificial rear-rangements that narrow meaning and value. For example, the word *selfish* is most often filed in a category of "not so nice" behavioral traits and is perceived as representing the opposite of giving, which is filed in the "good traits" category. But there are other contexts in which self-ishness operates positively.

A selfish activity that results in no discomfort or burden to others, es-pecially one that enriches and makes better the person indulging in it, can expand that person's value to others. By increasing what the person is, she or he has more to give to others, be it more energy because of a reinvigorated spirit or more wisdom because of a rich, new experience.

In one of our focus groups, marketing messages that urge a purchase "because you have earned it" were perceived by older people as a wan-ton appeal to "bad" selfishness. A message that urges a purchase by say-ing "because you will be more" still puts the message into an ego-based self-serving context, but one that promises the potential of benefits be-yond narrow self-interest.

## Why Possession and Catered Experience Aspirations Subside

We now come to a tenet of Maslow's that begins to explain why there is a limit, among normally developing people, to the duration of the Pos-session Experience years and later, the Catered Experience years. These are the years when people's energy is devoted to getting what they have not yet had. In other words, these years are devoted to curing the "deficits" in one's life that are found in Maslow's first four basic needs levels.

> **Maslovian Tenet 3**: The objective of behavior designed to fulfill deficit needs is the elimination or reduction of the appetites they drive. Substantial success in gratifying deficit-driven needs less-ens the potency of drives behind those needs, which then frees up psychic energies for growth needs.

Given the relentless need to continuously seek new experiences—to grow—that is built into us by nature, from where does this need arise once the aspirations for Possession and Catered Experiences that are prompted by this need have been largely met? The objects of Possession and Catered Experience aspirations are strongly related to the need for marking one's identity and providing evidence of one's accomplish-ments in a sociocultural context. Achievement of those objectives pri-marily addresses deficit needs; consequently, according to Maslovian te-net 3, the strength of urges to repeat those experiences will weaken as the need for establishing one's identity and accomplishments decline. It is almost as though a vacuum results from their satisfaction that attracts the category of aspirations that expand at the onset of the Being Experience years, thus reflecting the meaning of Maslovian tenet 4.

> **Maslovian Tenet 4**: As opposed to deficiency-driven needs, growth-driven needs (self-actualizing needs) do not seek to extinguish themselves, but rather tend to perpetuate and even intensify themselves.

There is a wonderful unfolding of self that happens as a person reaches the upper levels of human maturity. Released from many stifling inhibitions, because they are no longer heavily influenced by the opinions of others, mature adults more freely soar toward their greatest emotional potentials. Elsewhere I mention Connie Goldman's "Late Bloomers," older people she has identified as having moved into a higher phase of existence, according to their self-characterizations, relative to their earlier years. Late Bloomers have made life activity choices that have given them greater feelings of satisfaction and joy in life than ever before. Maslow, however, would not use the modifier *late*; he would just call them *Bloomers*, people who have unfolded in flowerlike splendor in accordance with their unique potentials. He would observe that to reach full maturity is to reach full flowering.

## Mature Adults Are Good Prospects for Repurchase Products and Services

Tenet 4 is good news for those in the business of selling to maturity markets those products and services that support a Being Experience-oriented lifestyle, especially products and services subject to periodic or continuing repurchase. Examples of repurchase or subscription-type products and services that support a Being Experience-oriented lifestyle include educational magazines, theater and concert tickets, travel, health club memberships, collector's-item subscription programs, specialty gift programs (for giving to friends and family), lecture programs, and college courses.

Many products, while not repurchase-type products, are so effective in contributing to a continuum of Being Experiences that maturity market consumers will want them as eagerly as people in their Possession Experience years want things. Books, records, clothes for Being Experience occasions, jewelry offered with a story, and antiques which tell a story are examples of non-subscription-type products that have high appeal to mature consumers.

## How to Market VCRs to Maturity Markets

If I were developing a promotional program for VCRs to maturity markets, a nonsubscription purchase, I would not focus on the benefits of watching the latest movies in the quiet of the owners' homes. I would focus on how a VCR would enable them to see movies they can no longer see in theaters, movies such as *Casablanca, Gaslight*, and *It Happened One Night*. The VCR, thus, is positioned as a gateway to a category of Being Experiences (nostalgia), but is also a product that invokes traditional values (entertainment without blatant sex and violence).

On the subject of "basic values," keep in mind that the currently growing *neotraditionalist* movement has been spawned by the children of the Age of Aquarius—the same self-oriented people whose youthful lifestyles engendered the atmosphere that led to unprecedented moral license in our society. Their current change in direction is, once again, consistent with Maslovian theory. Aquarians are seeing life a lot differently now from when they were younger, which leads us to the fifth Maslovian tenet:

> **Maslovian Tenet 5**: The higher a person's ascent in Maslow's hierarchy, the more expansive his or her cognitive powers and the more objectively realistic he or she is.

Mature consumers see things or, to use Maslow's word, *cognize* things differently than less mature consumers. When he writes that self-actualizing people are more "objectively realistic," he means, in part, that they *cognize* concretely rather than abstractly. Abstract cognition involves piecemeal-type thinking, while concrete cognition involves holistic thinking. Abstract thinking is seeing the trees, concrete thinking is seeing the forest. Ornstein says we cognize abstractly with left brain processes and concretely with right brain processes. Such differences as Maslow observed in the cognition patterns of mature people in comparison with less mature people have doubtless contributed to a great deal of the misunderstanding that abounds about older people.

## The Difference in Thinking Styles between Older and Younger Adults

While I was at a symposium on older markets held at the University of Florida, a researcher presented a paper on the cognitive differences between younger people and older people in reading ads. She observed that older people did not "elaborate" as much on ad content as younger people, and that to the extent that they did at all, they tended not to "elaborate" negatively on an ad's contents. By elaboration, she meant what is also referred to as *cognitive backtalk*—the conversations we have with ourselves as we are trying to figure out something.

Her conclusions from the findings in her studies led her to give the following advice: Keep ads short and simple (so as not to "overload" older minds, and "we must find ways to teach older people how to 'elaborate' negatively; otherwise, they will be subject to exploitation by inflated or false claims in advertising."

I have no doubt that her *findings* were correct. They square with Maslow's largely intuitive conclusions regarding mature people's cognitive patterns, and her findings also are consistent with recent findings in neuroscience about how the brain works.

But I disagree with her *conclusions*, based on those findings. I talked to AARP's Bob Forbes about her conclusions. He said, "All of our experience tells us to include more, not less, information in ads. And as to the ability of mature consumers to 'elaborate negatively'—they don't have to. They get to the point without having to go through a lot of thinking processes. They work intuitively."

The researcher drew from her thinking style and values (meanings) to conclude that for people who don't "think" much when reading ads, it is best to give them little to think about. Her conclusions were in direct conflict with Figure 2-2, the *Modern Maturity* educational ad exhorting, "Don't make a long story short."

## Defense Needs May Be the Basis of the Mind's Screening Processes

Forbes' comments are supported by Maslow, Ornstein, and others. The facts of mature life they represent are rooted in the concept, so well developed in Ornstein's *Psychology of Consciousness*, that a person's cognitive capacities and patterns are largely defined at any point in life by his or her defense needs. That means defense of ego, defense of belief systems, defense of self-esteem, defense of social position, defense against being seduced by an ad, as well as physiological defense.

Ornstein maintains that what is relevant to defense enters cognition and what is not relevant tends to stay in the unconscious. He suggests that the more one is defense-oriented, the more abstract (sequential reasoning) one's thinking is. Less defense-oriented thinking tends to allow concrete (holistic, intuitive) thinking processes to develop.

Maslow termed people whose cognitive patterns are largely defined by deficit needs as *D-cognizers* ("D" for deficit). He described those whose cognitive patterns are largely defined by growth needs as *B-cognizers* ("B" for being, that is, for people who approach "being all they can be."

Table 6-1 is adapted from notes of Maslow's lectures and writings, compiled and edited after his death by his wife, Bertha. It reflects a number of more detailed differences between D-cognizers and B-cognizers in their cognition patterns. I have reduced the original tabular presentation by more than half, eliminating some enumerated entries entirely and abridging others. Maslow's comments may occasionally be somewhat obscure to those unfamiliar with his work. Nevertheless, the essence of Maslow's thoughts about the differences in cognition patterns between the mature and the less mature comes through strongly.

## Mature Adults "Get the Picture" More Quickly

The differences between the ways in which D-cognizers and B-cognizers organize reality in their minds is roughly analogous to the differences between the ways a picture is formed in a 35-mm camera and on a television screen. As soon as the lens is opened on the 35-mm camera, all that comes within its field of vision is recorded instantly on the film in full detail, to the resolution capability of the film. The image on the television screen results from a stream of electrons that are fired at the back of the screen upon which the final picture emerges, dot by dot, like the pictures in the Sunday comic strips. The difference, however, between the dots or pixels making up the comic strip image and pixels making up the television image is that the pixels arrive on the television screen in a piecemeal, sequential fashion.

D-cognizers predominately organize reality in sequentially arriving bits, like the pixels of a television screen. B-cognizers predominately organize reality in instantaneous fashion like the 35-mm camera. D-cognizers rely heavily on what psychologists refer to as *secondary processes*, processes involving cognitive back talk, the processes that the young researcher claimed older people tend not to reflect in cognition patterns. She was right. Only her conclusions were wrong.

B-cognizers rely heavily on what psychologists refer to as *primary*, or *primitive, processes*. What we call *intuition* is a primitive process because it results in an image derived not from logic, but from feelings. Maslow

**Table 6-1.** Characteristics of Being-Cognition and Deficiency-Cognition of the World

| B-Cognition | D-Cognition |
|---|---|
| 1. (The World) seen as whole, as complete, self-sufficient, as unitary. | 1. (The World) seen as part, as incomplete, not self-sufficient, as dependent upon other things. |
| 2. Tends to de-differentiate figure and background. Richness of detail seen from many sides. Seen with "care" totally, intensely, with complete investment. Relative important becomes unimportant; all aspects equally important. | 2. Sharp figure back-ground differentiation. Seen imbedded in relationships to all else in world, as part of the world. Rubricized; from some aspects only; selective attention and selective inattention to some aspects; seen casually; seen only from some point of view. |
| 3. No comparing. Seen *per se*, in itself, by itself. Not in competition with anything else. Sole member of the class. | 3. Placing on a continuum in or within a series; comparing, judging, evaluating. Seen as a member of a class, as an instance, a sample. |
| 4. Human irrelevant. | 4. Relevant to human concerns; e.g., what good is it, what can it be used for, is it good for or dangerous to people, etc. |
| 5. Made richer by repeated experiencing. | 5. Repeated experiencing impoverishes, reduces richness, makes it less interesting and attractive. Familiarization leads to boredom. |
| 6. Object-centering. Self-forgetful, ego-transcending, unselfish. So absorbed and poured into the experience that self disappears, so that whole experience can be organized around the object itself. | 6. Organized around ego as a centering point, which means projection of the ego into the percept. |
| 7. The object is permitted to be itself. Humble, choiceless, undemanding. Taoistic, noninterference with the object. | 7. Active shaping, organizing, and selecting by the perceiver. Rearranges it. He works at it. This must be more fatiguing than B-cognizing, which probably is fatigue-curing. |

| | |
|---|---|
| 8. Seen as end in itself, self-validating. Self-justifying. Intrinsically interesting for its own sake. Has intrinsic value. | 8. A means, an instrument, not having self-contained worth but having only exchange-value, or standing for something else. |
| 9. Outside of time and space. Seen as eternal, universal. "A minute is a day; a day is a minute." | 9. In time and space. Temporal. |
| 10. Resolution of dichotomies, polarities; exist simultaneously quite different from each (yet) sensible and necessary (to each) other. | 10. Aristotelian logic, i.e., separate things seen as conflicts. |
| 11. Concretely (and abstractly) perceived. All aspects at once. Therefore ineffable (to ordinary language); describable, if at all, by poetry, art, etc., but even this will make sense only to one who has already had same experience. | 11. Only abstract, categorized, diagrammatic, rubricized, schematized. Classifying. "Reduction to the abstract." |
| 12. World and self often (not always) seen as amusing, playful, comic, funny, absurd, laughable, but also as poignant. Philosophical humor. World, person, child, etc, seen as cute, absurd, charming, lovable. May produce mixed laughing-crying. | 12. Lesser forms of humor, if seen at all. Serious things quite different from amusing things. Hostile humor, humorlessness. Solemnity. |

SOURCE: Abraham H. Maslow, *The Farther Reaches of Human Nature*, Penguin Books, New York, 1987, pp. 249–253.

observed that B-cognizers become more capable of emotional feelings than they were earlier in their lives.

## Misconceptions about Older People May Be Based on Inappropriate Tests

After hearing the presentation of the researcher at the University of Florida, I finally organized a conclusion in my mind: Much testing of older people may be leading to faulty conclusions because of testing instruments that are inappropriate tools to measure their cognitive processes. The tests also may contain numerous items irrelevant to many mature adults' existence (in terms of their survival and defense needs) which thus escape comprehensive cognitive processing.

I began to suspect that the low intensity of response might be related to irrelevancies when I observed focus group respondents struggling in their evaluations of certain concepts, concepts that, given their educational levels and career accomplishments, they should have been able to grasp more clearly.

In arriving at these conclusions concerning the inappropriateness of many survey and testing instruments, I am reminded of the standard intelligence tests recently found to have been biased in favor of white males of European extraction. Those earlier tests failed to take fully into account naturally occurring differences in cognition dynamics based on cultural values and certain gender characteristics. For example, males tend to be more proficient in spatial relationships, while females tend to be more proficient in verbal skills. These differences are detectable within a few weeks to a few months after birth and thus cannot be attributed to environmental influences.[6]

A considerable amount of research has compared various mental processes of older people with those of younger people. One finding is that there are some types of memory diminishment among older people. The seemingly apt conclusion is that such impairments represent a handicap. But the threshold question ignored by such a conclusion is, Does the diminishment of certain kinds of memory *necessarily* interfere with efficient functioning of an individual? A handicap could be deemed to exist only if the memory loss interfered with *appropriate* functioning. Remember, according to Ornstein, our psychological operations are primarily designed for survival and defense needs, not for test results.

[6]Richard Restak, *The Brain: The Last Frontier*, Warner Books, New York, 1979, p. 223.

## Use Mature People in Developing, Administering, and Interpreting Tests

Market researchers who employ psychographic research, be it in the form of surveys or focus panels, will greatly enhance the accuracy of the results by remembering that many older people will respond to questions and other stimuli according to their own unique ways of perceiving things. It is a good idea not only to have test instruments evaluated by mature adults, but also to have test results subjected to the interpretive review of mature adults. Mature people should be similarly involved in administration of focus panels and interpretations of the results.

## Decline in Some Skills May Be Offset by Improvement in Others

Marketing professionals as well as others need to avoid the trap of thinking that older people view their differences in cognitive patterns and overall mental acuities as deficiencies or handicaps.

There is indeed a slowing of the operation of the central nervous system in older age which increases the amount of time required to process information, with the result that less information is initially encoded into short-term memory.[7] Suppose, however, it was found that along with certain kinds of memory loss associated with aging, new and more efficient levels of mental skills emerged? Or suppose it was determined that the emergence of different, if not higher, levels of mental skills simply rendered peak skills in certain kinds of memory no longer necessary, so that a certain amount of atrophy comes to affect those skills, irrespective of the effects of a slowing of the central nervous system?

We have seen the difference in the ways Maslow's D-cognizers and B-cognizers organize their perceived worlds. Each has a different way of establishing concepts of reality. In both cases, there are things that members of the other group do not see. B-cognizers do not see the detailed picture seen by D-cognizers, and D-cognizers do not see the whole picture except (if at all) as a mosaic showing the boundaries of all the individual pieces, each of which is potentially submitted to a separate evaluation process.

---

[7]Donald Kline and James E. Birren, "Age Differences in Backward Dichoptic Masking," *Experimental Aging Research*, vol. 1, 1975, pp. 17–25.

## Adjusting to the Different Thinking Styles of Mature Adults

I would presume that tests given to older people are dominantly prepared by D-cognizers, administered by D-cognizers, interpreted by D-cognizers, and their meanings determined by D-cognizers—all of which may yield results about as useful as those produced by measuring water with a yardstick. I believe we owe it to ourselves and to older adults to stop looking at them in relation to younger people, and to start looking at them in relation to their abilities to accomplish what they need to accomplish to achieve a comfortable and life-satisfying existence.

In summary, many older people may sustain certain kinds of memory loss in part because what has been lost has been superceded by a more efficient method of processing information. What is not related to survival is not maintained in peak condition.

Ornstein makes a startling statement when he says, "Many people whom we consider 'unintelligent' or 'retarded' may in fact possess a different kind of intelligence and might be quite valuable to society." Applying Ornstein's logic, young people might perceive older people in terms of strengths which they, themselves, have yet to acquire, instead of perceiving older people in terms of deficiencies. The current societal perception of older people is analogous to calling human beings handicapped because they cannot fly. Surely a robin who can't fly is handicapped, because flying is essential to its being what it should be. Neither speed of body nor speed of mind is essential to an old person's being what he or she might best be. As observed before, age is never a handicap, unless it is perceived to be.

## Selfishness May Be Harmful to Your Cognitive Health

A corollary to Maslovian tenet 5 is that the extent of one's cognitive powers tends to be limited by one's degree of selfish orientation. This does not mean that an unselfish person necessarily has a greater scope of cognitive powers than a selfish one. It means that if a selfish person can grow beyond a lower needs level, he or she will experience an enhancement of his or her cognitive powers. The mind-clogging clouds of an ego-centered life begin to dissipate, giving a person a clearer self-image and a view of the rest of the world as more human. The selfish person is far removed, therefore, from the outer limits of his or her potential in many ways, including cognitive abilities.

## Why Mature People Tend Not to Elaborate Negatively on Ads

Mature people may not "elaborate" negatively on ads as much as less mature people do in part because their perceptions of an ad's meanings emerge full blown in the mind without the need for laborious sequential reasoning processes to come into play. They tend to *initially* recognize as valid or as invalid, appropriate or inappropriate, desirable or undesirable, truthful or untruthful, an ad's contents without much "elaboration." Their perceived image of the advertised product or service is formed in the consciousness at the same time as the values reflected in the ad. *Initial* value determination is not the product of logic, a process undergone *after* the product or service has been perceived, but is *holistically* part of the total picture at the instant that picture forms in the mind.

## Getting the Picture Quickly Can Lead to Faulty Conclusions

This is not to suggest that mature consumers immediately absorb all that is represented in an ad. Nor is it to suggest that the intuited, holistic impressions that mature consumers get from an ad are necessarily valid impressions. It is to suggest that mature consumers will often come to a conclusion about an ad more quickly than a person of less maturity, regardless of whether the conclusion is valid or accurate. Mature consumers may, for example, derive their entire perception of an ad from one graphic image, the headline, or a single statement. Consumers may then generalize the meanings perceived in that isolated statement to the entire offering.

For example, mature consumers might well view the claim in a travel ad that "You will never have another experience like it" as presumptuous hyperbole and immediately conclude that all other representations in the ad are similarly empty. The credibility of the company, as well as the remainder of the ad, has suffered, and justly so, for having ignored the Fifth Key Factor for Maturity Markets, The *Antihyperbole Factor*:

---

**FIFTH KEY FACTOR FOR MATURITY MARKETS**
The Antihyperbole Factor

Maturity market consumers have a strong aversion to embellished claims and to what they perceive as misleading imagery.

---

The use of hyperbole results in value-inflated statements, a standard tool in advertising. Telling a copywriter to avoid all value-inflated statements in ads directed to maturity markets is like tying one hand of a boxer behind his back before sending him into the ring. But it must be done. Maslow described mature adults as *resistant to enculturation.* That means they like to make up their own minds. Just give them the facts to do so—and be honest and complete with the facts.

Because of their generally more effective cognitive powers, maturity market consumers not only are adept at separating the wheat from the chaff, but also want facts, not fancy, to use in making purchase decisions. Messages that fail to respond to these desires are perceived as lacking credibility, as are the product or service being offered and the company offering them.

## Reality-Distorting Ads Do Not
## Perform Well in Maturity Markets

Despite tests showing a general inability of young adults to distinguish taste differences between most domestic beers, many young people can become downright feisty in defending the taste superiority of their favorite brand. Defense by young consumers of their favorite brew, or their choice of any other of numerous products, subtly involves the merger of peer group values and attitudes with the intrinsic attributes of the product. Often, peer group values owe much to the claims and image-laden suggestions of marketers. Reality thus becomes distorted by the consumers who define a product in terms of the values of their peers, irrespective of the product's intrinsic attributes. Marketers assist consumers in developing these illusory product attributes through verbal and graphic images. Thus, the ad maker can contribute as much to the taste of a beer as the brewmaster does.

Much of U.S. marketing theory and practice has been based on marketers' knowledge of how to create distortions of reality in legally, socially, and culturally acceptable ways. In a sense, the reality that the consumer attributes to a product is the consumer's *own* reality which he or she sees reflected in the product. And the younger (or rather, the less mature) the person is, the more his or her reality draws upon that of peers.

When Maslow said that B-cognizers have a greater sense of reality, he meant, in part, that less of their self-image enters into the formation of their perceptions of an object. (Again, see Table 6-1.) In other words, B-cognizers are more objective. This presents challenges to marketers used to positioning and promotional strategies based upon reality-distorting techniques.

Reality distortion is commonly employed in advertising to stimulate emotions. Among mature consumers, emotional pitches can be just as effective as among younger consumers. Because of the higher levels of emotional capacity that mature people have developed, emotion-stimulating strategies can have an even greater value in maturity markets. But since hyperbole has so often been used in stimulating emotions, the question arises, What techniques can be used in maturity market promotional efforts to evoke positive emotions? The answer lies in selling experiences, not the product, as initially discussed in Chapter 3 in the section on the Three Bases for Consumer Satisfaction.

### Why Younger Adults Generally Are Low in B-Cognition Abilities

The trip up Maslow's hierarchy requires many years and countless experiential opportunities. All human life begins with the dominance of physiological needs. Because human personality development is a product of heritable personality attributes, physical brain development, and environmental conditions, time and experiential requirements necessarily prolong arrival at the highest level, self-actualization, until later in life.

Maslow claimed his studies showed that self-actualization does not occur in young adults for numerous experiential reasons: "[The young have]...not yet achieved identity, or autonomy; not had time enough to experience an enduring...post-romantic love relationship, nor have they generally found...the altar upon which to offer themselves, nor have they generally acquired enough courage to be unpopular, to be unashamed about being openly virtuous, etc."[8] In that abridged statement, Maslow defined much about many older people by saying what young people are not.

## The One-Minute Guide to Understanding the Mature Consumer

My adviser on Maslow for this book, Dr. Lou Kopolow, (who was a student of Maslow's) told me that of all the Maslovian ideas I have presented in this book, none are of more all-encompassing importance to marketers than the ones I am about to set forth.

[8]Abraham Maslow, *Motivation and Personality*, Harper & Row, New York, 1970, p. xx.

## The One-Minute Guide to Understanding the Mature Consumer

In his classic book, *Toward a Psychology of Being*, Maslow listed 13 personality attributes of the self-actualizing person.

1. *Superior perception of reality.* Older people, on average, seem to be more discerning in evaluating advertising claims.

2. *Increased acceptance of self, others, and nature.* We sometimes refer to this as "mellowing out." This results in a higher capacity for humor, a highly useful tool in coping with stress, and permits marketers to present serious subjects in a palatable way in advertising.

3. *Increased spontaneity.* This is illustrated by the tendency of many older people to live day to day. Spontaneity enlivens any scene, including those used in advertising to make a statement.

4. *Increase in problem-centering.* This is opposed to self-centering, and it partially accounts for the significant increase in altruistic activities by older people. Images of older people doing good works in advertising catch their attention and are consistent with their self-images.

5. *Increased detachment and desire for privacy.* Many senior adults dislike the idea of "social directors" in senior housing. Similarly, many older people don't respond well to group-driven events, except when their peers have been the primary organizers. Advertising images should acknowledge the unique individuality felt by mature adults.

6. *Increased autonomy and resistance to enculturation.* Mature people know their own minds and what they want, and they resist efforts by others to change their minds. Those attributes account for many older people's aversion to value-inflated representations in marketing communications. Give them facts, not self-serving claims.

7. *Greater freshness of appreciation and richness of emotional reaction.* This is centered on the Big Things Become Small and Small Things Become Big Principle set forth in Chapter 5. Touch their hearts, and they will allow you to enter their minds.

8. *Higher frequency of peak experiences.* This is derived from Peak Being Experiences which are the most important kinds of experiences with which to associate a product or service. See Chapter 5 to review factors contributing to a Being Experience.

9. *Increased identification with the human species.* Older people really want to do for others—see the Four Faces of the New Senior in Chapter 2. In ads show older people wearing one or more of the Four Faces, and they will recognize themselves and thank you for it.

10. *Changed (the clinician would say improved) interpersonal relations.* Friendships are pursued for their own sake, not for what they can do to further self-centered goals. Avoid ego-centered activities, symbols, and characterizations.

11. *More democratic character structure.* An individual's sense of fairness and fair play increases with maturity. This enriches mature adults with the wisdom of Solomon, an easy image to symbolize in graphics and narratives.

12. *Greatly increased creativity.* This significant shift from left brain (rational) activities to right brain (creative) activities tends to occur among mature people. Invoke the *poet* in the mature consumer before you invoke the *philosopher*, but be sure to invoke both.

13. *Certain changes in the value system.* Values get reordered in terms of importance and priorities, a condition calling for significant re-evaluation of the values invoked in ads for young versus older markets, even for the same product.

Referencing each of these 13 attributes will assist marketers in developing symbols and messages intended to evoke positive responses among older consumers. The attributes offer a vitally useful framework for understanding the typical financially and psychologically independent older consumer. The better one understands each of those attributes, the better equipped one will be to achieve business success in product and service design and delivery, as well as in developing marketplace communications. And until one can grasp the full meaning of the first listed attribute, "superior perception of reality," it will be difficult to comprehend the others to any great degree.

## Implications of the "Superior Perception of Reality" Attribute

Could some of the attitudes about the foggy minds of older people come from the fact that a lot of older people, in addition to seeing things differently, see things that younger people *may not see*? To my knowledge, there have been no definitive studies to confirm what seems common sense to me, a phenomenon embodied in the Sixth Key Factor for Maturity Markets, a factor that provides one explanation for the achievement of a "superior perception of reality":

---

**SIXTH KEY FACTOR FOR MATURITY MARKETS**
The Brain-Shift Factor

As people mature, their cognitive patterns become less abstract (left brain orientation) and more concrete (right brain orientation), which results in sharpened sense of reality, increased capacity for emotion, and enhancement of their sense of connectedness.

---

The definition of Being Experiences set forth in Chapter 5, and research by Ornstein and Restak, suggest a strong psychobiological basis for not only the increased importance of Being Experiences, but also the changes in cognitive and overall behavior patterns of mature older people.

## The Possible Psychobiological Basis for a Shift to Right Brain Orientation

As people age, the slowdown in the central nervous system leads to a slower processing of visual and acoustical information. This, in turn, results in a lessened capacity for distinguishing between colors and light intensities as well as between acoustical tones, pitches, and volume. In initial attempts to compensate for these growing deficits, a person's internal processing of externally derived information may lead to excessive and uncoordinated neuronal firings. By shifting to more right-hemisphere-oriented information processing, a person may be reducing some of the neuronal overloading. Ornstein observes in *The Psychology of Consciousness* that the right hemisphere processes information with greater simplicity of operation. Jacquelyn Wonder and Priscilla Donovan report in *Whole Brain Thinking* that an overload of words, arguments, or demands for concentration exhausts the left hemisphere which then allows the right to take over.[9]

Evidence of increased dependency on right brain information processing also lies in the fact that while older people tend to suffer declines in the ability to recognize and recall nonsense syllables (analysis of verbal information is generally processed on the left), they retain without decrement their ability to recall visual images.[10]

[9]Jacquelyn Wonder and Priscilla Donovan, *Whole Brain Thinking*, Ballantine Books, New York, 1984, p. 119.
[10]Harlan E. Spotts and Charles D. Schewe, "Communicating with the Elderly Consumer: The Growing Health Care Challenge," *Journal of Health Care Marketing*, September 1989, p. 40.

Susan Whitbourne adds further evidence of a psychobiological shift to greater right brain dependence with her research that suggests that older people may compensate for decrements in short-term memory by using life experiences and repetition of stimulus trace (the *etching* of stimuli into memory).[11] Reminiscing and repetitive mental activity tend to invoke right brain activity or at least cooperation between both hemispheres.[12]

Providing there is significant validity to the idea about a hemispheric shift in cognitive patterns in later life, the conclusion emerges that this shift can occur without respect to levels of maturity, notwithstanding Maslow's characterizations of the ways in which highly matured people change in their cognitive patterns. It may simply be that the more mature a person is, the more pronounced the shift. In any event, it's a good bet that heavier use in marketing programs of stimuli designed to invoke right brain responses would generally lead to better market response from older consumers.

### The Case for More "Right Brain" in Consumer Research Instruments

I once saw a reference to Japanese society as "a right-brain culture." In research precedent to a recent lecture trip to Japan, I learned in more detail the meaning of that representation. Tokyo-based ASI Market Research (Japan) founder and president George Fields writes in *Gucci on the Ginza* about the difficulties Westerners have in communicating with the Japanese and vice versa.[13] He attributes this to the typical Japanese mind's greater visual facility compared to the typical Western mind's greater strengths in aural communications. He explains why these differences occur.

The Japanese have three forms of written communications: *kanji*, which is expressed in Chinese ideograms (visual), and *katakana* and *hiragana*, both of which are phonetic (aural). A case is mentioned in his book concerning a Japanese who suffered brain damage that resulted in 100 percent loss of memory in *katakana* and *hiragana*. Memory for *kanji* was retained 100 percent. Investigation showed that the location in the brain for memory of *katakana* and *hiragana* was the left hemisphere. *Kanji* is memorized in the right hemisphere.

Young Japanese students first learn *kanji*, which keeps the children in a heavy right brain orientation as they begin intellectual develop-

---

[11]Ibid.
[12]Wonder and Donovan, *Whole Brain Thinking*, p. 269.
[13]George Fields, *Gucci on the Ginza*, Kodansha International, New York, 1989, p. 121.

ment. Children in general begin life with a strong right brain orientation, but in Western societies they are literally schooled away from it. Keeping in mind that the two hemispheres take different approaches in organizing reality (the left brain organizes abstractly, the right brain organizes concretely), we easily see why, as Fields asserts, Western minds have difficulty in communicating with the Japanese mind and vice versa. Each simply sees things differently.

I have hypothesized that scaled questions (for example, "strongly disagree/strongly agree" and gradations in between) do not accurately gauge mature adults' perceptions or attitudes. Maslow's characterization of mature people as "nonjudgmental" further supports that premise. Scaled questions compel respondents to make precise, finite judgments. I feel that somehow this nonjudgmental attribute is connected with a shift away from the left hemisphere and toward the right hemisphere in the organization of reality.

Fields has observed that the Japanese approach scaled questions totally differently from Westerners. The Japanese begin at the center of the scale and work toward the extremes. Westerners begin at the extremes and work toward the center. A Japanese (you can substitute *mature adult*) is cautious about taking a fixed position without all the data (scaled questions have few data) that might lead to an accurate position. Westerners, with their penchant for defining things and relegating them into neat categories (a left brain skill), have no qualms—indeed seem compelled—to take fixed positions.

A great deal in the literature on Japanese culture and recommended protocol for communicating and dealing with the Japanese is eerily reflective of Maslow's and others' observations of the behavior and cognitive patterns of mature Western personalities. Might not the root of some of the difficulties younger people have in communicating with and understanding older people be the same root that Fields says underlies difficulties in communications between the Western mind and the Japanese mind—in the specialized functions of the brain's hemispheres?

## Don't Be Afraid of Maturity

Abraham Maslow was a good man, in the highest sense of the word, judging from various readings and from conversations that I have had with his students. He acknowledged the value of the darker, Freudian views of the human mind. He recognized humankind's capacity for doing infinite harm to itself as well as to others because of demons agitating for perverse action from deep within. He agreed that these had to be dealt with, but he was a champion of fighting bad with good. He believed that many of a person's problems would begin to wane if he or she were stimulated into growing, instead of focusing primarily on what caused the problems in the first place.

In *Toward a Psychology of Being*, he wrote:

> There are certainly good and strong and successful men in the world—saints, sages, B-politicians, constructors rather than destroyers ... such people are available for anyone who wants to study them as I have. But it also remains true that there are so few of them even though there could be more, and that they are often treated badly by their fellows. So this too must be studied, this fear of human goodness and greatness ... this fear of maturity....[14]

A very well-known author and consultant in marketing told me recently, "Seniors are like everybody else—they want to be young, so they buy young." For certain, some older people do. But most older people like being older. Countless ones have told me that they never have felt freer or more satisfied with life. "I would never want to go back," many say. They are the people who are relishing their maturity. But there are those, young and old alike, who fear maturity because of its ultimate association with aging. Some hold important positions in the field of marketing. To them I say this: I am confident that, were Maslow lecturing an audience of marketers involved with maturity markets, he would say,

> Do not strive to conform older consumers to your styles and values; better for you, and what you want to accomplish, to strive to emulate their styles and values.

[14]A. Maslow, *Toward a Psychology of Being*, Van Nostrand Reinhold, New York, 1968, p. iv.

# PART 3
# Perceptions

# 7
# Symbols

## Semiotics: The Spoken and Unspoken that Rule Markets

With due respect to Gertrude Stein, a *rose* is not always a *rose*. When the word *rose* is used as a descriptor for something other than a flower, as in a person's name or as a past-tense verb, it is not a *rose*. But even in reference to a flower, that which we call a rose can be much more than a biological specimen in the plant world. It can mean, "I'm sorry" or "You are special" or "Congratulations!"

The context in which the mind cognitively operates on the concept of a rose determines its meaning to a person. Some meanings are quite literal, as in, "What's that? Oh! It's a rose." Other meanings are symbolic of botanically unrelated meanings, as when a gift of roses is intended by the giver to say, "I love you." However, in some Arab countries, a man's gift of roses to a woman would be received with horror, for the rose is a symbol of death. These thoughts are grist for the field of communications study called *semiotics*.

**173**

## Understanding Semiotics Is
## Important to Success in Maturity
## Markets

Semiotics is gaining increasing recognition in the world of marketing. It involves the most important category of concerns in marketing—image making—and one that has particular significance in maturity markets. The reading of emotionally charged symbols involves cognition patterns widely associated with the right hemisphere of the brain, not only because of its specialty in perceiving visual patterns but because of its generally proposed linkage to emotions. Since mature personalities tend to sustain an increase in emotional capacities and tend to be more creative than at earlier times in their lives, the role and power of emotionally charged symbols in maturity markets are highly significant.

Bruce Myers, executive vice president for research at BBDO Worldwide, says, "Once you put pictures and music (music listening also is processed primarily by the right brain) in people's lives, they start making judgments in a different way than they would if they were reading."[1] (Reading is processed primarily in the left brain or in both hemispheres working together, with comprehension in the left and emotional surcharges in the right.)

There is another factor that drives home the importance of understanding how symbols work in the minds of mature consumers in order to induce them to make purchasing decisions, or at least move them to the point where they are willing to consider a purchase. The instantaneous responses produced by right brain oriented cognition, in comparison with the more time-consuming elaborate processes of left brain oriented cognition, mean that marketers to mature consumers need to work doubly diligently to produce marketing communications with quickly received message units (headlines, photos, graphics, etc.) containing symbols that are positively received by prospects and are devoid of negative symbols. A headline that fails to evoke positive emotional responses may never lead a reader into the body copy. Of course, a negatively emotionally charged headline can have the same result.

### The "Context" Subjects All Symbols
### to Changes in Meaning

The field of semiotics deals with symbols and symbol systems. It is far broader in scope than semantics and linguistics, which deal with verbal communications. Semiotics deals with both verbal (aural) messages and

---

[1] S. Stiansen, "Non-Verbal Messages in Ads Gain New Importance," *Adweek's Advertising Week*, Jan. 4, 1988, p. 23.

nonverbal (but involving all five senses) messages and the symbol codes and contexts that determine their meanings. There are symbol codes shared uniquely by given peer groups, symbol codes shared uniquely by age cohorts, and, of course, symbol codes that are unique to given cultures and ethnic groups.

There also are symbol codes that associate with psychological and sociological levels of maturity, and those that associate with experiential stages of life. For example, people in their Possession Experiences years are likely to interpret symbols used in promoting a racy sports car differently than will people in their Being Experience years.

Contexts that determine meanings include the time and place in which a message is given, the subject to whom it is given, and the style of its delivery. An instruction given to a rambunctious small child to go to his or her bedroom at 10:00 a.m. means something different from the same instruction given to the same child at 10:00 p.m., even though the action commanded is the same in both messages.

In a larger dimension of time, age represents contexts that can cause the same symbol to mean different things to different people. Compliment a man of 75 by saying to him, "My, George, but you are gay!" That statement will very likely be perceived by George as having an entirely different meaning from the same statement made to a 25-year-old. George can hardly be unmindful of more recent sexual meaning of the word, but when he first learned the meaning of the word (verbal symbol) *gay*, it meant something altogether different from its more common contemporary usage.

## The Basis of Symbol Systems Is
## Formed in Initial Maturation Years

Most of the symbols we draw upon in communications with others, and in *cognitive backtalk* with ourselves as we think things through, have meanings rooted in the experiences of our initial maturation years.

Age itself does not account for differences in symbol readings. It is a matter of the character of the external forces influencing a person's perceptions of the meanings of various symbols at the time the symbols first become a part of memory. The social and cultural milieu of the early 1900s was much different from the social and cultural milieu of the 1960s. Thus a young person can read significantly different meanings into a given symbol from an older person.

Experiences in later life can add to or somewhat modify those meanings, but the original interpretations of meanings tend to stay with us all our lives. It's like the aging of copper. As time passes, copper takes on the patina of age; however, scratch through the acid-formed patina, and the underlying copper is still the same.

I related the anecdotal comparison of the difference between how a 25-year-old and a 75-year-old could interpret the meaning of the word *gay* to a woman in her late fifties. Without a hint of humor, she responded, "Yes! And I resent how young people have ruined a perfectly good word!" She conveyed that the "original" meaning was still strong from her youthful years, but she was fully aware that, like the patina of aged copper, new appearances had added a veneer to the basic element.

Suppose that 75-year-old George *were* gay, in the more common sense of the word today. He would likely have a double set of feelings invoked by being called gay. He would not have an exclusive cognitive bias toward the older meaning, and certainly he would have no moral bias, as did the woman quoted above, against the newer meaning.

### A Symbol's Meaning Is Largely Determined by Ego Needs

Experiences do temper and alter the meanings of symbols; however, some psychologists would say that the meanings are most probably changed in favor of ego factors rather than for purely objective reasons. In other words, the meanings we ascribe to and derive from symbols reflect our values—which may or may not be coincidental with the meanings perceived by people around us or by society in general.

In *The Psychology of Consciousness*, Ornstein has much to say about the influences of the ego on cognitive patterns and the products of cognition. Maslow said it quite simply when he said, "Behavior is a defense against the psyche as often as it is a direct expression of it. It's a way of hiding motivations and emotions, intent, and purport, as well as of revealing them, and therefore must never be taken at face value."[2]

Maslow is saying, in part, that when you communicate by symbol (words or behavior) with another, the person's response may carry a different meaning from what you infer because that person was hiding something, consciously or unconsciously.

## The Complex Role of Symbols in Marketplace Dynamics

Consider a woman who asks her husband on the way home after an enjoyable evening out, "Are you thirsty? Would you like to stop for a drink?" He answers, "No, I'm not thirsty." To his dismay, he notices, after arriving at home, that she has become sullen. She was telling her husband in an

---

[2]A. Maslow, *The Farther Reaches of Human Nature*, Penguin Books, Baltimore, Md., 1976, p. 196.

oblique manner that she would like to stop for a drink with him. Linguists call the kind of message that the wife was attempting to deliver a *metamessage,* a message that transcends the literal meaning of the words used.

Had the wife asked the same questions on the way home from an outing in which, say, they had been laboriously moving furniture around in his office, her meaning as well as his response might have been different. Context makes the difference. She would not have been masking a motive, and he might have perceived her questions as the result of attentiveness to their mutual needs.

## Can Marketing Messages That Are Directed at Everyone Be Effective?

Given that there are significant differences in the way mature people and less mature people read symbols, can the same message be effective in all markets for a product or service? I think the answer is, "It all depends."

Traditionally, marketers of general-interest products have studiously avoided showing older people as serious consumers of those products in ads and broadcast commercials, for fear of alienating young consumers. I think such logic is often self-defeating, because I believe it is easier to target older people and pick up young buyers in the process than the other way around.

An ad showing a group of people in which older people play a key role can be done in such a way that young people will relate to the ad in a highly emotional and positive way. Young adults have parents and grandparents whom they love and admire. Seeing one's counterparts in an ad, in an attractive fashion, can evoke the positive emotions of family relationships. Basically, it is easier to transcend age with right brain messages and images than with left brain messages and images. Right brain values tend to be more egalitarian while left brain values tend more toward discriminatory ranking.

## Broad-Appeal Marketing Draws on Universally Valued Themes

The McDonald's commercials featuring older people have been received quite positively by adults of all ages, judging from the high ratings in ad recall surveys. The TV commercial showing the elderly man eyeing an elderly woman as he looks for a place to sit evokes genuine pleasure from people of all ages because it projects that universally desired opiate, romance. Therein lies the key to universally appealing ads and commercials: presentations based on those things all people have in common.

An ad or commercial showing a group dominated by young people, however, often gives older people little to relate to, as the values reflected are commonly age or life-stage specific. A commercial developed to the beat of break dance music is age-sensitive and life-stage specific, whereas a commercial that unfolds to the accompaniment of traditional or classical music can be perceived according to universal values.

### Seniors Should Play a Large Role in Designing Marketing Programs

Knowing when and how to use and develop broad-appeal advertising requires more than a passing understanding of the values of all groups. Generally, it takes a lot of living to develop such an understanding.

The seniors referred to in the heading for this section are not senior consumers, but senior personnel in marketing organizations. Young people in marketing who are crafting graphic and narrative communications for older markets run a high risk of either not capturing mature adults' interest or of offending them because of insensitivity to the differing meanings of symbols at various points in life.

Michael Jackson and his fans understand one thing when the word *bad!* is used to describe another person or an experience. Those born early in this century understand the word to mean something else. While that is a dramatic and rather obvious example of the differences that can exist in meanings of symbols from people of one generation to those from another, there are countless others, some of which are addressed throughout this chapter.

In an article published in *Advertising Age*, titled "The Decline and Fall of Advertising," Jack Trout and Al Ries, marketing strategists of Trout & Ries in Greenwich, Connecticut, and authors of *Marketing Warfare, Positioning*, and other books on marketing, wrote recently, "In law firms, high-priced senior partners try cases and work out strategies. The junior partners do the research. So it should be in advertising agencies. Solving today's tough marketing problems requires experience. *The thinking should be done by seniors, not by juniors.*"[3]

### Advertising Ethics Can Become Murky in Use of Principles of Semiotics

In marketing, semiotics is given special importance in the area of visual communications, for often what can morally be implied through visual stimuli cannot morally be stated verbally, as evident in the following story.

---

[3]J. Trout and A. Ries, "The Decline and Fall of Advertising," *Advertising Age*, June 26, 1989, p. 26. (Italics mine.)

A few years ago, Mercedes-Benz and several other automotive manufacturers that are highly regarded by consumers for engineering excellence, designed and installed extra-large taillights for safety purposes. Domestic car manufacturers soon followed suit, ostensibly with the idea that "Euro-taillights" on a Euro-sport Chevrolet suggested high tech performance. Consumers making such an association would be doing so regardless of the attributes of the vehicle in front of the taillights.[4] Imagery thus would be transcending reality, in a positive way for the vehicle's marketers, without their having to say anything that wasn't true.

Jay C. Houghton, writing on semiotics in *Advertising Age*, raises an interesting point: "While we are legislated to truthfully depict a product's performance or substantiate our claims, no legislation governs the depiction of what it stands for or is symbolic of. How often do we see products positioned as symbols of success or achievement or sexual prowess when, in fact, they can contribute nothing to those ends."[5]

Houghton's point may have more relevance to maturity markets than to other markets. If marketers represent a forced or unrealistic relationship between product or service and the experiences that are an implied potential consequence of the purchase, mature consumers, who place utmost value on honesty and integrity, likely will be repelled.

### How Sight Can Make Eggs Taste Bad

A client recently told me a story that is an equally good example of how symbols can unconsciously convey impressions that the facts may not support. The client had a custom of periodically staying overnight in various retirement communities that his company owned in order to get a deeper feeling for the attitudes of residents toward their community and its management. On one of his visits, residents came to him with complaints that the eggs being served for breakfast had deteriorated in quality, "ever since you changed suppliers and went with that low-cost outfit."

My client checked with management and found that there had been no change of egg suppliers. Instead, the egg supplier had changed trucks. Previously the eggs had been delivered in trucks clearly marked with something like, "Farmer Brown's Farm Fresh Eggs." Recently, "Farmer Brown" had been delivering eggs in a plain, unmarked truck. The residents had associated the symbol of an unmarked truck with cheaper, hence inferior, products which then translated into poorer-tasting eggs.

Houghton, who is marketing manager for Audi of America, refers to

---

[4]J. C. Houghton, "Semiotics on the Assembly Line," *Advertising Age*, Mar. 16, 1987, p. 18.

[5]Ibid.

the process involved in a person's perception of a product's design features that lead to assumed values as the *transformation process*. Perhaps a more descriptive term would be *meaning transference*, referring to the transference of values (meanings) between unrelated objects. (Its acronym, *MT*, carries an appropriate irony about it, when pronounced out loud.)

There is obviously no relationship between taillights and engineering excellence and no relationship between the taste of eggs and the appearance of the truck that delivers them. Yet, consumers can and often do draw such irrational conclusions. When this happens, "feelings" or emotions impede or overwhelm logic.

## Meaning Transference Is Driven by Emotional, Not Rational, Processes

The most dramatic example of meaning transference between unrelated objects that comes to mind was accomplished by Richard Nixon in 1952 when, as a candidate for Vice President, he was suddenly facing calls to step aside over a mid-campaign scandal. He appeared before the television cameras in a homestyle setting to answer his detractors. Beside him was a dog. Nixon:

> It was a little cocker spaniel dog in a crate ... sent all the way from Texas—black and white, spotted, and our little girl Tricia, the six-year-old, named it Checkers. As you know, the kids, like all kids, loved that dog, and I just want to say this right now, that regardless of what they say about it, we're going to keep it.

Keeping in mind that "they" had never said anything about the cocker spaniel because no one knew of it until the TV broadcast, what Nixon was *really* saying was, "Regardless of what *they* say about *it*, we are going *to keep Richard Nixon.*"

Nixon's creative employment of meaning transference was extraordinarily successful. Within the next 24 hours, over a million Americans registered their support of Nixon in an avalanche of phone calls, telegrams, and letters. A logical evaluation by the TV audience would have seen the fate of the dog as wholly unrelated to the fate of Richard Nixon. Nixon proved himself masterful in moving the issue from one invoking logical responses to one evoking emotional responses—a case of pure left brain bypass—in what has since come to known as Nixon's famous "Checkers speech."

Meaning transference between unrelated objects would seem to heavily involve B-cognition or right brain processes since D-cognition or left brain processes would disclose such a connection as meaningless or even silly—if not altogether deceptive.

Marketing messages designed to stimulate meaning transference have one distinct advantage over messages designed to invoke rational responses: The communication is instantaneous, and because it first registers emotionally, rather than logically, MT messages provide little for a person's left brain cynicism to take pot shots at. The capacity of MT messages to register instantly is obviously a benefit to marketers because such communications are not confronted with attention-span challenges. They register as first impressions rather than as the evolutionary impressions that D-cognition processes produce.

## Packaging Creates Assumptions about Product Performance

There is another phenomenon that is similar to meaning transference which Davis Masten, of California-based Chesken & Masten, a firm specializing in image consulting, refers to as *sensation transference*. He describes it as a process by which consumers transfer feelings from advertising and packaging to the product itself.[6]

No small degree of Steven Job's initial marketing success with Apple Computer is attributed to the trendy, forward looking design of the boxes containing the high tech electronics. It was a positive and powerful contrast with Big Blue's cool, utilitarian product design. Job's design responded strongly to the values inherent in the symbols vocabulary of the high tech generation that would be Apple's biggest users: the boomers. Big Blue's products were left for a more stodgy crowd.

Meaning transference and sensation transference are important concepts because strategies based on their invocation solve positioning challenges when consumers perceive few differences between competing brands. Because neither of those forms of *cognitive transference* initially involves rational thinking processes, both represent instantaneous or first-impression reactions.

## Mature Adults Are Not Opinionated, but Are Strong in Their Opinions

First impressions tend to be holistic impressions because the perceived object enters cognition simultaneously with the attributes assigned to it by the perceiver. This squares with Maslow's characterization of highly matured personalities as "non-judgmental." It is not that they lack judgment. They simply don't call on elaborated processes to arrive at judg-

---

[6]J. Motavalli, "Probing Consumers' Minds," *Adweek's Marketing Week*, Dec. 7, 1987, p. 8.

ments. Because judgments about relevance and values arrive in cognition as the object is being perceived, older people tend toward greater frequency of first-impression conclusiveness.

Although first impressions often lack support from follow-up verbal explanations, people forming quick conclusions from first impressions "feel" their decisions are as logical, complete, and correct as if their impressions (decisions) had been arrived at through logical processes.

Marketers to mature consumers, observing that their first impressions often appear to be their last, sometimes conclude that older people are opinionated and resistant to change. All evidence suggests that older people as a rule have neither less—nor more—certainty about the reality of a matter than a D-cognizer who has gone through all the elaborations of left brain analytical thinking. The mature will, in fact, readily change opinions—even subjecting the matter to analytical processing—if a different message "feels" right to them. So their alleged closed-mindedness is the result of a tendency toward quick decision-making—the product of experience and confidence in their judgments.

## Implications of Differences in Right and Left Brain Cognitive Patterns

When the occasion demands, the B-cognizer can, and often does, return to the use of the D-cognizer skills, developed and more heavily employed earlier in life. This is another example of what Maslow referred to as the "polarities and oppositions" of older self-actualization-oriented people which are often viewed by younger people as paradoxical or contradictory behavior. On one hand, mature older people make instant judgments, which often are resolute to the point of terminating desire to think any more about the matter; on the other hand, they can demonstrate considerable skill in sequential reasoning processes. This gives rise to the Sixth Principle for Maturity Markets:

---

**SIXTH PRINCIPLE FOR MATURITY MARKETS**
The Cognitive Processing Principle

Discretionary purchase decisions of mature consumers tend to originate with the more "instinctive" right brain processes (B-cognition), and conclude with left brain processes (D-cognition) in order to provide a rational validation of initial feelings.

---

Initial responses of mature consumers to a discretionary purchase offering tend to originate in the emotions, while final decisions are determined by rational processes. In other words, interest may be generated as a whim, but not many purchases are made on a whim.

## Putting the Right Brain/Left Brain Concept into Perspective

Before elaborating further on the Sixth Principle for Maturity Markets, I want to anticipate those readers who take the position, "This right brain/left brain thing is overplayed." Discussions of the concept have occasionally evoked such responses from individuals and seminar attendees, one of whom observed, "I think this right brain/left brain business will eventually be debunked."

For the purposes of the hypotheses expressed in this book regarding the purported roles of each hemisphere of the brain in cognitive processes, the ultimate validity of this "right brain/left brain thing" is immaterial. For my purposes, *red cognition* and *blue cognition*, or D-cognition and B-cognition, would serve just as well as *right brain* and *left brain* as labels for the dichotomy in the cognitive approaches and operations between fully mature adults (in the Eriksonian/Maslovian sense) and less matured adults.

While Maslow observed differences in cognitive patterns between highly and less highly matured adult personalities, he did not relate them to specializations of right and left brain hemispheres. That dichotomy was not recognized in his time. It is noteworthy, however, that the attributes of cognition that he assigned, respectively, to those he termed D-cognizers and B-cognizers precisely correspond to the cognition dichotomies that neuroscientists say characterize the specialized functions of the brain's two hemispheres.

## The Idea of Two Minds in One Is Ancient

That there are "two minds in one" has been subject to observations and speculations among psychologists for generations and among philosophers for centuries. Neuroscientist Joseph E. Bogen wrote two decades ago, "I hope you will believe Pythagoras and Plato, the wisest of the ancient philosophers, who, according to Cicero, divided the mind into two parts, one partaking of reason and the other devoid of it."[7]

---

[7]Joseph E. Bogen, "The Other Side of the Brain: An Appositional Mind," *Bulletin of the Los Angeles Neurological Societies*, vol. 34, no. 3, July 1969.

Bogen goes on to summarize the differences in specialties of the two hemispheres: "The left hemisphere of the cortex, which subtends [underlies or wraps around] language and mathematics, seems to process information primarily in sequential manner, appropriate to its specialties. The right side of the cortex processes its input more as a 'patterned whole,' that is, in a more simultaneous manner than does the left."[8]

With respect to the purported dominant role of the right hemisphere in our emotions, neuroscientist Richard M. Restak, author of *The Brain* (upon which the award-winning PBS series of the same name was based), observed, "Subjects have been shown to strongly favor the right hemisphere for the memory storage of emotionally charged material."[9]

Emotionally charged material—isn't that what marketers often try to infuse into their marketing messages? The fact that emotionally charged material tends to be processed first in the right hemisphere of the brain is a matter of more than just academic interest to marketers. Given that each hemisphere has its own distinct way of processing information, marketing effectiveness calls for the development and presentation of information consistent with the cognitive characteristics of the hemisphere being targeted. The challenge is to design programs which incorporate the fact that the two hemispheres operate interdependently, and often cooperate in determining a final course of action on a matter.

## How We Learned about the Brain's Hemispheric Specialization

The most compelling evidence of the "two minds in one" depiction of the upper brain's hemispheres derives from research begun in 1961 by Dr. Roger Perry, of the California Institute of Technology. That research took a dramatic leap forward in providing a fuller understanding of the human brain when Perry's neurosurgical colleague, Joseph E. Bogen, cut the *corpus callosum*, the wall of fibrous connections linking the two hemispheres, in 16 epileptic patients suffering from life-threatening seizures. Thus separated, the functions of each hemisphere could be independently studied.

The most startling discovery was made:

> Instead of the normally unified stream of consciousness, these patients behave in many ways as if they have two independent

8Ibid.
9Richard M. Restak, *The Brain: The Last Frontier*, Warner Books, New York, 1979, p. 201.

streams of conscious awareness, one in each hemisphere, each of which is cut off from and out of contact with the mental experiences of the other. In other words, each hemisphere seems to have *its own separate and private sensations, its own perceptions, its own impulses to act....*[10] (Italics mine.)

Underscoring the great significance of the research of Perry and Bogen in developing revolutionary new insights into the operation of the human brain is their award of the Nobel Prize in 1977. Since their early work, equally revolutionary findings have been made in a field described by some experts as the most rapidly advancing area of all sciences.

## Lead with the Right; Follow with the Left

The Sixth Principle for Maturity Markets reflects the greater capacity for emotional response (in relation to one's past capacities) experienced by members of maturity markets. It puts into perspective the recommendation to give older consumers "lots of facts." They won't look at the facts until they've been attracted by emotional appeals. So the marketer's first task is to create an opportunity by which they can vicariously experience or identify with the values associated with the product or service. If that experience elicits positive feelings, the consumer will want to look at the product or service with a sharper, more incisive sense of realism. At that point, the marketer had better be able to provide the facts that these Ph.D.s in consumer purchases will be seeking.

With respect to a right brain lead (emotional lead) in advertising or promotional materials, members of maturity markets are not intrinsically different from people in other markets. For a long time marketers have widely practiced the principle of "Sell the sizzle, not the steak." But with mature buyers, marketers must be prepared to sell the sizzle *and* the steak.

## Selling to Seniors Is like Selling to the Japanese

Targeting brain hemispheres in consumers' minds is a relatively simple task. Headlines and body copy that deal with facts and reasons to buy are processed primarily in the left brain. Mood pictures and graphics, along with copy that evokes emotions, are processed primarily in the right brain. Because of the apparent increase in right brain information processing

---

[10]Ibid, p. 196.

among mature adults, a right brain lead will often be more effective in getting an initial favorable response than a left brain lead. (See Figure 7-1.)

Earlier I alluded to the Japanese people's heavier orientation to right
brain cognition and skills in interpreting the "visual," due to early
schooling in *kinji*, a visually oriented written language. As a result of the
Japanese people's strong visual orientation, Japanese advertising is
more mood-oriented (right brain) than hard-sell-oriented (left brain).
Assuming the general correctness of my hypothesis about the cognitive
shifting of mature adults toward the right brain, selling to seniors may
be a lot like selling to the Japanese.

Mood advertising need not be confined to self-indulgent images. In
fact, Japanese mood advertising often reflects group rather than personal values. Products are often marketed in terms of right brain humanistic values. Ads appear that never describe the product but instead
promote the company's concern for a better environment, or that extol
"human values, peace, quiet, and return to nature."[11] Company integrity thus becomes attributed to the product through *meaning transference. The product becomes defined by values, not logic, and the relevance
of the product to a consumer's needs and desires is defined by the consumer, not the ad maker.* These dynamics employ the principles of conditional positioning described in Chapter 1.

### Grandma's House Is Nicer Than "Social Security Haven"

Figure 7-1, showing two advertisements for a senior housing community, clearly demonstrates the effectiveness of strategies that are based
upon the Sixth Principle for Maturity Markets. This chapter explains
how those ads reflect the operation of that principle.

An interesting background story involving those ads conveys the importance to marketers of the Cognitive Processing Principle. For reasons that will shortly become clear, one ad has what I would term a
"right brain" lead, the other a "left brain" lead. Gene Grace, of Grace
Management Company, the company handling the on-site marketing
and sales for the senior adult community promoted in the ads, gave me
copies of the ads, telling me that to his surprise, one ad produced four
times as much qualified traffic as the other. He asked me which ad I
thought was the winning ad. I picked what I thought was the one and
told him why it was the winning ad. With some surprise, he acknowledged my choice as the correct one. I put the ads in my briefcase, and in

[11]Boye De Mente, *How to Do Business with the Japanese*, NTC Business Books,
Lincolnwood, Ill., 1987, p. 202.

# GRANDMA & GRANDPA'S HOUSE.

Thanks to Tarrytowne, Grandma and Grandpa can spend the best years of their lives in grand style.

Tarrytowne is a unique community of elegant, well-appointed garden homes designed specifically with the active senior adult in mind. In fact, no other community offers such convenience, amenities and features in such a warm and friendly atmosphere.

- NO ENTRANCE FEE.

- 1 & 2 bedroom apartments available.

- 24-hour staff & emergency call security system.

- Delightful dining and social activities.

- Special "Commons" area with country club amenities.

Come out and reserve your special place on our residence list today. For more information, call and ask about transportation to our beautiful models. And bring your grandchildren. They'll love visiting Tarrytowne as much as you'll enjoy living here.

TARRYTOWNE WESTBRAE
10680 Westbrae Parkway
(713) 771-3707

TARRYTOWNE MEMORIAL
1815 Enclave Parkway
(713) 531-1905

Houston's Most Prestigious
Senior Adult Communities.

(a)

**Figure 7-1.** Comparison of (a) right brain and (b) left brain housing ads. (*Courtesy of Tarrytowne and Grace Management Company.*)

# SOCIAL. SECURITY.

More than just neighbors — the caring people of Tarrytowne invite you to come experience the friendship and the security of Houston's most exciting and prestigious senior adult communities.

Designed with senior adults in mind, Tarrytowne's elegant, well-appointed garden homes are unlike anything you've seen before. In fact, no other community offers such convenience, amenities and features in such a warm and friendly atmosphere.

- NO ENTRANCE FEE.

- 24-hour staff & emergency call security system.
- Delightful dining and social activities.
- Weekly housekeeping.
- Special "Commons" area with country club amenities.

Come out and reserve your special place on our residence list today. For more information, call and ask about transportation to our beautifully furnished models. Once you see Tarrytowne, you'll agree — retirement definitely has its benefits.

TARRYTOWNE WESTBRAE
10680 Westbrae Parkway
(713) 771-3707

TARRYTOWNE MEMORIAL
1815 Enclave Parkway
(713) 531-1905

Houston's Most Prestigious
Senior Adult Communities.

( b )

**Figure 7-1.** (Continued)

my travels began to ask other people involved in marketing similar communities which ad they thought was the one that produced four times as much qualified traffic as the other ad. I stopped counting the respondents at around 50. Only one marketer selected the correct ad.

I also asked a number of nonmarketers the question. About 60 percent selected the winning ad, which was the "Grandma's and Grandpa's House" ad. The marketers, in my polling, reflected a bias toward the belief that the left brain considerations—"Is there a good social life here?" and "Is the security good?"—were of greater value to older consumers than the right brain intangibles of feelings.

The "Grandma & Grandpa's House" ad, shown in Figure 7-1(a), reflects right brain values because human love and caring emotions, which are said to center in the right hemisphere of the brain, are evoked by the terms "Grandma" and "Grandpa." Even with the insertion of the period between the words "Social" and "Security" the other ad's headline still remains dominantly a left brain headline. Notice that the copy below the headlines is essentially the same; in both cases, the text is quite similar and dominantly left brain.

Another interesting aspect of the left brain ad, according to Grace, who ordered the ads from Fellers & Gadis in Austin, Texas, was that prospects who visited the project in response to the "Social. Security." ad were "tire-kickers." *Tire-kickers* is a term describing a left brain mental disposition and used derisively by marketers in referring to shoppers who show great skepticism. Also more children of older people were brought to the sales center by the "Social. Security." ad than by the "Grandma & Grandpa" ad, a clear reflection of young adults' left brain orientation in their current stage of life.

A representative of one advertising firm called me a while ago to tell me that she and others in her firm had seen a piece with those ads and comments I had written, but it did not identify the more effective ad. She wanted to know which ad was the more effective one, saying she was the member of a minority in her firm in selecting the "Grandma & Grandpa" ad. In fact, she said, based on her guesswork before calling me, she had a new ad crafted, based upon the right brain/left brain hypothesis of messaging, for a project that was suffering from poor traffic. The ad hit the mark; traffic significantly increased.

## Right Brain Ads Can Bypass Consumers' Skepticism

Right brain oriented approaches are more subtle than left brain approaches. Stuart Agres, executive of strategic planning for Lowe Marshalk, says, "A subtle approach works better because it has a chance to get past the consumer's barrier of skepticism." I might add that a sub-tler approach also frees up the consumer's imagination to define the product or service in terms of his or her own values, needs, and de-sires—the very essence of conditional positioning at work for the mar-keter.

Agres' company has conducted studies of rationally oriented (left brain) ads versus ads combining rational and emotional (right brain) messages, and the latter ads scored significantly higher in both recall and persuasion.[12] By combining elements that appeal to *both* the ratio-nal side and the emotional side of consumers' minds, the marketer is presenting a *cognitively holistic* message, one that will be more effective with more mature consumers. Alternatively, a consumer may resist buy-ing because of uncertainty about the total nature of a product.

The dilatory pace of some senior adults in coming to a decision to buy or rent in a senior adult community no doubt reflects the greater num-ber of perspectives they often incorporate in their purchasing behavior to arrive at a *complete* picture. In their earlier years, people commonly put more thought into the left brain values of a new home, for example, price, terms, financing, size, and conveniences. In their later years, they are more inclined to devote a great deal of attention to the right brain values of the new home, for example, who their neighbors are for pur-poses of socialization experiences, other experiential opportunities re-lated to their feelings, and the overall intangible ambient qualities of the community.

### Beware of Negative Symbols in Product Design

One day I was relating to a senior housing developer my ideas about the role of symbols in either attracting or repelling older people to senior housing projects. I told him of one senior adult community I had visited that consisted of one building laid out very much along the lines of a nursing home, but instead of single rooms contained apartments. Es-sentially, the building layout was in the form of a "Y," with quite long corridors. I had been called in by the client to try and diagnose the poor sales results of a project that was well styled and appointed, if reminis-cent of a nursing home.

At the end of the first day of my visit to the community, a company vice president escorted me down a long hallway to an elevator on the way to the apartment in which I was to stay for the night. The elevator

[12]K. Foltz, "Psychological Appeal in TV Ads Found Effective," *Adweek's Marketing Week*, Jan. 4, 1986, p. 38.

door opened and disclosed a cavernous space large enough to handle several gurneys (wheeled stretchers)—similar to the elevators you see in a typical nursing home or hospital. I commented on its size, and the VP smiled with obvious pride and said, "Yes, they are great. We use golf carts to transport residents from the lobby to their apartments, and these elevators are large enough to accommodate the golf carts."

I said to the developer to whom I telling this story, "You know, it never occurred to the project's designers or to my client that the golf cart service emphasizes the long nursing home type of corridors and that the gurney-sized elevator makes a negative statement about the place and the grim things that happen to some of its residents."

I then said to my developer friend, "Show that elevator to a 25-year-old and she will say, 'Great! Finally an elevator you can move furniture in!' But show the elevator to a 75-year-old, and he might think, 'This is where they carry the bodies out'."

The developer responded, "I know what you are saying. I learned the same thing, so I had Otis Elevator install the elevators that we need for gurneys sideways, and we put a small love seat in. Now our elevator just looks like a pleasant oversized elevator rather than a hospital or nursing home elevator."

## The Semiotics of Product Design Strongly Influence Perceptions

My developer friend and I had been discussing the semiotics of the project's architecture. Keeping in mind the words of French semiologist Roland Barthes that the discipline includes "any system of signs, whatever their substance and limits; images, gestures, musical sounds, objects, and the complex associations of all these,"[13] it becomes apparent that every detail of the nursing home–styled retirement community was subject to approval or disapproval by every visitor because every detail projects a message. The same is true of every detail of every ad, every detail of every design element of a product, and every detail, body language and all, of every sales conversation. In fact, any aspect of a product or service, including any aspect of the associated marketing activities, that can enter a person's mind through any one or more of the five senses has meanings to convey.

Perhaps now is a good time to recall the definitions of marketing and marketers used in Chapter 1. Drawing upon the definition of marketing adopted by the American Marketing Association, the architect of the

---

[13]C. Suplee, "In Search of More Perfect Persuasion," *Washington Post*, Jan. 18, 1987, p. C-3.

building with the gurney-sized elevators is a marketer. He injected negative marketing messages into his institutionally oriented design when he could have created positive ones. Unwittingly, the architect created a design that was replete with strong anti-Being Experience symbols.

## Studiously Avoid Anti-Being Experience Symbols

The first-impression messages projected by long hallways and gurney-sized elevators fall into the category of anti-Being Experience messages, which are defined as follows:

> **Anti-Being Experiences:** Experiences that discomfort a person, or tend to threaten or actually thwart attempts to be what he or she wants to be.

When a product's design or a service program conveys symbols of conditions that repel a person, it is conveying anti-Being Experience messages.

Every reader can easily relate to the idea of anti-Being Experiences. We all have been discomforted by reminders of some condition we fear or disdain. Each of us has dealt with countless incidents throughout life in which some event or some person has thwarted us from being what we want to be. A workplace superior who fails to acknowledge a dedicated and productive worker is subjecting the subordinate to an anti-Being Experience. The very essence of an anti-Being Experience is interference with a person's *being*.

I have seen countless ads and brochures for senior adult housing and health care facilities that show staff helping residents. Such images are anti-Being Experience symbols. Their visual character invokes right brain responses of negative emotions instead of the desired left brain logical response of "here is a place that is *right* for you for *these* reasons."

Marketing consultant Gordon French told me a story that strongly symbolizes the extreme sensitivity older people feel toward "helping hands." Headed for church one Sunday, French encountered a neighbor, who was in her eighties, arriving at the church steps at the same time as he did. He reached out for her arm, which she immediately withdrew with the command, "Don't take my arm. If I want help, *I will take yours*." She was putting him on notice that he was attempting to force an anti-Being Experience on her—by not letting her be what she wanted to be, or by assuming her to be other than she was.

Elias Cohen, president of Community Services Systems, Inc.,

Narberth, Pennsylvania, spells out the cumulative effects of "helping hand"–administered anti-Being Experiences. He proposes that caregivers, gerontologists, family members, public agencies, and others create and maintain conditions whereby "elderly with disabilities are the victims of low-goal formulation and underestimated potentials for self-realization." This results in what is commonly referred to as *learned dependency*, a condition whereby a person accomplishes less—is less—than his or her intrinsic capabilities would allow. Cohen suggests that servicers of elderly also suffer from learned dependency, in that they develop a need to have elderly depend on them in order to fulfill servicers' agendas.[14]

Cohen's indictment of servicers of elderly people as a major cause of diminished autonomy among older people has dramatic implications. He basically is saying that greater autonomy means decreased roles for servicers, thereby posing a threat to servicers' roles and importance.

I have long believed that those who ostensibly have had the best interests of older people in mind have, in fact, been a primary source of the flawed images of older people's competence and self-reliance. This is true for organizations that serve as advocates for older people as well as for individuals. After all, one stands a better chance of getting public funds or new laws passed to benefit older people when one convincingly draws a picture of widespread need. Much good has been accomplished by that approach, but it has been a double-edged sword. The good accomplished has been offset somewhat by the promotion of false images about life for those in their later years, which have subjected countless older people to undeserved anti-Being Experiences. Unfortunately, marketers have widely bought into those images, and they end up creating marketing messages that often repel older people because of the anti-Being Experience connections.

Anti-Being Experience messages are the very antithesis of the First General Principle of Marketing. People do not want to be ill or dependent. People do not want to be surrounded by reminders of what they do *not* want to be. And people, in general, don't like messages that tend to group them with people who are being what they would rather not be.

Some people argue that life insurance ads are inherently anti-Being Experience ads. However, typical life insurance ads mostly convey a right brain focus on happy survivors whose welfare has been secured by a thoughtful, caring, and loving family provider; or the ads make a straightforward appeal directly to the left brain in selling the benefits of

---

[14]Elias S. Cohen, "The Elderly Mystique: Constraints on the Autonomy of the Elderly with Disabilities," *The Gerontologist*, vol. 28 (suppl.), 1988, p. 24.

prudent financial planning. Most people want to be thoughtful providers, a right brain value; and most people want to think of themselves as prudent, logical thinkers and planners, both left brain attributes.

## "Snake-Check" Marketing Materials for Anti-Being Experience Symbols

The imperturbable Alexander Haig, when he was Secretary of State, frequently insisted upon documents being "snake-checked" before they left the State Department. He appropriated the term from his military experience. When soldiers on bivouac return long after sundown to their sleeping areas, they are advised to check their sleeping bags for any snakes that may have slithered in. Haig's use of the term in State Department communications meant orders to his staff to double-check documents for "hidden snakes" that could create untoward results.

Marketing communications directed at maturity markets should be carefully snake-checked for untoward readings of symbols that to less mature people might carry altogether different meanings. In Chapter 10, you will read about Ted Marzac who organized his Silver Foxes program using retired marketers to snake-check marketing communications. Older people are the best snake-checkers, because they understand the idioms and semiotic values of other older people better than most younger people.

## Chronic Illness Can Be Good for Your Mental Health

"It's now time to take our medicine, Grandma." To a nursing home resident, that statement is an anti-Being Experience. It underlines Grandma's presumed dependency and suggests that she has entered into a state of being where she no longer deserves a more respectful manner of address. No one has told the administering nurse that she is a member of the marketing team, a member of the postsales service group. Her attitude is not likely to contribute to the building of a referral market for the nursing home.

Such attitudes derive from a presumption that older people who are in a state involving some degree of dependency are often best treated as another dependent group is treated—children.

There is a widely prevailing belief that a chronic illness, or even acute illness, necessarily interferes with mental well-being and life satisfaction and makes a person more dependent. However, a longitudinal study carried out in Bonn, Germany, between 1965 and 1983 found that the opposite is often true. In comparisons made over time between healthy subjects and subjects that sustained a chronic disease, psychologists Andreas Kruse and Ursala Lehr discovered the following:

> Contrary to our hypothesis, in the group of healthy persons, the dependency in everyday life was significantly *higher* than in the group of ill persons. *Illness and dependency do not go together.* There has been the tendency to classify the elderly generally as being dependent. Our analysis *totally* contradicts this generalization. Even in cases of serious diseases, most elderly people are able to live a self-reliant and independent life.[15]

Kruse and Lehr reported that their healthy participants also showed more depression as well as a wish for more help in their lives. In view of estimates that two out of three people aged 65 and older have some form of chronic condition, the findings of these two researchers are highly important to anyone involved in *any* capacity with older people. In accepting Kruse's and Lehr's findings, a person who has held more traditional views can hardly avoid viewing older people in general and chronically ill people in particular in a different and more positive light.

## Physical Conditions Are Unrelated to a Person's Sense of Well-Being

How is it possible that many people who become chronically ill can be so upbeat, while many healthier people in the same age cohort register less happiness and life satisfaction? Isn't that contrary to common sense? Common sense is experience-based intuition. So until a person has experienced what the chronically ill older person has experienced, his or her common sense will arrive at conclusions based upon speculation, not experience.

A man who has never sustained a prolonged chronic condition looks at another person who is sustaining such a condition and vicariously experiences it in the context of his current state of wellness. The man suddenly sustains an anti-Being Experience: He is discomfited by the prospects of losing his good health to a persistent illness. Sympathetic emotions then color the perceptions of the chronically ill person. What has happened is that the healthy person has effected a *sensation transference*. He has projected his values upon the chronically ill person in analyzing the ill person's condition, and then, having drawn a conclu-

---

[15]A. Kruse and U. Lehr, "Longitudinal Analysis of the Developmental Process in Chronically Ill and Healthy Persons—Empirical Findings from the Bonn Longitudinal Study of Aging (BOLSA)," *International Psychogeriatrics*, spring 1989, pp. 73–85.

sion about the nature of the condition, further projected his values in presuming to know the nature of the ill person's state of mind and general outlook.

In the meantime, according to Kruse and Lehr, the ill person has been reappraising life and forging new adjustments which involve the setting of newly defined expectations and goals, both of which are defined in realistic terms reflective of any limitations imposed by the illness. Kruse and Lehr found that the ill subjects in their research were generally more oriented toward planning and forming new thoughts about the future than were healthy subjects.

With new expectations and goals in hand, the person is ready to tackle life anew. To achieve and maintain a sense of well-being, all that person has to do is to see expectations realized and goals met. For a stroke victim who was initially paralyzed by the stroke, walking down a 100-foot-long corridor in less than 10 minutes can induce a high as great as that of a climber on reaching the top of Mt. Everest.

Well-being and life satisfaction are inextricably linked with the realization of expectations and fulfillment of goals, regardless of one's physical capabilities. Physical condition has ultimately little to do with a person's ability to feel good about self and life. Recalling Maslow's comments about the principal role of behavior being the "defense against the psyche," it is natural for a person who has sustained impairment of certain abilities to adopt a new style of behavior that "defends against the psyche." When that happens, the person has successfully converted what was initially an anti-Being Experience to a Being Experience: the successful surmounting of a major challenge.

When a marketer has created a marketing message that brings to mind limitations, based on the marketer's value system, someone who has overcome an anti-Being Experience can be powerfully repelled by the message. It is always the better course in marketing to any target group of consumers to assume that they have no limitations in achieving their goals. It is not even wise to make light of or humorously refer to limitations.

## Misplaced Humor Often Results in Anti-Being Experiences

The stereotypical images from which older people have suffered for so long are as demeaning as those images of blacks created from their predominant casting in pre-World War II movies as housemaids, handymen, town clowns, and "born-to-be" dancers. They were nearly always cast in those images with strong doses of humor that conveyed a societally reinforced inference that blacks could not be serious human beings with serious roles, serious needs, and real concerns in the "white man's world."

The effect—*not the purpose*—of such humorously proffered role portrayals was mass imposition of anti-Being Experiences on an entire race. Anti-Being Experiences, cloaked in humor, made it easier on a person's conscience to keep blacks in "their place," a place without dignity in white society. Humor is often used to dull the effects of human prejudice on otherwise decent spirits, for prejudice diminishes both the bigot and the victim of prejudice.

## Misplaced Humor Helps Create Stereotypes of Older People

We have seen and laughed at, from the time of our first memories, portrayals of old people in ways as unseemly and unkind as those suffered by blacks in earlier movies. Think of the bulbous-chinned toothless old man that we still see in cartoons, or the cranky, toothy old woman with bedraggled hair. Cartoonists reflect society's attitudes and values in their work, especially in their caricatures. Their object often is to communicate serious ideas in amusing ways. Their success is evidence of both their ability to communicate in ways that amuse and the attitudes of those who are amused.

No better than the visual caricatures of older people by cartoonists are the depictions in other forms of older people as neuter (no capacity for or interest in sex and romance), indolent (a lifestyle of full-time leisure, "doing nothing,") and impaired ("Let me do that for you, Grandpa." "Eh? What's that you say, sonny?").

It is important that marketers not read these as moralizing comments. These comments are straight talk about the reason for many older people's hypersensitivity to symbols that are strongly rooted in age-based contexts. It is not that older people have a diminished capacity for humor. To the contrary, Maslow found that highly mature people experienced an increase in capacity for humor. What I am talking about is the kind of humor that may help younger people deal with their own fears of aging, but robs older people of their sense of purpose, dignity, and value in society.

When an ad or broadcast commercial shows an older person in a position of curtailed or defective functioning, that ad or commercial is mirroring images that have long been projected in caricature in cartoons, comics, movies, television, radio, and even children's literature. When the prospective purchaser of a product sees an ad with images of older people expressed in disrespectful caricatures, that person's likely emotional defense reaction is to ignore the ad, and the *logical* defense reaction is simply not to buy.

### Negative Meaning Transference Jeopardizes Marketing Success

It is irrelevant that there is no logical connection between a product's value and the social statements implicitly or explicitly made in its marketing activities. When those statements carry elements of caricatures of aged people, *negative* meaning transference takes place: The negative meanings reflected in the marketing activities are transferred to the product or service being marketed.

Because of the phenomenon of meaning transference between unrelated concepts, stereotypical image projections are not limited to graphically explicit expressions in narrative or graphic marketing communications. For example, conventionally designed grab bars in the bathrooms of a senior adult housing apartment that is being shown to fully ambulatory and able prospective residents shout, "Stereotypes live here!" and so alienate potential residents. Some designers have gotten the message and either create "designer" editions of hand assists, or are blocking walls for later possible installation of hand assists at the occupant's request. As useful, practical, and sometimes necessary as they are, the image projected by grab bars is one of personal diminishment.

Advertising messages that say, in effect, "Be selfish, you have earned it" associate a product or service being offered with people who suffer from vacuous self-absorption—an image reflecting what few older people want to be, but an image consistent with past caricatures of older people. Remember that commercial in which the closing statement is made by a pain-racked, unsteady old man who complains, "Is this what getting old means?"

## Countering Anti-Being Experiences with Positive Images

Getting old is not what a lot of young people think it is. It will come as a surprise to a lot of 30-year-olds that when they are in their sixties, seventies, and beyond, they will see themselves as still basically the same persons. Many of today's older people have been delighted to learn that about themselves. In essence, they have learned that although the body ages, the person does not. Dr. Lou Kopolow, my adviser in interpreting

Maslow, suggested that a pearl might be an apt analogy for describing the passage of the person through time. "The pearl," he noted, "grows layer by layer, each layer having a higher luster than those preceding." Beyond some point in time, many people—the more mature ones— think more about pearl-like growth than about age.

Not all older people, of course, look at being older in the same sense as Lou Kopolow does. They dwell too much on the pearl as "the product of a grain of sand and a lot of irritation." Nevertheless, studies show that most older people have a more quiescent, happier view of aging.

Consider a highly subjective view—my view of my own aging:

At age 56, the world still looks more or less the same to me as it did when I was 30 or even 20. I believe I have grown a bit wiser, but I am still the same person. The reality I perceive now is not all that different from the reality I organized in my mind 30 years ago. The sky, the earth, and the creatures of the earth all look pretty much the same. And they all act much the same as before. I sometimes muse: "Nothing much has changed out there. I wonder if I have changed much in the view of others? I see an attractive young woman; I wonder if she thinks of me as handsome. Why not? I am still me."

Anything that suggests that I am different simply because I have grown older is offensive. It is an assault on my identity. It took me years to find out and define who I am. Now some people want to redefine my identity for me. I resent it. And I will not buy their products.

## Show Mature Consumers Enjoying Self-Esteem

It is not very difficult to determine how mature adults would like to see themselves represented in communications, whether in the form of statements that buildings make or that advertisements deliver or in the attitudes conveyed by people dealing with or serving them. Maslow's listing of 13 key attributes of self-actualizing people lays it all out. But his fourth, and last, deficit-need level is the central focus of older people in terms of self image: self-esteem and the esteem of others.

Until self-esteem is strongly etched into a person's psychological being, the finest rewards that could be his or hers for having productively lived much of life will stay out of reach. Those rewards are the peak feelings one can continuously enjoy only when one is beyond striving but is still vitally involved in life. That defines the "farthest reaches of human nature," according to Maslow. But without a full complement of self-esteem and the knowledge that one enjoys the esteem of others, those reaches are inaccessible.

## Sustained Self-Esteem Has Only
## One Source: Productivity

There is only one source of sustained self-esteem: individual productivity. Self-esteem cannot be derived from consumption; it can be derived
only from the products of one's efforts. Nor can self-esteem be be-
stowed on one person by another. If a person lacks self-esteem, no
amount of flattery or testimonials by others can develop self-esteem in
that person. Yet marketing messages are replete with exhortations to
older people to live a "carefree life" because "you deserve it." Moreover,
association with symbols of dependency, losses of vitality, and lack of
clear thinking tend to compromise people's sense of self-esteem.

Self-esteem needs are like the needs which must be met to maintain a
healthy body: More or less daily sustenance must be provided. No quantity of awards or statements of recognition for past accomplishments
can secure self-esteem for the remainder of one's life any more than a
single meal can suffice for an entire life.

## Picture the "Little Old Lady"
## Helping the Boy Scout across the
## Street

Depictions of older people in commercials and advertisements should
always clearly convey that these people have strong feelings of self-
esteem. Showing them in roles where they are dependent or being
served in some patronizing fashion works in the opposite direction. Pictures showing older people in activities that are contributing to their
own inner growth convey self-esteem, as do pictures showing older people helping others. What is wrong, for instance, with showing that "little
old lady" helping the Boy Scout across the street?

Sedentary poses of older people are symbols of nonproductivity, the
annihilator of self-esteem. If a picture includes older people sitting,
there should be a healthy purpose to their sitting other than resting or
being involved in mindless prattle with other "old" people. Productive
and meaningful existence can be equally well conveyed by showing a
person honing his or her mind with a Great Book, observing in childlike
wonder the majesty of the Taj Mahal on a travel tour, or giving time
and attention to others—the opposite image of that often seen in seniors housing brochures, where others (the *professional staff*) are giving
to the older person.

The mature person's productivity patterns flow in two directions:
inner-directed and outer-directed. Inner-directed does not necessarily
mean self-absorption, but rather an *introspective*, self-enlarging orientation, an orientation toward internal growth. The healthy-minded

older person never stops growing until he or she has achieved that point which is beyond striving. Even then, while personality growth has reached its summit, experiential growth continues.

# 8
# The Ageless Market

## The Altered Sense of Time
## Experienced by Mature Adults

This chapter validates the title of this book in ways that carry practical implications for marketers. In so doing, it draws an image of the mature psyche that may, to some younger people, seem like an idyllic romanticizing of age. However, the resulting images also represent a system of reality.

This chapter does not offer bulleted, easily grasped principles for applying new knowledge about mature psyches in the marketplace. Rather, it is a thoughtful inquiry into one attribute of the *fully* mature personality: the different way in which mature adults sense and regard time. Marketers can gain valuable insights into the psychological origins of the cognitive patterns that do, in fact, lead many older people into a frame of mind where time loses its value to the point that they essentially become *ageless*.

## Mature Adults Operate in a Zone of
## Relative Timelessness

Recently, in preparation for a presentation in Tokyo on the topic of marketing to older people, my host and translator, Shigenobu Ueoka and I were going over key words to determine their closest equivalents in Japanese. Mr. Ueoka was struggling with the term *Ageless Market*, stating that he was having difficulty coming up with the right word. Finally, he said, "Timeless; the Japanese word for *timeless* is the best word to use in the translation."

*Timeless Market* will do just as well in English, as it conveys just what I mean in using the term *Ageless Market*. Fully mature people tend to move through life in ways whereby time loses much of its meaning. Without time, there is no aging. Thus, the term *Ageless Market* is *not* a poetic or romantic substitution for *senior market* or *elderly market*. It is even possible for consumers who by no one's definition are either "senior citizens" or "elderly" to be members of the Ageless Market.[1] However, most members of the Ageless Market have celebrated their sixtieth birthdays.

This intriguing sense of timelessness, when "a day is a minute, a minute is a day" (Maslow's characterization), makes possible a broader perspective on life as well as the mitigation of many of its travails.[2] People operate in a timeless milieu in which one can become more tolerant and secure about self and can develop a greater sense of cosmic connectedness. Timelessness is an aspect of *being* that, at least in U.S. society, appears to be accessible primarily to young children and older adults.

## The Young Confront Age; the "Old" Integrate It into Their Being

It is noteworthy that Erik Erikson made major revisions to his famous eight stages of human development theory *after* he entered "old age." Like Maslow, who had difficulty understanding self-actualizing personalities and their "polarities and oppositions" until he reached the same age range of his subjects, Erikson apparently did not fully understand "old age" to his satisfaction until he became "old." After becoming old, he found *being* old to be a more remarkable and enjoyable experience than he could ever have conceived of in his earlier years as one of the twentieth century's great students of the human mind.

Helen M. Luke, an indomitable personality in her eighties as of this writing, has recently written a book called, simply, *Old Age*. This remarkable book, enjoyable and easily read in a short afternoon, is probably fully understandable after at least several enjoyable readings. It is a poetic validation of Erikson's theories about the Eighth Stage of human development, the "integrity vs. despair" stage, which after having been successfully experienced leads to fullness in the psychological strength of "Wisdom."

[1]The first work leading to the concept of self-actualizing personalities was done not by Maslow, but by psychologist Kurt Goldstein. Goldstein's initial work on the subject involved brain-damaged soldiers. There were incidents of brain damage among young soldiers that resulted in the kind of concrete cognition that underlies "agelessness."

[2]At this time the reader might want to return to Figure 6-1 to review its summary points in Maslow's ideas about the pattern of timelessness in the cognitive patterns of mature personalities.

Luke teaches us in *Old Age* that we have a choice between "getting old" and "growing old." *Growing old* means developing into a personality that transcends chronological age and, to a large extent, our physiological selves that defined so many of our needs earlier in life. The later years of life are therefore a time when mind finally does take a position over matter for those who have the grace and skills to *grow* old.[3]

To young people, age is a thing to be *confronted*. To the healthfully developing older person, age is a thing to be *integrated* into one's total reality. We confront the unavoidable that we believe can be mastered; we integrate the unavoidable that we know cannot be mastered. Wisdom enables us to know the difference and to determine appropriate courses of action. Lacking such wisdom, we can be driven to despair by futile efforts directed at the unchangeable, driven to disdain and cynicism about the world because it fails to respond to our wishes and efforts. This is what Erikson teaches us about the Eighth Stage of human development, marked by him as beginning around the sixties: It is the time when we should be getting our experiential house in order, the time when we should discharge pettiness from our lives, along with disenchantments, regrets, and second thoughts about our worth and the worth of all life.

### Mature Adults Grow Beyond the Capacity for Regrets

The Eighth Stage is the time, if we are continuing to develop psychologically, when we come to accept with grace and equanimity not only the unchangeable past but also the present and future. With the holistically patterned mode of thinking that is enabled by full maturity, we are able to take both good and bad episodes of our life history and integrate them into a whole that makes sense, and even come to view our lives as having unfolded as they should have, despite all the earlier frustrations, disappointments, and times of grief, despair, and sadness. This is what aging for many older adults is about: It is a period, or rather a state of being, beyond striving, beyond scorn, beyond regrets about what might have been.

It would be too much, and entirely inappropriate, to suggest that young people should love the idea of *growing* old. But it is not too much to exhort young people to accept the idea that *growing old* is another one of the wonderful, even exhilarating experiences life offers us. The fact that there may be little time left on earth does not necessarily diminish one's deeply felt pleasures in experiencing life. In fact, many older people, in their sixties and beyond, have told me that they have

[3]Helen M. Luke, *Old Age*, Parabola Books, New York, 1987, p. viii.

never found as much enjoyment in life as they have found in its later years. The old saw "Life begins at 40" should perhaps be amended to "Life begins *again* at 60."

## Why Mature Adults Often Appear to Live for the Moment

I have heard marketing lecturers talk about how seniors live for the moment, and make the value judgment that such a lifestyle attitude evidences self-centeredness and frivolity, implying a lack of serious intent. That observation usually leads to the conclusion that living for the moment is the older person's way of avoiding thoughts about his or her perilous future as an old person, and ultimately death. The evidence that I have drawn upon to forge my own views on the matter of seniors' living for the moment leads to different interpretations and conclusions.

First, how is it possible that as a person approaches his or her last dawn, life can be more beautiful and satisfying than ever? It is hardly because thoughts of future sickness and death have been blurred from consciousness by entering a lifestyle that distracts such thoughts. Instead, I propose that the mature person undergoes a change in cognitive patterns by which perceptions of possible future catastrophes become less relevant to current existence.

The term used above, *last dawn*, is a left brain concept, for it represents the last calibration in a series of calibrations marking the time allocated to a person's life. Calibrations of time and other concepts are the specialty of the left brain, which orders the construction of reality in a measured linear fashion. The right brain lacks that capacity because it orders the construction of reality in an unmeasured, holistic, nonlinear fashion. The left brain "takes time" to construct its pictures of reality, developing the picture detail by detail, each detail a potential subject for analysis.

In the right brain, pictures of reality take no time for construction because all the details of the picture arrive simultaneously. This accounts for what has been termed the *present-centeredness* of the right brain, a state of mind when neither the past nor the future figures prominently in awareness.

Centuries of religious, philosophical, and poetic writings give testament to the idea that the mind is quite capable of entering into a state in which the present is ever-present. Ornstein suggests that we "regard these 'present-centered' moments as shifts toward a right brain dominance."[4] He has studied and written about how mind-altering drugs, periods of deep meditation, and losing oneself in the majesty of

[4] R. Ornstein, *The Psychology of Consciousness*, Penguin Books, Baltimore, Md., 1986, p. 138.

existence reflected in a beautiful sunset over the sea all have the capacity to induce present-centeredness. Each of those experiences is driven or affected by the right brain.

## Older People Don't Need as Much Time as Younger People

We have all heard older people talk about how the passage of time seems to accelerate as they get older. They are indirectly expressing a sense that in later life time begins to lose the urgency it often had in the earlier years of life. The sole reason for awareness of time is the marking of the duration of events and where we are between events. When family-rearing years are past and careers have been concluded, fewer events occur that have strong connections with time.

With lifestyles and mental dispositions that tend to ignore time, older people are often surprised by how much time has flown by. It happens when grandparents, not seeing a toddler grandson for a few months, upon seeing him again are amazed at how much he has grown. The parents hadn't noticed their son's growth because he is a part of their daily lives. For those whose daily lives are heavily marked by time calibrations, the passage of time is less noticeable than for those whose daily lives are largely uninfluenced by the clock or the date. So, in a sense, rather than speeding up for older people, time slows down. Only reminders such as the inch and a half added growth of a grandson or changes in a friend not seen in years jolt them back into the "real time" in which the rest of the world operates. Otherwise, the mature older person's sense of time redefines his or her conception of reality.

We have all commonly experienced a sense of time and motion that alters our conception of reality. While sitting in your car in a distracted frame of mind at a traffic light, the car next to yours moves, but you feel that your car is moving. You snap out of your distracted mood, check your brakes, and thus are jolted back to the reality of the situation. For a moment, your sense of time was altered.

## Common Examples of Time-Altering Experiences

People who meditate seriously speak of experiencing such jolts back into "real time." A meditator looks at the clock just before beginning to meditate. It is 8:25. She closes her eyes. At 8:45 she opens her eyes and experiences a strange sensation that no time has passed, but the clock's minute hand has somehow moved 20 notches.

You are on your way to an important meeting and an accident on the road ahead brings traffic to a stop. You look at your watch. It's 15 minutes before your meeting—just enough time if the traffic were moving at a normal pace, but traffic shows no sign of moving. A wave of anxiety begins to sweep over you, your body becomes taut, and your heart begins to beat faster. You are stuck between the event of getting to your meeting and the event of being at your meeting.

The stalled traffic has not created your anxiety, but time—or at least your perception that not enough time remains to get you to your meeting on time—has created your anxiety.

In the car behind you is a retired couple in their sixties. By coincidence the couple is going to the same building as you. It has a nice restaurant where they have been wanting to have lunch. You, of course, are not aware of that when you look in your rear-view mirror and see them talking and laughing. You muse, "Wouldn't it be great if I could be so carefree and unconcerned?" But the real difference between you and the couple is time. It has great value to you, therefore its depletion can be traumatic. For the couple, it is only kind of a background phenomenon, a kind of ether in which things take place, rather than a driver of action.

## The Pleasures of Later Life Alter
## Older People's Perceptions of Time

That older people sustain a diminished sense of time may also be evidence of higher levels of satisfaction with life than ever experienced before in their lives. Time is an event-based concept whose sense is determined by the nature of the events experienced. The sense of time collapses or expands according to the character of the events being experienced. Einstein once joked, "When you sit with a nice girl for two hours, it seems like two minutes; when you sit on a hot oven for two minutes, it seems like two hours. That's relativity."[5]

We all have experienced occasions so pleasurable that time seemed to whiz by. It seems that the more enjoyable the experience, the faster time flies. The older person whose life is blessed with a continuum of life satisfaction talks about how time flies. But he or she is really talking about sensory perceptions, not reality. In fact, it is not so much that time is flying as it is that time has become less a factor in lifestyle, activities, and *moods*.

In the objective sense, time cannot be speeded up or slowed down. But we do not sense and live life objectively. Because of that, we can

[5]Ibid., p. 134.

sense time as moving rapidly, slowly, or hardly at all. Ernst Poppel, in *Mindworks: Time and Conscious Experience*, says the differences that occur in our subjective perceptions of the passage of time are a matter of *mental content.*[6] The less content there is in the mind, the longer an increment of time seems to be. Boredom slows time to a crawl. An imminent car accident causes a driver's sense of time to decelerate in the fractional seconds before the accident. The only thought in the driver's mind is the impending event.

Transcendental and other forms of meditation which seek to eliminate all content from the conscious mind result in a sensory perception that time ceases to exist altogether. When time has ceased to exist cognitively, all cognitive activity in the left brain has stopped. The right brain has taken over the controls of consciousness. Its brand of consciousness is devoid of time because it cannot sequence events. Something either *is* or *is not*. It cannot be what *was* or what *will be*.

We know through studies of split-brain patients that the right brain cannot measure time or even demonstrate an awareness of it: "It has been found that left hemisphere damage interferes with the perception of sequence [time order of events], while right hemisphere damage does not. These 'timeless' experiences [present-centered moments] ... overwhelm the linear construction [of the left hemisphere] and allow an infinite present to exist."[7]

## The Psyche-Serving Aspects of a Sense of Timelessness

The reason that the sense of time changes so dramatically for many older people may be strongly linked to the mind's dedication to a person's survival and defense needs. As long as the timekeeper left brain dominates perception and cognition, perceptions of current and future events will carry a time context that can be psychologically unsettling. As a person passes through the final quarter of life, the possibility of physical and psychological impairments, and even death, in the near future increases day by day. Growing anxieties would seem to be a predictable result. It's like some people who become increasingly nervous as the time for a dental appointment approaches: The closer the time of the "big event," the greater the anxiety. But extensive testing of older people, especially among those who already suffer from some chronic

---

[6]Ernst Poppel, *Mindworks: Time and Conscious Experience*, Harcourt, Brace, Jovanovich, New York, 1988, p. 86.

[7]Robert Ornstein, *Psychology of Consciousness*, p. 138.

illness, shows lesser levels of anxiety over the prospects of a dire future than "left brain common sense" would suggest.

Could it be that a growing sense of timelessness serves to protect the psyche? I think so. I believe that the mind stimulates the appetite for Being Experiences in order to increase right brain cognitive operations, which in turn decrease a sense of time and, thereby, mute awareness of the future in the context of any dire possibilities.

## Mature Adults Have Fewer Anxieties as They Age

Why do studies show anxieties over health and mortality to be greater for people in their fifties than for people in their sixties, seventies, and older? At least in Western society, most people in their fifties still operate heavily in the timekeeper left brain world. Having lived more than half their lives, they are, timewise, aware that the candle begins to grow short. They perceive that fact sometimes with grim apprehension. But the older, mature person doesn't clearly perceive the base of the candle. *Intellectually*, he or she knows it is there, but it rarely comes into focus. For all the mature person knows, the candle may extend to the center of the earth.

Maslow observed that to the B-cognizer all things are infinite (see Table 6-1). The ultimate sense of safety, security, and well-being that we can feel lies in a strongly felt sense that we are a part of infinity *now*. By definition, the present is without end in the ethereal dimension of full infinity, because there are no endings, not even an ending of the present. In such a context, Being is without compromise or ending. Logically, of course, the timekeeper left brain won't tolerate such nonsense. But the right brain gets heady over it.

## "Time Is of the Essence" Pitches Don't Work in the Ageless Market

Marketers of senior adult housing have been frustrated by the time it takes older people to come to a decision. Many senior housing marketers report that prospects will visit six to eight times over many months or even several years before they decide to rent or buy. Exhortations to buy because "there are only two apartments left like the one you want," seem to have no effect on most prospects.

Because mature adults tend to operate with less sensitivity to time as a value factor in decision-making, the age-old marketing strategy of creating urgency in the prospect's mind has limited effectiveness in the ageless market:

---

**SEVENTH PRINCIPLE FOR MATURITY MARKETS**
The Timelessness Principle

Time is usually *not* of the essence in the decision-making processes of the mature consumer; therefore, attempts to instill a sense of urgency in a purchase consideration generally are ineffective.

---

The more the present seems *ever-present*, the less influence the future has. A sense of urgency is literally a sense that time is running out. With the present always being present, time can't run out because it doesn't exist to do so.

Mature consumers have the same desire as all other buyers to make decisions that make them feel good. The difference is that mature consumers, in being generally happy with their lives, do not perceive any single purchase as essential to their life satisfaction. They already have it, while younger consumers are still looking for it. If they miss one opportunity because they failed to buy in time, they know that other opportunities yielding equal levels of enjoyment are close at hand.

Because older people's sense of timelessness has reduced their anxieties about what the future holds, marketing pitches that expressly or implicitly suggest that they should buy now, before it is too late, will fall on deaf ears. One of the principal sales points in senior adult housing has been to "move in now, while you are *still* independent. You may avoid going into a nursing home, if you do." Since not all older adults are *fully mature* adults, that will appeal to some. But I believe that even many of those will not respond positively to such a sales pitch.

No product should be sold to older people on the basis of avoiding dire consequences. If there is a potential for dire consequences in not buying, the mature personality is usually going to be quite capable of figuring that out without assistance from others. Appeals based on images of dire consequences violate the First General Principle of Marketing.

### Is Timelessness a Source of Older People's Increased Spirituality?

Common wisdom holds that older people are more spiritual because, having "done it all," they are less subject to temporal temptations and appetites, and, being closer to their own deaths, they begin to think more about what comes next. But could it not be that diminishment of time perception, which engenders a sense of infinity, is a major factor in the increased spirituality of older people?

God is of the infinite, and when time ceases, the infinite is all that exists. In such a perception of things, the B-cognizer feels a part of the infinite Being, the Being that is "outside of time and space" that is seen as "eternal, universal," observed Maslow. Anyone who feels this way and has personified the "infinite Being" is quite likely to incorporate an active religiousness in his or her lifestyle.

Even those mature adults who are not religious, in the conventional sense, usually reflect a deep spiritualism in their lives. This greater spirituality among older adults is an important influence on their consumer behavior:

---

**SEVENTH KEY FACTOR FOR MATURITY MARKETS**
The Spirituality Factor

The increased spirituality of mature adults causes them to have a higher regard for traditional basic values that are commonly perceived in a society as being universal and eternal. Marketing messages should avoid images that are contrary to such values and invoke images that reflect such values.

---

Some familiar icons and symbols of those values that are held in high regard by mature adults, and that can be effectively drawn upon in positioning and marketing activities, will be identified later in this chapter.

## The Phenomenon of Cognitive Age

What are the practical marketing consequences of considering the connections between aging and timelessness? To begin, a sense of timelessness decreases a sense of aging. The mature older person remains aware of a body slowing down, but does not perceive significant corresponding decrements in his or her psychological being. Since advanced age is generally associated with decrements, a mind that suffers none remains somewhat ageless, that is, it remains basically in the same state of competence as always. The body ages while the person doesn't.

A great deal has been written in marketing literature about *cognitive age*, the age one feels in contrast with one's chronological age. I have seen no literature on the subject of cognitive age that attempts to explain why there is such a phenomenon. I believe that until some rationale is provided for the concept of cognitive age, its full significance will not be grasped. It is not enough to say that it exists. To best devise strategies for responding to consumer behavior that is influenced by perceptions of age other than "real" or chronological age, one must develop an organic understanding of its origins and purpose.

## Use of Younger Models Doesn't Effectively Deal with Seniors' Age Bias

It is commonly stated in marketing literature that older people "feel" 10 to 15 years younger than they actually are. Follow-up advice to that claim usually tells marketers to show people in ads who are 10 to 15 years younger than the target market. I don't subscribe to that view.

I have found something more definitive than the widely purported "feel-age" differential between cognitive age and chronological age of 10 to 15 years. I have asked individuals and entire seminar audiences, "If you did not know how old you were, how old do you think you would be?" Typically, three-quarters or more of those asked respond with an answer that ranges from 75 to 85 percent of their chronological age.

I have a suspicion that the stronger a person's sense of overall well-being, the greater the gap between cognitive age and chronological age; that is, the more mature a person is, in a Maslovian/Eriksonian sense, the lower that person's cognitive age. That suspicion is supported by the views of Elaine Sherman who together with Leon Schiffman has extensively studied the phenomenon of cognitive age.

Sherman and Schiffman reported to me in an interview that their studies show a close linkage between degree of life satisfaction and cognitive age: The stronger one's sense of life satisfaction, the younger one feels. This supports the proposition advanced earlier that

- The greater one's life satisfaction, the greater one's maturity.
- The greater one's maturity, the more dominant right brain influences become.
- The more influential the right brain is in one's life, the less sense of the passage of time one feels.

It may be that cognitive age is somewhat determined by the right brain's inability to tell time, thus accounting for the disparity between cognitive age and "real age."

## Cognitive Age Is a Multidimensional Phenomenon

Ours is an intensely time-oriented society that places a premium on fast food, "timely" results, and quick answers. We operate as though time were *really* running out. Unfortunately our time values reinforce not only quick answers but also shallow and often misleading answers. As a general note, I believe that the development of truly practical insights of older consumers cannot be achieved through shallow thinking that tends to overvalue the obvious and devalue the subtle. The issue of cognitive age in older markets is but one of virtually countless issues that have been subjected to such shallow and misleading thinking.

Sherman and Schiffman, in a more thoughtful evaluation of the issue, have come up with a more complex construct of cognitive age by defining it as a composite of several perceptions of one's age:

- *Feel-age.*     The age one *feels, independent* of physiological conditions.

- *Look-age.*     The age that one believes he or she physically appears to be.

- *Do-age.*     The age that corresponds to associations of certain activities with specific age groups.

- *Interest-age.*     The age that corresponds to associations of certain interests with specific age groups.[8]

Sherman and Schiffman arrive at cognitive age by averaging the midpoints of each decade a respondent has identified as being his or her perceived age for each category. For example, if 68-year-old Mary Erskine says she feels as though she is in her thirties, looks as though she's in her early sixties, participates in activities typical for people in their forties, and has interests that are generally perceived as characteristic of those in their child-free late forties, then her cognitive age will be 47.5 (35 + 65 + 45 +45, divided by 4).

If Sherman and Schiffman have, in fact, pointed out a better way to determine cognitive age, then the old saw about "showing models in ads who are 10 to 15 years younger than the target market" is indeed flawed advice. Even before I learned of Sherman and Schiffman's way of determining cognitive age, I thought that was bad advice. If you took the usual advice and lopped, say, 15 years off 68-year-old Mary Erskine's chronological age, you would need to use models in ads who are in their early fifties. I am not very confident that that ploy would necessarily increase Mary's interest in the product being advertised.

## Age of Models in Ads Is Relatively Unimportant

Mature consumers are less positively influenced by the age of models in ads than common wisdom supposes. However, there is a high capacity

[8]L. Schiffman and L. L. Kanuk, *Consumer Behavior*, Prentice-Hall, Englewood Cliffs, N.J., 1987, p. 531.

for the age of models to create *negative* reactions. If you use 50-year-olds in ads for a product or service to be purchased primarily by much older people, you run the risk of making the consumer feel duped. Recall the earlier discussions concerning mature people's resistance to enculturation (indoctrination) and their ability to see through ploys? It seems to me that the reflection of feel-ages, do-ages, and interest-ages in marketing is more important than worrying about how to handle the look-age. Focusing on the latter can be a no-win situation.

Show a model who is "the right age" to Mary Erskine, and you may alienate another viable prospect whose attitudes on look-age are different. On the other hand, if Mary thinks she looks as though she is in her early sixties, then seeing a model in an ad who is her early seventies might be positively received if the model were Barbara Stanwyck. However, seeing an unknown model who is 15 years younger may be displeasing to Mary if the activities with which the model is involved are alien to or nonreflective of Mary's activities, values, and interests. In Chapter 10 you will read of the health maintenance organization (HMO) that successfully used a centenarian, 103-year-old Jane Stovall, as a model. At 103 she flies her own plane, reflecting a do-age at least a half century lower than her chronological age.

Too much emphasis has been put on the "right" age for models in ads and brochures aimed at maturity markets. The issue of aging, perceived and otherwise, is too complex to be resolved cosmetically with the faces of models in ads and brochures. I do believe that responding to feel-age, do-age, and interest-age images is a better approach. The key to doing that appropriately is to focus on those images that invoke timeless right brain responses.

## The Transcendence of Time through Being Experiences

It may be helpful to look at time as operating in two cognitive modes: *event time*, which unfolds in a sequenced experiential sense, and *being time*, which is relatively *timeless*. Neither contradicts the other, because the first is *temporal* in orientation (left brain), with finite beginnings and endings, while the second is *spatial* (relationships without respect to time) in orientation (right brain) and has only a present tense.

Since I advised marketers earlier to "lead with the right, follow with the left," the concept of "being time" is an important concept to note. Those symbols that trigger right brain oriented responses tend to invoke or be associated with timelessness. Ornstein argues that we incorporate into our picture of reality those things that support and embellish that reality. That being the case, symbols and icons that reflect concepts and values we tend to regard as *timeless* are important ingredients of marketplace communications directed at the Ageless Market. Such symbols and icons, all of which symbolize or facilitate Being Experiences, are represented in Table 8-1.

The camera's eye or artist's brush aimed at such symbols and icons should be soft and gentle and should seek expression with the delicacy of a child's wonder, rather than by amazing and startling the senses. Only the left brain needs to be shocked into yielding to emotions; they come naturally to the right brain. Sensitivity and good taste outweigh the circus barker's command to come and experience the extraordinary. For B-cognizers, everything is extraordinary. They don't need someone to advertise the extraordinariness of a product or service in outsized images and claims.

### Ideas for Being Experience Vignettes in Advertising

Table 8-2 is a list of activities with a particularly high Being Experience potential, hence positive appeal to right brain values. Certain activities in Table 8-2 have been marked with an asterisk to indicate that they in-

**Table 8-1.** Symbols and Icons of Basic Values

| | |
|---|---|
| American flag, state flags | Child with doll |
| Church or temple | Child with dog |
| Civic buildings (capitols, opera houses, museums, etc.) | Grandparent with grandchild |
| School | Family gatherings, especially on traditional occasions, birthdays |
| College, university | Neighbors, especially doing things together, e.g., chatting across a fence |
| Historical place, monument | |
| Scene from the past | |
| Fireworks | Friends doing traditional things together |
| Patriot | |
| Home | Nature views (especially panoramas) |
| Neighborhood | Flowers |
| Traditional small town | Animals (especially in anthropomorphic vignettes, e.g., animals in humanlike socializing, caring of young, etc.) |
| Corner drugstore | |
| General store | |
| Bandstand | |
| Mother and child | |
| Father and child | One person helping another |

**Table 8-2.** Being Experience-Oriented Activities for Mature Adults

| Sharing products of skills with others 1 | Sharing wisdom with others 2 | Entertaining others 3 | Caring for others 4 |
|---|---|---|---|
| Composing | Collaborating* | Acting* | Assisting |
| Creating | Consulting* | Arranging* | Caring |
| Decorating | Cooperating* | Demonstrating* | Catering |
| Designing* | Educating* | Hosting* | Counseling |
| Drawing | Influencing* | Joking* | Curing* |
| Fixing | Proposing | Performing | Encouraging* |
| Painting | Teaching* | Public speaking* | Helping* |
| Writing* | Training* | Singing | Humoring |
| | | Staging | Nurturing |
| | | Story telling* | Petting |
| | | | Supporting |
| | | | Tending |

*Activities involving significant contributions from both hemispheres of the brain. The other items involve primarily right brain functions.

SOURCE: Adapted from Jacquelyn Wonder and Priscilla Donovan, *Whole Brain Thinking*, Ballantine Books, New York, 1984, p. 268.

volve significant contributions by both hemispheres of the brain. The nonstarred items are primarily or dominantly right brain in operation.

Also note that the activities in Table 8-2 align very closely with the Four Faces of the New Senior, described in Chapter 2:

- *First Face.* Creativity and intellectual involvement.
- *Second Face.* Wisdom and experience and the desire to share them.
- *Third Face.* Productivity and vitality.
- *Fourth Face.* Compassion for others and concern for the world about them.

Column 1 is primarily first face oriented, while column 2 is heavily oriented to the second face, column 3 to the third face, and column 4 to the fourth face. The activities in both Tables 8-1 and 8-2 relate to or represent images of mature adults as they generally perceive themselves. Drawing upon these images will be more effective in positioning a product or service for mature markets than seeking the "right age" models to use in advertising and other marketing materials.

## Intergenerational Scenes Are Highly Attractive to Older People

Many of the activities listed in Table 8-2 reflect intergenerational scenes. There is a great aversion to age segregation and to symbols of age segregation on the part of many older people. I have often heard older people say, "I wouldn't move into a seniors community. I couldn't stand being with no one but people of my age or older."

Mature people, especially those who are full-fledged members of the Ageless Market, take a holistic view of life and of themselves as part of life. The idea of being segregated into an enclave of people all more or less of the same generation is to be only part of, and thus less than, the whole.

Most older people want to stay in touch with the commonalities they share with all people, regardless of age. Each wants to be regarded as an individual in his or her own right, but doesn't want age to be a major factor in how he or she is perceived. Remember, a key element in the definition of Being Experiences is a greater sense of *connectedness*. Scenes in advertising that emphasize separateness deny the element of connectedness.

The Ageless Market is composed of people who are not comfortable with the idea of separateness. They see things all of a piece. Maslow observed that when he said B-cognizers "tend to de-differentiate figure and background, [and that] relative important becomes unimportant; all aspects [are] equally important."[9]

Members of the Ageless *Society* are truly remarkable people. The spirit they show toward themselves and life is remarkably like many of the ideals often promoted by young people at the very beginning of adulthood. It is the nature of our social and cultural milieu that most young people lose touch with their ideals in their quest for identity and accomplishment in a very left brain dominated world.

How wonderful it is that many of those young people will someday see life as they did in their youth, when they saw a great need for things to change. This is not to say that mature adults become unrealistic. To the contrary, said Maslow, they become more realistic. It is to say, however, that while the ideals of youth are frequently not in balance with reality, the ideals of those who are members of the Ageless Society are nearly always so.

---

[9]Abraham Maslow, *The Farther Reaches of Human Nature*, Penguin Books, Baltimore, Md., 1971, p. 249.

# PART 4
# Implementation

# 9
# Method Marketing

## The Practical Value of Empathy in Marketing

A friend of mine tells of the time when he, in his early forties, was giving his views on old age to a man in his eighties. The elderly man suddenly grew impatient and cut off my friend midsentence: "Young man, I know what it's like being 40 because I've been there. But you don't know what it's like being 85 because you haven't been there yet."

## You Cannot Be Wise until You Have Aged

To best understand another person, one must have directly experienced the kinds of life-shaping events that the other person has known. One cannot fully understand what being married is like, until one has been married; one cannot fully understand what it is like to have a baby until one has given birth; one cannot fully comprehend the psychology of an older person until one has become older. Deep life wisdom, which is so much a part of an older person's behavior, is not accessible to the young. It is not even accessible to all older people. Joan Erikson put it this way: "Not all old people are wise, but you can't be wise unless you have aged."[1]

[1] D. Goleman, "Now in Their 80s, Eriksons Develop Fresh Insights into Psychology of Aging," *Baltimore Sun*, June 13, 1988, p. F-1.

A 10-year-old may have all the facts about a matter, but odds are that in matters requiring life wisdom a 15-year-old will process the same facts more competently. The same will be true for a 20-year-old who is processing the same facts as a 15-year-old, and for a 30-year-old who is processing the same facts as a 20-year-old.

It is an inescapable condition of life that our present is largely defined by our past and that the more history we have behind us, the more enriched is the library of experiences we reach into for the life wisdom to interpret and act upon the events that have meaning to us. Growing physically takes place during barely a quarter of our lives; growing psychologically takes place all our lives.

## Wisdom Is Not the Exclusive Property of the "Educated"

If we accept Erikson's and Maslow's ideas that personality development continues well past the half-century mark in life, meaning there is progressive improvement in our ability to cope and to achieve satisfaction with life, then it seems reasonable to assume that there is more life wisdom in the head of a 60-year-old than of a 30-year-old. It is not an absolute certainty, of course, but surely more likely.

As observed in Chapter 6 in the discussion of Maslow's ideas about mature adults, the person who continues to grow psychologically adopts differing patterns of cognition in later life. Until a person has grown enough to see the world by utilizing the same cognition patterns of Maslow's B-cognizers, he or she will never be able to see the world in quite the same way as the B-cognizer. Ultimately, much of what we call wisdom is tied not so much to experience per se as to *how that experience is interpreted*. A man with little book learning who has never moved very far beyond his neighborhood theoretically has as much potential for wisdom as a Nobel scholar.

Perhaps the greatest challenge for people in a sociocultural context is to communicate to others what they mean and to interpret what others say to them. That defines the ultimate challenge in marketing to older people, particularly the denizens of the Ageless Market—the psychologically mature.

## To Understand Mature Consumers Requires Holistic Perceptions

This book provides a great many facts on older people, but there is one thing it cannot give. No book can give—and possibly no one can teach—*empathy*, that capacity for feeling what another person feels. Empathy is not the same thing as intellectually understanding what another person is experiencing. Intellectual understanding is a product of different processes than emotional understanding and ultimately is only partial understanding of any person or any scenario involving human beings. The intellect, no matter how competently it is used, is insufficient to produce a full and well-rounded understanding of any other person, regardless of age or level of maturity. How often have we observed of another, "He understands it *intellectually*, but not *emotionally*." Not until the emotional coloration of an event, a person, etc., is integrated with an intellectual perception does a full—or, better, *holistic*—understanding emerge.

*Holistic* is a better modifier of *understanding* than *full* because one can never develop a "full" understanding of another. In holistic perceptions, all the basic attributes of an object are represented in the picture that has been formed by one's perceptions of it. But holistic perceptions are like holograms: Their degree of fullness and clarity of image depend on the quantity of the input that gets projected.

If you cut a 35-mm slide film in half, you still get just as sharp an image as you will in projecting the whole film; you just get half of the picture. If you cut a holographic film of an object in half and then project it, you still get the whole picture, but it is much paler in resolution than if the full original film is projected. Each part of a holographic film plate contains a memory of the content of every other part of the film.

In a holistic understanding of another person, each attribute is seen not alone, but in a context that reflects the "memory" of all the other attributes. Hence, with a holistic understanding of mature consumers a health care provider sees consumers as more than "sick" people. Similarly, a financial services provider will regard consumers as more than people with money to manage, and a travel agent will perceive consumers as more than just people who want to take a trip. Mature consumers see themselves as experientially enlarged personalities with many facets. They tend to resent being pigeonholed. They are themselves holistic in the way they organize their realities, and they want to be perceived holistically by others.

## Empathy Flows More Fully from Holistic Perceptions

Maslow's characterization of mature people as being "more realistic" recognizes the greater clarity in perceiving an object that holistic cognition permits. After the time of Maslow, neuroscientists identified the capacity for holistic cognition as being a specialty of the right brain. My hypothesis that older, more mature people tend to shift toward greater right brain influence in their cognitive processes is compatible with both views. And perhaps a strong imperative for caring for others, a greater richness of emotions, and "more democratic nature"—all of which Maslow observed as emergent in the mature—would logically seem related to the greater capacity for holistic perceptions and lead to a greater capacity for empathy.

Empathy is a product of the emotional self. Importantly, empathy is not to be mistaken for sympathy, although they both share the common mother of emotion. Sympathy involves feeling *for* someone; empathy involves feeling *as* someone feels. One can have a strong capacity for sympathy without a comparable capacity for empathy.

Older people frequently complain about being patronized by younger people. Patronizing is action based on sympathetic feelings, not empathetic feelings. We respond positively to empathetically based actions on our behalf, but most of us are repelled by sympathetically based actions, however charitable they may be. Pictures in advertising that show older people being helped by younger people are likely to be perceived as patronizing. Copy that focuses on care or other services clearly aimed at compensating for "the effects of age" are read similarly.

A better way of showing the "care that counts" in an ad might be to show one resident of a nursing home or senior housing community helping another resident. In reality, such scenes often take place. Research has indicated that a person suffers less anxiety when aided by a peer than when assisted by a care giver or even a family member (other than a spouse), at least as measured by blood pressure. Further, the peer who is rendering the aid tends to become healthier, often experiencing an increase in infection-fighting lymphocytes in the bloodstream.[2]

The health care facility that fosters the development of buddy systems may be doing more for most residents' health than all the nursing care it can provide. In any event, images of residents aiding residents make a more attractive picture than that of traditional institutional care.

## Self-Orientation Tends to Inhibit Empathy

The greatest obstacle to developing a capacity for empathy lies in people themselves. Maslovian tenet 2 (see Chapter 6) holds that the less mature people are, the more self-oriented they are. A corollary to Maslovian tenet 2 is this: The more self-oriented people are, the less their capacity for empathy.

---

[2]Robert Ornstein and David Sobel, *The Healing Brain*, Simon & Schuster, New York, 1987.

Maslow said that the more self-oriented a person is, the less able that person is to perceive others in terms of who they are, *independent* of their capacity to aid the self-oriented person in gratifying some need. Thus, the less mature a person is, the more subjective that person is in measuring the value of someone else. When someone else no longer is perceived as being able to contribute to the needs gratification of the heavily self-oriented person, then the relationship will be severely diminished in strength, if not altogether broken. Empathy, according to this thinking, would seem to be strongly tied to degree of psychological (specifically, emotional) growth. It seems to me, then, that the younger a person is, the greater the challenge in developing a strong capacity for empathy, simply because self-orientation is a natural and potentially productive attribute of younger people on their path toward higher personality development.

There may also be a strong relationship between the brain hemisphere of dominant influence and levels of empathetic capacity. Since, as previously observed, the right hemisphere appears to play a larger role in emotions than the left hemisphere, a person with right brain dominance might have a greater natural capacity for empathy, even though immaturity could inhibit its operation.

Empathy, holism, and intuition are all said to be primarily products of right brain operation. They all aid a person in reading body language and discerning metamessages and their meanings. We often say of children, "They have a knack for cutting through the rubbish to get the real meaning." Young children in U.S. society tend to be much more dominated by right brain influences than will be the case throughout most of their adulthoods. But, as previously suggested, most will return to those patterns as they reach higher levels of human maturity in their later years. Consequently, the older person with greater capacities in empathy, holistic perceptions, and intuitive reasoning will subject marketing materials to scrutiny in ways quite different from other consumers. Marketers who enhance their skills in the same areas are better able to communicate with older consumers on their terms.

## Method Marketing: An Empathetic Approach to Maturity Markets

It seems apparent that much of the consternation about how to solve the riddles of so-called senior markets stems from the difficulty we all have in getting beyond ourselves in analyzing matters and in relating to others. And, as just discussed, the less mature we are, the more difficult it is to leave our subjective, self-oriented selves behind and get into the psyche of another from a *feeling* perspective, as distinct from an intellectual perspective.

In theater, actors are taught to get out of themselves and into their characters through the device of empathy. The injunction, "If you want to convince the audience that you are a tree, then you must 'feel' like a tree" symbolizes the central tenet of the school of acting known as *method acting.* You don't *act* like a tree; you *feel* like a tree. Only then can you project in the vernacular of trees.

What could be better for the marketing industry than the establishment of a new school of thought called *method marketing*, a marketing philosophy shaped by emphasis on the empathetic understanding of consumers? And just as method actors must escape the bonds of their own egos to immerse themselves in a character, so method marketers must get beyond their own egos to be able to feel as their prospects feel.

*Method marketing* could pose challenges to one's overall belief system. For instance, if a marketer believes "old people" are so handicapped by the aging process that they want all the help they can get, a discovery to the contrary could threaten a whole belief system as it relates to seniors. To *feel* as an older person feels, such a marketer might have to unravel a fabric of faulty preconceptions.

### An Ad Maker's Ego Can Be
### Ill-Suited for Maturity Market Ads

As previously noted, Robert Ornstein, armed with the current-day research in neuroscience unavailable to Maslow, concurs with Maslow that behavior is dictated initially by survival and defense needs. Ornstein uses the word *defense* in its broadest possible sense to encompass not only the physical self, but also the ego, social position, and belief systems. The defense system is operating continually, in every environment, coloring all with which one interacts.

A classic defense strategy for certain people is to choose companions over whom they feel superior; they experience a kind of safety in feeling superior and temporarily overcome feelings of inadequacy. This type of "defense" strategy is the basis of much social and racial prejudice. A young person operating from this mode of defense is not likely to exclude older people from such judgment.

For example, such a person might view older people not in terms of their accomplishments, abilities, or potential, but in terms of their perceived vulnerabilities and weaknesses. This perspective serves a defensive purpose for some individuals. Such prejudicial attitudes need not preclude kindness. One may extend kindness more fully to those perceived as inferior, and even encourage dependency to satisfy the need to feel superior. One whose interactions are strongly influenced by such perspectives and attitudes could be said to be operating at a less actualized Maslovian level, at which basic safety and security needs remain substantially ungratified.

This all refers to the role of ego in our behavior and how ego needs can shape our thinking. We most often use the word *ego* colloquially as an indicator of the strength of projection of an individual's persona. But the term *ego* refers to *all* that a person is at the cognitive level. It embodies one's perception of self. All that a person does carries the marks of his or her ego. When copywriters or artists are shaping a marketing piece, they are putting their egos on paper. The more mature the person, the less likely the work is to reflect ego defenses. That is the reason the senior people in a marketing organization should be totally involved, up to their elbows, in the creative output.

### Maybe It's Time for Ad Agency Executives to Get Back into Advertising

Jack Trout, along with his partner, Al Ries, was referred to earlier as believing that principals in marketing companies (ad agencies, in particular) should be more heavily involved at the creative level than is currently the case, especially in large organizations. Trout elaborated on that theme during a recent interview:

> Senior people have gotten so caught up with the business of the marketing business that they have abandoned the creative work to less seasoned people who put novelty and uniqueness of creative output ahead of where the market is.
>
> In my opinion, marketing is becoming so tough that clients are going to *demand* involvement of principals, and they are going to be asking firms to share in the risks of the marketing programs they are designing. Entrepreneurial-type advertising firms like Hal Riney's are going to be better suited to client demands in the nineties, because those firms tend to be better in touch with changing markets and can make course adjustments a lot faster than firms run by business managers.
>
> Beyond that, the entrepreneurial-type agency head is likely to give junior staff transfusions of their wisdom and experience and thus make the creative work of juniors more on target.

There are small firms, of course, whose principals are relatively "unseasoned" in terms of needs for maturity markets. My advice to those firms is to form advisory committees of mature consumers for the testing of creative product. It is best to do as Ted Marzak (see Chapter 10) has done: He recruited people from retirees who had careers in marketing and communications. Another recommendation follows, one that all firms of any size might be well advised to follow.

## Psychological Tests Can Identify Best "Creatives" for Maturity Markets

My former firm was the first in the nation to specialize in condominium and homeowner association management. We were nationally recognized for being in the forefront of our field, a reputation that should have served us well in client relations. We placed an unusual amount of emphasis on staff training as well as educating our clients (boards of directors) for more effective conduct of their responsibilities. We were the first community management firm to automate accounting activities, which yielded a much higher level of accuracy and permitted uncommonly detailed cost analysis. In short, the firm pioneered a number of innovations for which it became widely recognized. However, despite our innovative management style and enviable reputation, we still experienced contract fallout that was bewildering, sometimes losing out to firms that were poorly regarded throughout the industry.

I began to suspect that we were losing contracts for reasons other than issues of price and competence. In some cases, our best managers were losing contracts while less competent managers were retaining contracts. I ordered a psychological testing program for all managers. What I found out was that the managers who were most successful—consistently—in contract renewals were not necessarily those whose technical skills were the best, but those who showed the highest capacity for empathy on the tests.

It appears that if a person is so tied up in his or her psychological survival and defense needs that development of empathy with mature consumers is greatly inhibited, then the communications product of that person will be off target. To help identify those people most capable of empathy, the marketing company responsible for accounts involved in maturity markets might consider giving psychological tests to those charged with developing marketing communications.

## A Psychological Contract Exists between Providers and Consumers

We learned that those with high levels of empathy were better able to "read" each board member and therefore were intuitively able to effect strategies to meet individual board members' expectations. Importantly, we found those expectations were as much psychological as technical. We began to realize (and tested later for this fact in surveys of boards) that we had, in effect, two contracts with every client: the legal contract and a *psychological contract*.

In our introspective research, we found that we could perform to the letter on the legal contract but fail to get a renewal. But we also found out that when we fulfilled the psychological contract, even though we might come up short on the legal contract, renewals were virtually ensured. Satisfaction of the psychological contract, we learned, went a long way toward creating the perception that the legal contract was being fully honored. It was another example of sensory transference, the transference of feelings about one object or condition to another object or condition irrespective of the lack of a logical connection.

The product or service offered by a marketer is the basis of the legal contract, while the purchaser's experiential expectations of both the transaction and the "ownership" of the product or service form the basis of the psychological contract between provider and consumer. Understanding the law of warranty is vital to fulfilling the legal contract; understanding the consumer is vital to fulfilling the psychological contract.

I have made several references to the similarities of marketing to Japanese and to mature adults in the United States. There are also similarities in that price considerations are frequently less important than certain intangible considerations. Both the Japanese at large and mature U.S. adults consider a company's concern for social and individual human values relevant to a purchase decision. The legal contract deals with the functional performance of a product or service. The psychological contract often deals with issues wholly unrelated to the functioning or intrinsic qualities of the product or service. The psychological contract frequently involves a kind of bonding between the provider and the consumer because the provider has evidenced endorsement of the consumer's basic values. Such a bonding arises from the provider's empathetic understanding of what is important to the consumer. This empathetic understanding leads Japanese—and mature adult U.S. consumers—to often pay more for something than its intrinsic value alone would justify.

## The "Game of Life" Technique for Enhancing Empathy

One technique used for developing empathy with older people is what some have called the *game of life*. It has been widely used in sensitizing staff in senior adult housing to some of the problems older people may experience.

The game of life consists of exercises whereby players are placed in positions that replicate conditions experienced by many older people. For example, vision is dimmed by smearing petroleum jelly on eyeglasses, or the effects of strokes are simulated by tying a person's dominant hand behind the back or by "forbidding" a player to speak. Thus handicapped, players may be asked to feed themselves with their secondary hand, read an advertising brochure with dimmed eyesight, or try to ask for help without speaking.

The owner of one life care community who had all his staff introduced to the game of life calls it "a humbling experience." He says that when the game is skillfully administered, players can become highly frustrated by such simple tasks as eating or communicating with others or downright angry with fellow players for their lack of understanding—and *empathy*.

The purpose of the game of life is to get players to escape the boundaries of their ego-centered selves in order to enter vicariously the psyches of older people. Because it is an emotional, more than an intellectual, experience, the empathetic capacities of many players are enhanced or at least become more highly developed.

## The Game of Life Can Lead to Flawed Impressions of Elders

There are problems with the game of life and similar sensitivity programs, according to gerontologist Nancy Peppard, of AgeAware, a Rockville, Maryland, consulting firm. Peppard said in a recent interview that such programs tend to perpetuate stereotypes of older people.

> Most companies interested in older markets will not have many dealings with the frail elderly to which these programs are oriented. A problem is that these programs carry an implication that at some point in life, most people are going suddenly to have the kinds of problems that are supposedly emulated by vaseline-smeared glasses and cotton balls in the ears. The reduced acuity in sight and hearing may shock those young people experiencing sensory decrements for the first time, but for those older people who do have those kinds of problems, they have the benefit of years of gradual decline of acuity which allows them time to compensate.

Peppard says that the sensitivity training programs she administers are directed toward a much more serious problem—ageism.

More older people suffer a great deal more from psychological problems stemming from ageist attitudes than from physical problems. It is a lot more challenging to sensitize younger people to the feelings an older person has about these issues, than to issues involving reduced levels of physical abilities.

## Few Know How to Market Effectively to Older Consumers

I asked Peppard if she could name any companies exemplary in their marketing approaches to older markets. She said that none came to mind, expressing her frustration about how marketers are making marketing to older people more difficult than it should be.

Take hospitals, for example. All over the country, hospitals have been sold on the idea of setting up membership programs for older people, ostensibly, those 55 and older. The problem is that their services are aimed at frail and much older health care consumers. The market they would like to get, they are not going to get. They not only are showing a misunderstanding of younger seniors, but they don't even understand older seniors. The older person about ready to go into a hospital is not going to pressure his or her doctor into going to this hospital or that.

Peppard favors an approach in sensitivity training that draws on panels of older people. Importantly, she recruits some people with stereotypical problems, others without. She maintains that younger people gain a much more realistic view of older people and aging in that way. Asked about role playing with marketing and service staff, she says she uses role playing exercises extensively with training staff, but unless a client is willing to put out a greater sum of money than most, "role playing can be counterproductive because abbreviated uses of the technique tend to center on stereotypes."

## Bring Mature Consumers to Marketing Meetings to Enlighten Staff

Another way of helping young people to better understand older people is incredibly simple. It consists simply of putting a group of older consumers in the same room with art directors, copywriters, researchers, account executives, and others involved in planning and executing marketing programs for maturity markets. So here is yet another opportunity for marketing professionals to gain from "employing"—in the fullest sense of the word—senior consumers.

This discussion of the game of life and other techniques to expand empathetic capacities is not meant to imply that disability is the key issue among members of the ageless market, even among elderly mature consumers. The extreme conditions reflected in the Game of Life, for example, make a point by exaggerating a point. But between the conditions of one specific older person who suffers great limitations and the conditions of one specific 30-year-old who senses no limitations lie many degrees of conditions which, while not seriously limiting a person's capabilities, nevertheless are important enough to be taken into account by marketers.

More important, however, than empathizing with older consumers who suffer from limitations is to gain an empathetic understanding of their psyches. They do generally operate from different frames of reference than young people, and they tend to have markedly different ways of organizing their realities. So let the person who is 30 years old think about how his or her outlook on life might be different if suddenly that person had a sense of being ageless. Certainly one's frame of reference in viewing life and the patterning of one's lifestyle would undergo great changes.

## Physiological Changes of Marketing Significance

Early in this book, I stated that the dominant age range of maturity markets should be considered as beginning at age 50, despite the fact that some consumers, who are younger, reflect consumer behavior patterns more commonly associated with people past the age of 50. I preface the next discussions with this thought so that readers will continue to think of the fundamental ideas of this book in terms of maturity markets as already defined, rather than in terms of age of life and the physiological attributes commonly associated with advanced aging processes, the subject of the next part of this chapter.

There can be no ignoring the fact that significant physiological changes take place in the aging body that have a number of important implications in marketing, from product design, to promotional and selling activities, to postsale servicing of consumers. These changes affect all five sensory systems of the human body, as well as manual dexterity and mental operations. For the most part, these changes normally do not affect people in ways that suggest a major impact on marketing activities until people are in their sixties, although for some people the changes will begin more dramatically and earlier. But at that time, changes in most people's physiology do become significant enough that marketers need to take them into account.

## Eyes

The eyes begin to show the effects of aging at age 8. Not 80, but 8! At age 8, the human eye reaches its optimum ability to maintain a crisp, clear image in constant fashion regardless of the vergence of light. At 50, that ability is virtually zero: the clarity of an image is altered by the differing angles of light.

Without going deeply into the physiology of human sight mechanisms in terms of changes due to time, suffice it to say that there are three areas of change that marketers need to take into account:

- Short-term vision deficits.
- Increased problems with glare.
- Slower response to light.

These changes should dictate special consideration for such marketing elements as type size, finish of paper stock, color of paper and inks, and calibrations on measuring devices (automobile gauges, oven settings, etc.). A brochure may win an award for creative excellence but fail in its primary purpose if the type size, ink choices, and glare due to high-gloss finish make it difficult to read.

While distance factors in visual acuity can often be corrected with glasses, there are no prosthetics to compensate for deficits in responding to illumination-related stimuli. Because of this, special consideration must be given to ambient lighting, both directed and backlighting of displays, and modulation of lighting in movies and television projections. Rapid contrast in scene changes, for example, creates problems like those experienced by people suffering from night blindness in adapting to the sudden appearance of oncoming headlights.

Subtle gradations in color will be lost on most aging eyes, as can pastels and combinations of colors at the green-blue-violet end of the spectrum. Any undertaking to redecorate a store should draw upon experts who understand the effects of aging on visual acuity. Similarly, those involved in preparing advertising materials and television commercials should get knowledgeable advice on visual response to various aspects of the materials being prepared. And most certainly, architects, interior designers, and others involved in determining the character of the visual environments of senior adult housing and health care facilities need to follow the guidelines of experts to address the visual challenges created by aging optical systems.

Because of several conditions, including differing response to light and changes in the curvature of the lens of the eye, depth perception decreases with age. Thus the lighting near steps and the use of color breaks to mark changes of elevation in public areas are very important.

These visual changes begin for most people around their early forties, so we are not talking about the "geriatric crowd." Marketers have never really concerned themselves with these issues in the past because they have focused predominantly on consumers in their forties and younger. The seriousness of accommodating these changes in marketing may be underscored by one observation that has been made in tests for measuring various responses to glare. The distractions that glare produces can affect balance, orientation, attention span, and even short-term memory, all of which are effects that should concern marketers.[3]

### Ears

Inevitably hearing loss occurs with age, some characteristics of which are not correctable. Men have hearing loss problems more commonly than women, thus businesses catering to older men, with or without spouses in their company, should be aware of this fact.

Generally, there are decreased sensitivities to tones in the higher ranges, which result in a fusion of sounds. Amplification of sound in such instances only amplifies the resulting confusion. Poor acoustics in restaurants and other places of patronage can so increase both physiological and psychological stress that a discomfited consumer will never return.

In television and radio commercials, time-compressed commercials are more difficult for older ears to follow, and competition from background sounds or parallel messages results in less effective communication.

In taking into account the visual and auditory deficiencies experienced in aging, marketers should keep in mind that a person who believes he or she is getting less out of a message than other people can become so discomforted that anxiety develops, pulse rate and blood pressure increase, perceptions of others can take on aspects of paranoia, and any potential interest in what is being said in an "unnecessary" message (a commercial is an "unnecessary" message) does not develop. Moreover, irritation over the source of discomfiture can alienate a person irrevocably from its perceived source.

---

[3]C. D. Schewe, "Marketing to Our Aging Population: Responding to Physiological Changes," unpublished paper, School of Management, University of Massachusetts, 1987.

## Mouth

Taste buds are designed to respond to four categories of stimuli: salt, sweet, sour, and bitter. In later life, the sensitivity to each of these categories decreases. Exacerbating the problem is a decrease in saliva. However, food tastes are also affected by subjective responses to color, temperature, and tactile sensations (for example, the texture of food as perceived in the mouth), and, of course, smell. Smell may account for as much as 80 percent of the overall taste sensation.

Food is socially and personally such an integral part of a satisfying life for most people that any organization which hopes to be successful in marketing food products for retail outlets or directly serving prepared food to older people will learn to accommodate the sensory system taste changes due to aging. Hospitals and nursing homes are commonly criticized for their failure in this regard. But what about restaurants, airlines, bowling alleys, and other businesses that sell and/or serve food? Those who secure the repeat business of older customers should be studied carefully, for they will undoubtedly have found unobtrusive ways to accommodate the physiological decrements of their customers.

## Nose

Our sense of smell becomes compromised by the loss of olfactory cells at as early as age 30. Older people can find themselves in life-threatening situations as a result of a steady decline in ability to smell, for instance, a gas leak. But marketers of products ranging from deodorants, perfumes, toothpastes, and other personal products to foods, flowers, and certain household products have a potential interest and set of challenges in dealing with altered states of smell in older people. Some food preparation firms add chemicals to enhance the aroma—and thereby taste appeal—of foods. While purists may object to one more chemical addition to the food, it may be a reasonable trade-off to make eating a bit more enjoyable for, say, residents of a nursing home by restoring some of a lost sense of taste in food through artificial means.

The sense of smell has also been identified as the sensory system most powerful in inducing nostalgia. A word or a picture reminiscent of one's childhood may not do as much for pleasant reverie as the smell of a home-baked apple pie or a patch of honeysuckle. Think of what this might do for prospects in a senior adult community as they tour the dining room or kitchen, or walk in the garden.

## Other Physiological Changes

The skin, source of most of our tactile sensations, declines in sensitivity as it ages. At the same time, older people tolerate extremes in temperature less well. The ambient temperature and humidity conditions in stores and other public places frequented by older people should be maintained with concern for the differences between young and old in terms of tactile responses to environmental conditions.

Beginning between age 40 and age 50, a measurable loss in strength in the body's various muscle systems becomes noticeable, though not severe. However, strength reduction begins to accelerate in the sixties, with severe reductions commonly occurring in the seventies and beyond. As of yet, however, very few products on the market take these facts into account. From bags of peanuts handed out on planes to tamperproof medicine bottles, it seems that the older person is waging a continuous battle against muscle discrimination, although many younger people have difficulty opening such containers for various reasons as well.

## Correcting for Age Discrimination in Marketing Benefits All

Even after this brief review of some of the physical changes that occur in the aging body, it is not difficult to understand why many older people feel more and more alienated from society as they age. Very few places suitably accommodate the changes just described. For the most part, we have tended to think in terms of accommodating for highly obvious forms of handicap, rather than for differences in varying sizes of people who have varying degrees of motor skills and strengths, and varying degrees of sensory acuity.

There are places where designers have attempted to accommodate diminished physical capacities, but have done so with insensitivity. For example, a hollow wooden wheelchair ramp beside a stairway screams out that this is the entrance for people who have some condition which renders them different from "normal" people. An attractive spiraling ramp that fits in with the landscape and architectural design will more sensitively meet the needs of those who cannot use stairs, and such a design may attract children and others who want to walk in a leisurely fashion to their destination.

The design and incorporation of bathroom *grab bars* provide another opportunity for creativity. Instead of mounting unattractive utilitarian fixtures that serve as continual reminders of people's handicaps, planners can incorporate the bars into the design aesthetically so they are viewed as conveniences for *anyone* who might want a little assistance in changing positions.

The design of products and facilities that better accommodate people with physical limitations addresses only one aspect of those consumers' needs and desires. According to the Consumer Satisfaction Principle, the Third General Principle of Marketing, only the consumers' *functional expectations* are being addressed.

The Second Basis for Consumer Satisfaction, *Social Reinforcement Expectations*, is neglected when such accommodations are designed with little empathy for people's sensitivity to being singled out for special design considerations because of age or handicap.

## What's Good for Older People Often Is Good for All People

Most of the changes discussed in this chapter on product and package design, on the development and rendering of marketing messages, and on the delivery of services will result in better marketing decisions for those in markets of all ages and character. A good example of this point has comes from the makers of Whirlpool home laundry units. They designed a washer-dryer unit with oversized dials and backlit controls, and found that they had come up with a product equally appealing to young homemakers and older people.

Perhaps someone will figure a way to redesign medicine bottle labels so that after enduring the indignity of fighting to remove the cap, people won't have to spend untold minutes squinting and turning the bottle in an attempt to read the microscopic directions. One needn't be old, frail, myopic, or arthritic to have experienced such problems.

Fortunately for all of us, the current trend to de-stigmatize products and services for the mature market offers a likely payoff in the form of designs that will prove universally valid. We're discovering that what's good for older people will generally be good for younger people as well.

## Method Marketing "Gestalt" Requires Open-Mindedness

It is not within the scope of this book to discuss all the major physiological and psychological changes that are, or tend to be, associated with aging. However, anyone who is seriously interested in the maturity market will be well served by consulting other sources and, in the process, by assuming that he or she is starting from zero in necessary understanding. Participants in brainstorming sessions are instructed to assume that nothing is beyond questioning in order to emancipate the imagination and free the truth from the shackles of bias and preconceptions. Such a disposition is valuable for working in maturity markets.

It can be a challenge for intelligent, hardworking, creative people to lay aside their preconceptions about how things should be done, especially when their biases have been fortified by past successes in markets other than maturity markets. For example, even highly talented copywriters will often insist on compressing all copy into terse phrases or incomplete sentences. The expression of ideas in short phrases, as is commonly done in advertising copy, does not provide the sense of rhythm that is necessary for comprehension by many older minds, for whom flow, rhythm, and syntax enhance comprehension. In addition, older people often react adversely to what they consider to be poor grammar. They may even perceive single words, phrases, and nonsequential images as valueless (meaningless) because of fractured or nonexisting contexts.

According to an AARP guidebook on communications,

> Reading continuous copy or following a coherent sequence of images makes fewer demands on the visual ability of the audience because context and perceptual clues aid understanding. In print, indentation of paragraphs and the use of standard capitalization also provide visual clues, which improve reading. When faced with single words or phrases, or nonsequential images, these context clues are lost.[4]

Thus, the use of ad copy styles that might work very well in younger adult markets can severely inhibit cognition and comprehension in older markets.

The American Marketing Association's comprehensive definition of *marketing*, cited in Chapter 1, is consistent with the idea that designs which take into account the physiological and psychological changes occurring in later life are not tangential but integral to the marketing process.

The concept of *method marketing*, which is based on an empathetic understanding of the consumer as a *whole* being—in every sense of the word—encompasses *all* aspects of marketing. *Method marketing* calls for an empathetic approach to more than just the design of advertisements and brochures and the training of staff; it calls for an empathetic approach to the entire *gestalt* of products and services offered to older people.

---

[4]"Looking Good for the Aging Person," *Talking about Aging; Guidelines for Accurate Communications*, AARP, Washington, D.C., 1984, p. 28.

# 10
# Winners in
# Maturity Markets

## The Health and Fitness
## Club Industries

In this chapter, we take a look at some of the success stories and some of the many opportunities that exist in maturity markets. The opportunities that are identified are neither exhaustive for any specific industry nor do they encompass all industries. But there may be some surprises for some readers. For example, an industry that has not been widely identified as having lucrative possibilities in maturity markets is the health club industry.

## Age Does Not Preclude Interest in
## Health and Fitness Clubs

I recently authored several chapters of the book *The Forty Plus Market: How to Capture and Keep Full-Life Members*, published by IRSA, a trade association for racquet and health clubs. In the course of the research and writing, I learned that many in the health club business believe that older people have little interest in health club activities. The reason most commonly given is that, in the past, older people have not shown great interest. Others in the business think older people represent a market potential, but one developing only in the future, concurrent with the aging of the baby boomers, the population group that gave birth to the modern-day health club industry. The thinking is that narcissistic boomers will simply retain their memberships as a weapon against the ravages of aging. Echoing this view, one writer on boomer trends said, "You can expect boomers to be dragged into old age, kicking and screaming all the way." I don't believe such views accurately reflect the typical aging boomer. I will argue that point later.

## To Capitalize on Older Markets, Club Operators Must Make Many Changes

The health club industry stands to reap considerable profits from the growing markets among older people—provided club owners develop an understanding of the key personality motivations of older people *as mature older people*—not in terms of the self-oriented looks-and-fitness-conscious jocks and jills to which they are accustomed.

Understanding the social imperatives and inclinations of older people will lead smart club operators to change their facilities and operations a great deal. Decor, floor plans, and ancillary facilities will be designed to facilitate the kinds of social interaction sought by older people. Staff demeanor will change to accommodate the differing social interaction styles of older people. Clubs that will be successful in maturity markets will be less exclusively "sweat-oriented" and more oriented to the whole person.

There will be reading rooms and music rooms (to "work out" the head and to rest the mind as well as the body). Some clubs may team up with local colleges, where the enrollments of older students are increasing, to further promote the development of the whole person, fit in mind, body, and soul, which the mature—freed from the narrowing constraints of a single-focused career and family demands—can now pursue. As more and more older people enroll in health clubs, the massage business will increase as will stress and pain management clinic enrollments.

The *New Age* spirit and philosophy will increasingly bring about change in the character of health and fitness clubs because of the meaning of the one word that most fully symbolizes New Age thinking: *holistic*, frequently spelled *wholistic* in New Age literature, to emphasize *whole*ness. New Agers view the body as inseparable from the mind in all regards. Fit bodies cannot exist without fit minds; and minds are made more fit by fit bodies.

Health and fitness club operators who begin to place more emphasis on *total* fitness of the *whole* person will be better positioned to retain aging boomers as members and to recruit new members from people who never before considered health and fitness club membership. Essentially, those health clubs that can adapt to both the psychological and the physiological needs and desires of older people have a great future.

This will, however, involve a change in attitudes of a lot of club operators and club personnel.

One young executive (29 years old) in a major national club equipment supply firm told me that he saw no future in older markets because older people were not interested in "exercise" and besides, "People over 50 aren't interested in learning and doing new things." He actually said that. I hope he reads this book for the sake of his company. There will be a significant decrease in the market of people from their middle twenties to early forties in the next few years, and his company can make up for the decline in the current core market only by finding consumers in other age groups.

There already is strong statistical evidence that today's older consumers warrant special marketing attention in the health club business. A recent study by the Daniel Yankelovich Group[1] found that among the 39- to 49-year-old respondents, 50 percent reported that they exercised regularly in comparison with 41 percent of respondents aged 50 and older. When one discounts those in their middle seventies and older, who are generally not heavy exercisers (at least current ones), then the 9 percentage points of difference between the two groups of respondents lose all significance.

Another study[2] found strong correlations between levels of education and income and how much older people exercise. Presumably not a coincidence, the quality of health conditions reported by respondents had the same correlations with education and health. Among the 50- to 65-year-olds in the study, only 1 percent with annual incomes greater than $35,000 reported poor health. By comparison, 47 percent reported excellent health, and another 41 percent reported good health. For those with annual incomes between $20,000 and $35,000, 29 percent reported excellent health and 46 percent said their health was good. On the lower end of the income spectrum, those with annual incomes $15,000 or less, 15 percent reported experiencing poor health. Because of increasing higher-education levels among older people, it is a good bet that more and more older people will be serious candidates for health club memberships.

[1]*The Mature Americans*, Daniel Yankelovich Group, Inc.; study conducted for the Maturity Magazines Group, New York, a division of the American Association of Retired Persons, Washington, D.C., 1987.

[2]*The Prime Life Generation*, a joint study of the American Council of Life Insurance Association of America et al., Washington, D.C., 1985.

### How One Club Operator Has
### Succeeded in Older Markets

In 1986, Roger Grady's Newport Athletic Club, in Newport, Rhode Island, began consciously to target the 55-plus market for the first time. Two years later, nearly 10 percent of the club's total membership was from this group. Discounting those in the population in their middle seventies or older, Grady's "Inner Circle" membership holders are a greater percentage of the total club membership than their age group is of the total population.[3]

Grady quickly learned that ads that were effective for recruiting younger members did not play well in initial attempts to secure older members. And there were big differences in media selection for advertisements. "The folksy radio station in the Newport area was a perfect vehicle, consisting mostly of talk shows during the day, as well as 'swap shop' and 'potting shed' programs." He stresses the importance, however, of combining newspaper ads with radio commercials.[4]

He reports that, through experience, he learned not to stress *athletics*, because the term suggests one has to be athletic to join, and that overuse of the term *club* can be intimidating because of its overtones of exclusivity. He claims that his term *the Inner Circle* suggests "an accepting and accessible group," yet one that has an appealing specialness about it.

What Grady has discovered is that there is money to be made in older markets for fitness club operators—provided they learn to speak the language of older people and design the facilities' operation around older members' self-image characterizations, characterizations that are "lean" on athletic and narcissistic images and "fat" on folksiness and overall well-being.

### Travel and Hospitality
### Industries

Travel has long been recognized as a popular activity among older people. That won't change, and the sheer numbers in the boomer generation ensure a healthy market for travel services directed at older markets for many years to come. However, *per capita* expenditures among the older population can be increased, assuming the continuation of a reasonably healthy economy. How? The means used include these:

---

[3]*The Forty Plus Market: How to Capture and Keep Full Life Members,* IRSA, Boston, 1988, p. 38.

[4]Ibid.

- More innovative programs based on a better understanding of what older consumers respond to.

- The teaming up of corporations in noncompetitive partnerships, such as in the various frequent-flyer programs.

- Introduction of such innovations as Cunard Lines' "Weeks to Wellness" program, a cruiseship service for people to renew both body and mind while they enjoy the experience of travel.

In marketing travel programs to older people, marketers need to examine the differences in motivation between young travelers and older travelers. The former are strongly motivated to escape, to *get away*. Older consumers of travel services, by contrast, show a strong interest in the learning and personal growth opportunities that travel can provide. Marketing literature should present travel-specific programs as *gateways* to educational and personal growth experiences, not opportunities to escape—thus reflecting the First Principle for Maturity Markets, set forth in Chapter 1.

### *Choice*, the Most Important Word in Marketing to Mature Adults

Nearly all the major airlines now offer special age-based discounts, but a number of restrictions are usually placed on "senior-citizen" privileges. However, in November 1988, British Airways launched a comprehensive travel membership program for people 60 years of age and older that put a major emphasis on *choice*, the most important word in marketing to older consumers. British Airways' use of *choice*, as defined by older people, contributed to a jump in the enrollment figures in the first six months of the program to twice the goal for the first year.

The program is not marketed for senior citizens, but for "Privileged Travelers," people who have implicitly achieved a special status in life by passing through their family-raising and career years and now have the time and means to enjoy the special privileges accorded those of laudatory accomplishment. Importantly, those ideas are more *implied* than articulated in the promotional literature. Older people generally don't respond well to advertising pitches that exhort them to buy a product or service because they "deserve it."

The Privileged Traveler program has no hidden costs, no exceptions, and no restrictions on times when members may travel. In addition to choice, British Airways has put simplicity, another of the most important words, in maturity markets. "Flexibility and choice are key considerations for older consumers," according to Walter Klores, a principal of LifeSpan Communications, a New York firm that was a consultant to British Airways on the development of the program.

"Forcing older travelers to plan trips for off-peak hours to take advantage of special fares can backfire. If you make off-peak trips more attractive, they will choose them, but don't design a program that restricts them from going at other times if they choose," Klores advises. "No one likes to be restricted."

The Privileged Traveler program also keys into British Airways' *Privileged Vacation* program, which has been specifically designed for mature, more affluent, independent travelers, who often have more time at their disposal. Privileged Vacation programs give travelers opportunities to participate in imaginative, unusual programs such as English Walking Tours or London Study days, outings notable for their lack of tour-guide pace.

## Hotels Are Discovering "Prime Timers"

Hotels are also getting into older markets. They are preparing for these markets not only by offering special discounts, but also by offering special-accommodation features in room design for the less physically able traveler. Quite a number of older people, despite serious physical limitations, will travel if they have confidence that their conditions can be comfortably and unobtrusively accommodated.

Bill Todd, marketing director for Quality International, the world's third largest hotel chain, launched the company's "Prime Timers" program several years ago and reports that the results outstripped projections. He says that the company chose the term *Prime Timers* after consumer studies indicated that lots of older folks don't particularly like being classified as "senior citizens." My own research has found *senior adult* to be a more frequently preferred term. Apparently, many older people—especially those on the young side—associate a number of the attributes of stereotypical images of older people with the term *senior citizen*.

Todd attributes much of the success of the Prime Timers program to its simplicity and lack of restrictions on the times when members may take advantage of its benefits, in much the same manner as British Airways' Privileged Traveler program is structured. *Simplicity* and *choice* delivered older consumers once again!

Reporting that there was some initial corporate skepticism when he proposed the program, Todd's first marketing budget was only $400,000. Several years later, however, the program's success had earned it a $4 million marketing budget. But the small initial budget did not daunt Todd. He teamed up with American Express, Hertz, Avis, and other noncompeting companies that looked like natural partners and tapped into their marketing budgets.

### Age or Condition Takes No "Senior" Out of Discretionary Markets

Recently I encountered a woman sitting in a wheelchair in the Washington, D.C., National Airport, who appeared to be in her eighties. I noticed her when I overheard her asking an airline employee to wheel her over to the smoking section of the waiting lounge so that she could, in her words, "have a few 'pops' " before she got on board. Not finding a place with an ashtray, she said, "Never mind. I have an ashtray in my purse," and with that she deftly produced one. I wanted to meet this spicy lady.

She introduced herself as Dorothy New, a retired business school professor from Stanford University. She told me that she was returning from a long trip and was headed home to California—alone. Widowed for two years, Dr. New said that nothing could hold her down but her own mind—not even her body. She said that she had visited every country that she had ever wanted to visit except Israel and South Africa— and she wasn't finished yet.

Dorothy New is a vibrant testament to the idea that marketers should avoid looking at age as a handicap and avoid looking at "handicaps" as barriers to doing things for fun that involve buying someone's products and services. AARP's travel services director, Hal Norvell, says that AARP counts many people like Dorothy New among its travelers.

## Financial Services Industries

Financial institutions "adore" older people. Older people tend to speculate less with their investments, which means they put more money into institutions that insure their money against loss. And while things may be different among the boomers born from the late 1950s to 1964 (the end of the birth boom and the beginning of the birth dearth), boomers born earlier have considerable affluence through their own efforts, and many will benefit from substantial inheritances from their parents. In other words, for all the talk about the wealth of today's older population, prospects are good that the wealth and income of older America will be significantly greater in another 10 years or so than it is today.

The great unknown of the future, regarding money management habits of older people, is how boomers will handle their money as older people. Boomers' attitudes on money have not been influenced by living through the Great Depression. They may be willing to take greater risks in their investments later in life than earlier generations of older people. It is anyone's guess at this time as to what aged boomers' attitudes on money will be, but marketers of financial services should watch for signs of differences between the traditional attitudes of older people and emerging attitudes of boomers.

### Today's Older People Don't Like Installment Debt

You can count on financial service industries' becoming more competitive in wooing older consumers for deposits and other financial services, but one area of financial services that still has not found the key to widely expanded business in older markets is the credit card business. Surveys have disclosed that older people have fewer credit cards on average, use them less frequently than younger consumers, and pay off credit balances more quickly. According to Elaine Sherman, a professor of marketing at New York's Hofstra University, one survey found that only one senior citizen in six had a store credit card. The reason is simple: Why pay 18 percent on money you don't need to borrow because you have enough in the bank to cover your purchases? When it comes to money management, the reputation older people have for being prudent money-handlers is well earned. Installment debt at typical credit card rates is not good money management. It is better to take out a home equity loan at 1 or 2 points above prime.

### Reverse Annuity Mortgages May Become Big Business

One area of borrowing that does seem to represent significant business potential is the *reverse annuity mortgage*. Offered in a variety of forms, a reverse annuity mortgage is essentially a loan based on the equity held by owners in their homes, with the loan paid out in monthly installments over a fixed term.

A better deal than the reverse annuity mortgage is its cousin, the *lifetime reverse mortgage*. William Texido of San Francisco founded Providential Home Income Plan, Inc., to provide income for life for homeowners aged 62 and older, by using this approach. Texido is, in effect, betting that the actuarial statistics on the life expectancy of his borrowers are borne out and allow him to share in appreciated home values when the home is sold upon death to pay off the outstanding principal.[5]

[5]"On the House," *Inc.*, March 1989.

Texido, already a multimillionaire from his entrepreneurial successes (he built a $500 million company in the early 1980s in another line), has convinced a venture capital group of the future of a new business seeking to tap into the $750 billion of home equity held by heads of household aged 62 or older.

Texido and others believe that there are tens of thousands of older people of modest income whose net worth is composed primarily of the equity in their homes. Better than 70 percent of homeowners aged 65 and older have fully paid off their mortgages. Reverse annuity mortgages and lifetime reverse mortgages allow homeowners to tap into their home equity on an incremental basis to supplement other retirement income. Already there are trade groups, such as the National Center for Home Equity Conversion of Madison, Wisconsin, to help develop the field.

Leo Baldwin, president of LEO, Inc., a consulting firm based in Washington, D.C., says, "It is a very substantial market, but it's got to be cultivated slowly. The idea of a person 'eating' into his home equity is not an easy thing to get used to at first, regardless of the financial benefits on a month-to-month basis."

## Insurance Potential in Maturity Markets Has Yet to Be Defined

Long-term care (LTC) insurance is one of the biggest topics of conversation in insurance circles today. Most major personal insurance companies today either have developed a program or are in the process of creating one. Prudential has entered into an agreement with the American Association of Retired Persons. Aetna, Travelers, Chubb, and others have been working with operators of congregate and life care facilities to provide insurance for residents. But, as in so many other industries seeking to capitalize on the graying of America, projected market results have frequently been disappointing.

The Financial Institutions Marketing Association (FIMA) reported that a major Midwestern savings institution pulled out of the market after only five months. Instead of the projected one sale per day, the institution realized barely one sale per month. FIMA's analysis of the failure indicated that the program was too complicated, the premiums too expensive, and the market not properly targeted.

Another, brighter story, however, can be told about UNUM Corp., based in Portland, Maine. Like British Airways, UNUM has learned the powerful meaning of the word *choice* in maturity markets. "The biggest barrier to selling long-term care insurance is that people don't want to go to a nursing home. We're giving them the ability to stay independent in their homes or other settings for longer periods," says Donald

Charsky, the UNUM vice president in charge of developing the program.

Unlike the typical LTC policy which requires institutionalization as a prerequisite for payment, the UNUM approach is modeled after disability insurance, which has long been the company's main emphasis. In some of its programs, UNUM issues a check directly to insureds, allowing them to use the money as they see fit.

UNUM's research disclosed that there is a great deal of distrust of insurance companies despite most people's feelings that they are a necessity for many areas of their lives. To counter such feelings, UNUM relies on a third party to evaluate claims. That firm is LifePlans of Waltham, Massachusetts, which has a national network of professionals who evaluate functional disability and cognitive impairment.

UNUM's experience holds lessons for all companies seeking business in the maturity markets: Marketers need to find out what consumers are thinking and what they want, and tailor the products and sales messages to those answers. It seems simple, but what could account for all the shortfalls between marketing projections and marketing results, in industry after industry, except failure to do just that? If there were not such success stories as those of UNUM, British Airways, Quality International, and others, then questions about the business potentials of older markets would be well posed. However, the reverse appears to be the fact.

## Retail Industries

Unrecognized by many people is a trend toward more intimate and personalized sales environments that have a natural appeal to older consumers. This development is gaining much of its impetus from the boomers. Older boomers have arrived at a point in their lives where price often is less important than personal attention. Older people have long felt this way. That is one reason they will stand in line for a warm, friendly human bank teller rather than use the generally more efficient electronic fund transfer (EFT) machines. This is not to say that aging boomers will turn away from EFT machines as they age. They have become accustomed to them and will continue to value the convenience they provide.

During the 1960s, 1970s, and early 1980s, we saw the "chaining of America," with the rise of The Gap, Benetton, Laura Ashley, Banana Republic, and numerous other chains of specialty stores. Specialty store chains were the product of shrewd market segmentation–based strategies directed at specific age and gender segments—unlike traditional department stores which broadly positioned themselves for the general population with a special focus on family markets. Specialty stores have skillfully exploited the persuasive powers of peer group–derived values, a factor, as discussed in Chapter 1, that loses much of its potency in maturity markets.

The specialty store chains took much of their market share from the department stores, which routinely used to operate in 300,000 square feet or more, but are now frequently operating in the range of 100,000 square feet of retail space in many new stores. But as the pendulum swings back, the national specialty chains need to be alert to the possible threat of a new wave of "mom-and-pop" retailers who rely less on peer group–derived values and more on old-fashioned style and service to attract and keep customers. More and more, people are rebelling against the "You are a statistic" kind of retailer who employs clerks without commitment to the store or concern for the satisfaction of the consumer.

Older people tend to like people, and they like interaction with other people who seem to like people. Many are willing to pay the price differential between the chain store price and the mom-and-pop price in order to have pleasing experiences with the salespeople. Price advantages achieved at the expense of warm, friendly service compromise the perceived value for many older consumers. I suspect that over time there will be a backwash effect that moves younger consumers toward such attitudes, as older consumers increasingly demand more attention and friendlier service.

## Sears' Shift to "Everyday Low Prices" Position Is a Wrong Direction

Sears' much-hyped campaign, launched in 1989, signaling its joining the ranks of chain discount department stores might just prove to have been a major mistake, because it has pushed price to the fore as the presumed number one priority of its customers. It was a strategic decision that runs counter to the consumer psychology trends of the nation. I believe this venerable institution's very survival will be challenged because it decided to stop being what it has always been—a clear reflection of the middle-class society on which it has always centered its attention. Sears will survive and regain vitality only by making major changes that get the stores back into the mainstream of Middle America.

Others share the opinion that Sears has made a mistake. In a special supplement to a spring 1988 issue of *Advertising Age* that focused on "Retailing in the 90s," a chart of projected "Winners and Losers" in the retail business in the 1990s was presented. Sears was listed in the *losers'* column. Montgomery Ward, by comparison, was listed in the *winners'* column. Montgomery Ward has been "boutiqueizing" its stores, creating little stores within the big store in order to convey specialty store images. That would seem a logical approach to combat the inroads of the specialty store chains, which have probably done the most damage to the market share of department stores. But Sears elected to take on the discount stores instead.

Today there is a great craving in U.S. society for "old-fashioned" customer-seller friendliness. It is part and parcel of the *neotraditionalist movement* that descended on the nation in the late 1980s. The tones of that movement are reminiscent of times when department store clerks sent personal letters or even made phone calls to their best customers to inform them, in advance, of newspaper ads or special sales. Store employees counted store customers among the friends they had and valued in life. And customers counted store clerks among their friends. We may well see a return to such a social ambience because older people like that kind of individual attention, and it will be no more apparent than in retailing industries.

## Senior Adult Housing

The middle 1980s saw a tremendous rush by traditional real estate developers, health care providers, insurance companies, hotel chains, and others into the field of "senior" housing. These times also saw many outright marketing failures of senior housing projects, along with a host of mediocre performers that somehow never earned the consumer acceptance expected by their sponsors.

As the 1980s come to a close, the euphoric expectations of just five or six years ago have given way to anxieties and pensive sobriety in the industry, depending on whether one is trying to figure out how to save a failing project or is fearful that the one under development may not make it into big-time success.

Views on why there have been so many failures and mediocre performers in senior housing run the gamut from the theory that there is not so much of a market after all to the idea that the market is enormous, but the pool of talent who know how to design, market, and operate senior communities is not.

One of the big problems in the senior adult housing industry is that it has not yet defined itself. Is it an industry for the elderly consumer? For the "active" older person? For the "need-driven" older consumer? For the consumer who is looking for "continuing care services" *when* he or she *might* need it sometime in the future? The answers to these questions would suggest that the term *senior adult housing industry* is no more specific than the term *high tech industry*. Both terms refer more to land use than to any *specific* market.

## Many Senior Adult Housing Developers Don't Know Who Their Market Is

I have seen many senior adult projects planned and built with the idea of selling to "anyone 55 and older" whose new residents turned out to be 78 to 80 years old, on average. Common sense should suggest that the 25-year span between 55 and 80 is generally too much time to bridge in a single housing style project. Most of the seminars on senior adult housing talk to the 65-plus market, yet the advice showered upon seminar attendees is for housing that nationally reflects an average age at the time of entry of 78 to 80.

Mark Steiner, president of General Health Management, Inc., of Hartford, Connecticut, seems to know how to put together his senior adult communities with better definition of his markets than most. He attributes his company's success to a very simple rule: Market to older people on the basis of their desires, not their needs. This means, according to Steiner, "responding to the desires of a very heterogeneous and demanding group who will insist on a wide variety of choices and options."

A preponderance of senior communities are marketed on the basis of how they can take care of you "in the event of...," a condition that, by definition, severely limits choices. The rational side of an older person's nature might argue that having someone around "just in case" makes good sense. But the emotional side argues, "It probably won't happen to [us], so let's not move into a place that has all those old, sick people."[6]

Those senior communities that have on-site health care services are commonly called *continuing (health) care residential* (or *retirement*) *communities*, or CCRCs. Steiner asks, "Why emphasize care? It would be just as misleading to call it [a CCRC] a recreational community. If we only want to attract people who need 'to be taken care of,' this industry will never attract more than 3 or 4 percent of the possible market."

Referring to one commentator, who refers to older consumers as *veteran consumers*, Steiner says, "I like this idea. After 50 years of jingles, deals, and pitches, they have seen and heard it all. It is time for us to listen."

---

[6]"Viewpoint: It's Time to Respect the 'Veteran Consumer,' " *D. B. Wolfe's Maturity Market Perspectives*, September-October 1989, p. 5.

## The Boom in Senior Adult Housing
## May Come Yet

Gary Solomonson, of Minneapolis-based Sage Company, developers of senior living environments, predicts that within five years the retirement housing model in vogue today will begin to become obsolete. Its obsolescence is already being proved by the millions of older people who spurn marketers' attempts to induce them to move into a retirement community. A survey by Roche Associates, Inc., a Springfield, Massachusetts, research firm, found that only 13.8 percent of respondents had any interest in a CCRC—and interest is not tantamount to a decision.

Senior adult housing will be very different in 10 years from what it is now. Many of today's retirement communities will become what is presently referred to as *assisted-living communities*, communities for people requiring assistance in daily living activities, but not the more intense kinds of care provided in traditional nursing homes. In the meantime, I believe some of the major corporations who have made a lot of noise about their entry into the business will quietly fold their tents and go home, selling off senior housing divisions that failed to perform as their business planners predicted. The cosmetic giant, Avon Products, after investing close to $500 million in the industry, has done just this. Others will follow.

## Home Health Care Poses a Major
## Challenge to Retirement Housing

One major competing influence that could dampen significant growth in the full-service type of retirement community is the probable explosive growth in home health care. Home health care enables people to remain in their homes, a more attractive prospect for most than moving into a more institutional type of living environment. Kelly, the big temporary employment agency, saw the possibilities in home companionship services and has made a major commitment to the business. For between 50 and 65 percent of the cost of one day's care in a traditional nursing home, a frail, elderly person can *age in place*, the phrase that is becoming the catchword for a major social objective.

## Biggest Opportunities Lie in More
## Traditionally Designed Communities

A widely overlooked area of housing for older markets, with vast potential, is housing—rather, communities—for those whose family-raising years have recently concluded and who are near retirement or have recently retired. This group ranges from about 50 to 70 years of age, a cohort measured by about 20 years' time. Only four states—New Jersey, Florida, Arizona, and California—have any significant amount of housing development enterprise for this age group. One says, "Of course, California, Arizona, and Florida—they are Sunbelt states, which are ideal for retirement. But how did New Jersey get in there?"

Not all older people in the Snowbelt think in terms of moving to the Sunbelt, much less moving from the area in which they built careers and raised their families. Many would seriously consider a new community within their present geographic area if the right community—according to their lifestyle aspirations and value systems—were built. But the development industry has widely overlooked these consumers. New Jersey's success story seemingly would indicate that other non-Sunbelt states might have big markets waiting for the developer with "the right stuff."

Since maturity market consumers tend to be much more experientially oriented than "things" oriented in their lifestyle aspirations, the idea of just moving to another house, even to a smaller one to reduce household chores, does not have an overwhelming appeal. But design a community in the spirit of the discussion in Chapter 6, where residents "can be all they can be," a community that offers opportunities for continuing personal growth and opportunities and thus validation of their being, and many will order the moving vans.

Think of the people whose children are grown and careers concluding or actually ended. The idea that most such people breathlessly seek a life of full-time leisure after an exhausting adulthood spent with jobs and children does not square with the psychological facts of adult development and being. With little of value to do, most people suffer self-esteem problems. Communities that enable a life of continuing productivity can be the answer to such people's self-esteem needs and a boon to housing developers.

## Going Back to the Farm Could Be a Dream Come True for Many

Coming out of the ground, as of this writing, is a new community oriented toward older markets called *Worman's Mill.* Located just north of Washington, D.C., it is an intergenerational community that focuses on continuing productivity and personal growth throughout life, rather than on leisure, which has been the hallmark of "retirement" communities.

Worman's Mill, planned for about 1300 households, has a 40-acre farm that will be operated by residents. Many older people today have fond memories of farm life in their childhoods, especially when those memories are of visits to grandparents' farms.

In its town center, Worman's Mill townhouse owners can operate shops on the ground floors of their homes. This will, for example, enable a person to turn what was an avocation during the career years, say woodworking or painting, into a postcareer vocation. A 1987 study commissioned by AARP found that 37 percent of those 60 and older who were still working would like to open a home-based business. Of men living alone, 33 percent wanted to open a home-based business.[7]

## The Advent of the *Fourth-Wave* Senior Adult Community

Gerontologist Dr. Brian Hofland, of the Retirement Research Foundation in Park Ridge, Illinois, predicts the emergence of the "self-actualization community." He calls the first "senior" communities "social rejection" models, meaning housing that involves the "avoidance, repression and neglect of old people as a result of industrialization and its heavily materialistic values," where "old age is devalued and old people are considered expendable...[being viewed as] primarily production units to be discarded when their usefulness is over." County homes and earlier church-sponsored housing for elderly accounted for many examples of the social rejection model.

Hofland terms the next model that emerged the "social services" model. It expresses "the aim of political liberalism and the mechanisms of the welfare state." The hallmark of the social services model is the rendering of services by professionals in a highly paternalistic way that "often subtly leads the patient or client to become more passive and dependent, a phenomenon known as 'learned helplessness.'" Like the first model, the social services model results in a segregation of older persons. They are not seen as "whole" people, but rather as full-time leisure consumers living off the community without giving anything back.

Hofland's third model is the *"participation"* model. It involves a broadened view of the issues of dignity, self-determination, and integration within a community. Its aim is to make possible the avoidance of a nursing home or other highly dependent living environment for as long as possible. It begins to recognize that older people do not relinquish their human needs as a price of aging.

The third model represents a growing awareness that "the leisure pastimes and consumer role of the second model are seen as increas-

---

[7]*Understanding Senior Housing*, American Association of Retired Persons, Washington, D.C., study by Hamilton and Staff, Inc., 1987, p. 27.

ingly untenable and demeaning. There are only so many golf games you can play," says Hofland.

While the third model is a significant improvement over the first and second models, it still falls short of being fully reflective of what Maslow called the *humanness of people*. Hofland terms the fourth model the *"self-actualization" model*, but in looking around, he observes despairingly, "We may see an exemplar in 2020."[8] However, there are already communities emerging in the mode of the fourth model, communities that I refer to as *Fourth-Wave communities*.

Fourth-Wave communities are not necessarily designed *exclusively* for "seniors." They may be intergenerational. Essentially, a *Fourth-Wave community* is one that has been specifically designed proactively to provide diverse opportunities for each person, "to be all he or she can be." Communities for all ages, as we have known them, that have been developed by single development entities, have rarely taken on such a humanistic direction. Hofland believes (and I agree) that we will see such communities in the future.

## Media and Entertainment

A host of new publications targeted to older people has been launched within the last several years. Some will fold, and others will grow big. Those who understand that simply being older does not mean *a priori* that a person will develop an affection for a publication devoted to older people will enjoy higher prospects for success. Despite the new publishing entries into the "silver media," I believe that most of the market will ultimately be grabbed by existing publications that will knowledgeably change their styles to respond better to older people's tastes.

As with most other products and services intended for older markets, publications that stay away from strong identifications with age will generally do better. One magazine aimed at older female markets that is

[8]Brian Hofland, Ph.D., "Value and Ethical Issues in Residential Environments for the Elderly," in David Tilson (ed.), *Aging in Place: Supporting the Frail Elderly in Residential Environments*, Scott, Foresman, Glenview, Ill., 1990, pp. 241–247.

Hofland's concept of the 4 housing "models" is based on terms first used by Rick Moody in developing an educational curriculum for aging adults, which Hofland adapted to the elderly housing industry using Powell Lawton's work. Hofland's two principal sources in these regards are:

Harry (Rick) Moody, "Philosophical Presuppositions of Education for Old Age," *Educational Gerontology*, vol. 1, issue 1, 1976, pp. 1–16.

Powell Lawton, M. Greenbaum, and Bernard Liebowitz, "The Lifespan of Housing Environments for the Aging," *The Gerontologist*, vol. 20, 1980, pp. 56–64.

doing very well at this writing and is avoiding an age label is *Lears*, which has the tag line "The Magazine for the Woman Who Wasn't Born Yesterday." The magazine, founded by Francis Lear, former wife of television producer Norman Lear, was announced to the public via a series of provocative full-page ads depicting older women (see Figure 10-1). The magazine is a celebration of maturity, not a reflection of age and issues and challenges commonly associated with age.

The magazine exceeded its ad revenue and circulation projections in the first year and moved from being a bimonthly to a monthly publication at the end of the first year. Time is required to prove its durability, but early indications are that Francis Lear understands her market and that her market likes her product.

### Age-Titled Publications May Face Struggles in the Future

The market is being flooded with age-titled specialty publications, many in the form of tabloids. Many of these will fail, I believe, because their titles are too strongly tied to age.

Some traditional age-titled publications, such as the former *50 Plus* magazine, will gain a new lease on life by deemphasizing age and repositioning themselves in conditional terms, rather than the absolute terms of the past. When *Reader's Digest* acquired *50 Plus*, one of the first orders of business was to change its title to *New Choices*, with a title extension *For the Best Years*. *New Choices* is on the upswing as of this writing, with a projection of reaching the 1 million mark, up from about 500,000, two years from the time it was retitled.

### TV: Minnow's "Vast Wasteland" Will Become Greener in a Grayer America

Television represents another category of silver media where there will be winners and losers. Although the television industry at large may not gain additional revenues as a result of the graying of America, individual units of the industry will have a more profitable future because they had the good sense to shift the tone, style, and content of programming to conform to the values and interests of the older population.

TV *is* aging, along with its audience. From the days of *Leave It to Beaver* through those of *Father Knows Best*, representing the quintessential American family, to the days of the broken-family situation comedies, to the current days of *The Golden Girls*, TV has been both a

**Figure 10-1.** Ad for *Lear's* magazine. (*Courtesy of Lear's.*)

shaper and a mirror of U.S. society. Today TV is reflecting the aging of America and America's growing acceptance of that phenomenon. *Modern Maturity*, flagship publication of AARP, now has its own TV programs on public television, while new cable channels devoted entirely to older markets are opening up.

In Oklahoma, TEMPO TV, with over 14 million subscribers, has enjoyed great success. The Nostalgia Channel in New York, with more than 2 million subscribers, is cashing in. Others are being created. Cable offers advantages over the commercial network systems in that cable operators can afford to devote an entire channel to a single market if it is big enough. Older markets in the United States today are big enough for them to do just that.

But the commercial networks, too, will be dramatically affected by members of maturity markets; in fact, the changes that will take place in response to the graying of America are already occurring. Newton Minnow, former FCC chairman and famous for his characterization of TV some years ago as a "vast wasteland," might be pleased by some of the changes. For more than a decade and a half, television has been dominated by so-called reality-based programming and situation comedies about people coping with their insecurities in a morally altered and heavily fractured family-oriented society. A rebellion is underway that augurs change in all that. Note the headline and the first paragraph in the March 27, 1989, issue of *Advertising Age*:

*Advertisers "Up in Arms"*

> The "New Puritanism," an attitude of consumers that network TV has gotten too lenient in its treatment of sex and violence, is starting to hit advertiser, agency and network executives hard.

Such consumer attitudes became highly visible when a Michigan woman, Terry Rakolta, made headlines by calling for advertisers to pull commercials off Fox Broadcasting Co.'s *Married...with Children*, because of its "adult" themes and dialogue. Terry Rakolta's views were not unique, but they came to the public eye at a time when enough other people held the same views to effect a revolt. Many older people have long felt that network TV has become "trashy." But it was only when the generation whose moral values had encouraged such TV fare reached a level of maturity placing them in agreement with "the older folks" that a call for a reversal of this trend in entertainment became possible.

Although many of the players may be different, it is the boomer cohort, that highly socially activist generation in the 1960s, that is embarking upon a newly directed social activism in the 1990s. It is an activist-driven movement aimed at restoration of traditional values, hence the term *neotraditionalism*, which is frequently invoked to describe the emerging mood in the United States about lifestyles and moral values. The neotraditionalist movement will have tremendous impact in all areas of popular entertainment, from TV and radio to movies and popular music. Its thrust may be coming from the middle-aged boomers, but it is finding great support among members of older audiences. In these changes in the national mood lie significant business opportunities for those who observe, listen, and act on what aging consumers are saying they want and *don't want*.

Even among today's 55-plus population, the preference is clearly for less sensational and more factually oriented programming, as reflected in the following list of favorite shows, in order of popularity, taken from a 1988 Neilson Media Research survey:

| Favorite shows of men aged 55 or more | Favorite shows of women aged 55 or more |
| --- | --- |
| *Murder, She Wrote* | *Murder, She Wrote* |
| *60 Minutes* | *Matlock* |
| *Matlock* | *Golden Girls* |
| *In the Heat of the Night* | *60 Minutes* |
| *War and Remembrance*, part 12 | *Empty Nest* |

That survey also found that network news was the second most popular category for men aged 55 and older, as contrasted with its sixth-place position for adults aged 18 to 54. Comedies, as a category, placed fifth and sixth, respectively, for men and women 55 and older. Among the general population, comedies placed third with men and second with women.[9]

With the boomers moving into the ranks of older viewing audiences, bringing with them their neotraditionalist values, it is a good bet that there will be a great deal more of what today's older people would call "quality programming."

## Health Care Industries

Everybody expects the health care industry to boom until around 2015, when the last boomer will have celebrated his or her fiftieth birthday.

[9]"Over 55 TV Viewers Watch More News, Less Comedy," *D. B. Wolfe's Maturity Market Perspectives*, July/August 1989, p. 7.

However, health care delivery systems, venues for service, and the content and style of programs will bear little resemblance to what we see today.

Take nursing homes. Detroit area nursing home operator Horace D'Angelo, Jr., president of Caretel Corporation, said in an interview:

> About a decade ago, I began to question why the nursing home was the most socially rejected concept in our society. Whether care was good or not, people were embarrassed to place parents in nursing homes because the environment was so institutional and uninviting. The problem was less in *quality of care* than in *unimaginative presentation of care.* I realized that to improve the presentation, we had to change the model. Nursing homes operate under the Department of Public Health, and developers are hemmed in with regulations that force them to build *health care institutions,* which the public doesn't want. What they want is a place where Granny lives! I saw the correct model as a residential hotel with first class nursing care. From that insight grew the Caretel.

And D'Angelo built the place where Granny and Grandpa live! He threw out conventional designs with their long corridors, sterile room design, and overall institutional appearance, and he created the first *Caretel,* a name he has registered with the U.S. Patent and Trademark Office. Caretel, pronounced *"care-eh-tel,"* is a contraction of *care* and *hotel.* It represents a fusion of the best of the health care and hospitality industries.

D'Angelo has successfully broken away from the pack and created a new kind of long-term health care facility, with a fresh programmatic approach that patients and patients' families love. As 40-year-old William Rescorla, president of the hospital group that went in on the joint venture for the first Caretel with D'Angelo, says, "Peachwood Inn [the name of the first Caretel] is a harbinger of the future. It will be the model for the twenty-first century because we boomers, who have changed everything we encountered as we grew up, will change the nation's health care system. What our folks and grandfolks tolerated, we will reject."

Gerontologist Nancy Peppard, also a boomer, echoes Rescorla: "Health care people had better soon realize that boomers are taking control of their lives in ways that people in the past haven't, and that as we grow older, we intend to stay in control. We won't tolerate being patronized and put aside like older people of the past."

## How to Design Nursing Homes That Relieve Family Guilt

So unique and attractive is Peachwood Inn that residents of less expensive and more independent living facilities have moved into Peachwood

Inn. It is a rarity: a nursing home that is a delight to visit and one that people actually want to move into. Proof of Peachwood's appeal lies in D'Angelo's claim that not only do visitors come more often to see residents, but also there are more visitors and they generally stay longer on each visit. The ultimate testimonial came from a woman who said, "Peachwood has taken away my guilt about putting Mom in a nursing home."

Like other success stories already recited, much of D'Angelo's success can be attributed to his emphasis on that magic word in maturity markets, *choice.* There are no visiting hours; families can visit registered "guests" at any time. Designated family members are even given a key to enter Peachwood at a location other than where the reception desk is. D'Angelo calls it "the key to Grandma's house."

Peachwood residents have not only restaurant-style menu choices, to the extent that dietary requirements permit, but also a choice of dining rooms, one of which has been specifically designed as a pleasant place in which Grandpa can entertain visitors without exposing them to the more pathologically colored scenes that are inevitable in a long-term care health facility.

What D'Angelo has set out to accomplish in Peachwood, others will do in other kinds of health care facilities, including hospitals. They will do it because, as Rescorla warns, "We are the boomers, and we are coming to change the way you do business."


## Other Growth Centers in Health Care Industry

Other health care operations or subbusinesses that will grow enormously over the next 25 to 30 years include special facilities for people suffering from dementia (especially Alzheimer's patients), respite centers, convalescent centers (in other than long-term care facilities), home health care programs, and "assisted living" or "personal care" facilities (facilities for people who do not need the intensity of care and supervision available in nursing homes, but who need some help). In fact, the growth in home health care programs and assisted living facilities will result in nursing home populations being sicker than now because of the siphoning off of less frail and less dependent residents.

The question is not so much whether there will be significant growth in the health care industry, but who is going to do the best job of tapping into it. The determination of who will be most successful will be based on providers' willingness to throw out old ideas about health care. Increasingly, health care is less about helping people become less sick and more about helping people become more well, psychologically as well as physiologically.

The growing personal activism about one's larger role in one's own health management is altering the traditional relationship between health care provider and health care recipient. More and more of today's health care recipients are demanding that they be more in charge of their health care–related issues; that the professionals serving them be less patronizing; and that professionals be less directive and more consultative in their approaches. It's all a matter of electing to have choice over one's life's events, whatever the setting, rather than submitting to someone else's choices.

## Communications and Information Industries

Cellular phones were invented for business, but Nynex Mobile Communications has discovered that older people are buying cellular phones. With prices now as low as $600 to $700, older people find cellular phones a good investment for safety and security reasons. On the open road, a cellular phone provides instant communication with help in an emergency. Nynex is specifically targeting older people through ads that stress safety, showing how car phones can be a godsend in the event of a breakdown on the road. Nynex has also tapped into one of the more important attributes of most older people's value system—a strong desire to help others. By promoting the phone for use in a Good Samaritan role, Nynex is appealing to older consumers in terms of their self-images in full consistency with the First General Principle of Marketing.[10]

Given the *continuity theory of aging*, which holds that most people continue the basic patterns of their lives as they age, boomers will be the first high tech generation of senior adults. With the current pace of technological advancements in communications and information devices and systems, it seems safe to project greatly increased household usage of products and services in those areas by maturity market consumers.

George P. Moschis, director of the Center for Mature Studies (CMS) at Georgia State University, says business may not have to wait for boomers to get older to find big markets for high tech products. A recent CMS news bulletin reported that the long-held idea that older people will be resistant to high tech products may be wrong. New studies by

---

[10]"New Directions," *D. B. Wolfe's Maturity Market Perspectives*, March/April 1989; p. 2.

CMS found that among older consumers with lower education, either lack of interest or unfamiliarity with a high tech product's function may be the key factor behind poor responses. However, older consumers with higher education levels were as likely to use high tech products as younger adults.

## Educational Services Loom Large in Maturity Markets

Education is not commonly thought of as a business enterprise. However, each educational institution is a business enterprise in the sense that it provides services in exchange for payment. The role of educational pursuits in latter life is becoming so significant that failing to discuss what is taking place in the field of education, as it relates to maturity markets, especially those that constitute the Ageless Market, would leave a large void.

The idea of a society involved in lifelong education is not new. What is new, however, is the ability of so many older people to pursue lifelong education. Younger minds may have difficulty understanding why a 91-year-old man would want to undertake a new course of study after his career years have ended. Franklin Roosevelt obviously wondered about that when, upon visiting the venerable 91-year-old Oliver Wendell Holmes shortly after taking office, he asked the great man why he was enrolled in a new course of study. Holmes succinct answer was, "To improve my mind."

Many colleges and universities have designed special programs for older people whose expanded interest in returning to school offers those institutions a welcome compensation for declining enrollments from among new high school graduates. In some cases, exemplified by Eckerd College, St. Petersburg, Florida, the emeritus class of citizens is being tapped to act in *pro bono* roles as mentors to the traditional student body.

One of the better known educational programs specially designed for *emeritans*, as retirees are sometimes referred to, is Boston-based Elderhostel. With more than 280,000 members, Elderhostel offers retirees unique travel opportunities that combine the traditional pleasures of travel with innovative and exciting educational opportunities. Today the program, which was begun in 1975 by Martin P. Knowlton and David Bianco in cooperation with five colleges and universities in New Hampshire, is tied into some 1200 colleges and other institutions in all 50 states and in 40 foreign countries.

The list of higher learning institutions around the nation with special programs for senior adults is growing by leaps and bounds. Harvard

University has established its Institute for Learning in Retirement, a program of courses specially created for and taught by retirees. Eckerd College in St. Petersburg, Florida, not only has educational programs for retirees, but also has enlisted them as mentors for undergraduate students and has provided housing in the form of a 133-person senior adult community on campus. The University of Michigan has 1300 retirees enrolled in its special program, and in Allentown, Pennsylvania, Cedar Crest College is studying the feasibility of following Eckerd College's example. In short, colleges across the United States have discovered maturity markets in a big way.

## Educational Opportunities Increase Appeal of Many Products

For reasons that should be clear from the discussion in Chapter 6 of Maslow's theories and observations of older adults, the role of education in the lifestyles of many older people has tremendous influence on their overall consumer behavior. Successful marketers and purveyors of travel, financial, entertainment, housing, and other services and products in the 1990s will be among those who appreciate the educational imperatives of older people and why and how they affect consumer purchase and consumption activities.

AARP's Hal Norvell, who manages the largest senior travelers' programs in the nation, talks about the role of educational opportunities in AARP's success in offering travel programs: "The older traveler is heavily motivated by the historical perspective of a particular destination. He'll buy for the value of learning more about history and what it means to him right now, what it will mean to him in the future, and what it really meant to him in the past."

Norvell also reports that travel brochures that particularly emphasize educational aspects of a trip or destination attract more single seniors than those that emphasize luxury accommodations and service.

Of course, the educational imperatives of older people are not exercised solely in institutional settings such as a classroom. These imperatives drive older people to ask for more information on a product than is customary among younger consumers. And these imperatives influence the shows older people watch on television, what they listen to on radio, and the printed materials they read.

To be able to market well requires either a product whose success is virtually guaranteed because of widespread overwhelming need or an understanding of a given group of consumers so comprehensive that what is designed for them and how it is marketed speak effectively to their desires, cognitive world, and values. Most purchases by financially, physiologically, and psychologically independent older people fall into the same category of desire, hence a better understanding of their psyches measurably enhances success potential. The older person's quest for learning goes to the core of his or her essential being in later life.

## Key Factors for Projecting Growth Potential in Any Industry

A number of other industries have the potential, though not necessarily the assurance, of making it big in the aging population segment of the market. In fact, since older adults make purchases in virtually every category of consumer products and services, just as young adults do, there is no reason for any industry to ignore older consumers any longer, given the demographic shifts in markets today. In many categories, older consumers don't buy given items as much or as often, but the fact that they buy any products in a given line makes them important consumers.

Most of the more common categories of products and services considered growth industries in the graying of America have been identified above. A few areas not generally listed as growth industries are discussed later in this chapter. In addition, some industries not usually thought of as older market growth industries can nevertheless benefit from a better understanding of older consumers. Take food-related industries. Clearly, older people are already important food products customers. In fact, Figure 1-1 shows that food expenditures per household are highest in the 45-to-54 age cohort and third highest in the 55-to-64 age cohort.

When households are broken down into *per capita* figures, the second highest food expenditures are made by the 55-to-64 cohort, although their households have fewer people on average. It seems that while total quantity of food purchased by older households may be less, older households are prone to spend more on quality and more on dining out.

### The Three Categories of Choice in Consumer Purchases

In examining the growth potentials for various industries, one should think in terms of three categories of choice that influence consumer behavior:

1. *Wholly discretionary choices.* Purchases of such nonessentials as jewelry, travel, restaurant dining, magazines, flowers for the home, etc.

2. *Partially discretionary choices.* Purchases of "unnecessary" additions to basic or essential items already owned, such as extra shoes, dresses, etc., and items that are quality upgrades of basic items from what is necessary to maintain the consumer's ordinary standard of quality.

3. *Nondiscretionary choices.* Purchases essential to maintaining health and well-being and to meeting the basic food, shelter, and clothing needs in a socially conventional manner. Nondiscretionary items fall into two important subcategories: those products and services over which the consumer has highly limited or no choice as to provider or brand (for example, household utilities, prescription medicine, medical attention) and those over which the consumer has a wide latitude of choice as to the provider or brand [for example, food items, housing (except for low-income consumers), and basic clothes].

Understanding how each category fits into the older consumer's behavior is key to realizing market potential, for the consumer's decision-making processes draw upon different factors and values according to whether a prospective purchase is wholly discretionary, partially discretionary, or nondiscretionary with opportunity for a choice of provider or brand. Let's look at a few more industries and some factors that need to be taken into account to expand business in maturity markets.

### Is Planned Obsolescence Obsolete in Maturity Markets?

In general, companies not accustomed to older consumers need to redirect marketing and sales strategies for effective results in maturity markets, because of many differences between young adults and older adults in assessing need, desirability, and value in making a purchase. Among older car owners, for example, maintenance, economy, and overall durability and safety assume a greater role in value determination, especially since older people tend to keep their cars longer before replacement. A Chrysler vice president in charge of Chrysler's Motor Parts Division told me that Chrysler had a significant interest in older markets because older people accounted for some 68 percent of their auto parts sales.

It may be a difficult adjustment for automobile companies—which have always counted on cars' wearing out to make more new sales—to shift to a strategy of encouraging people to repair their cars and keep them longer. But the fact is, older people are inclined to do that anyhow. No amount of marketing effort is going to alter that behavior substantially; therefore, the smart automobile company will capitalize on such behavior rather than futilely try to change it.

## Fast-Food Restaurants for People Who Don't Need (or Want) Things Fast?

I have seriously wondered what a McDonald's will look like in the year 2010 and what its menu and service will be like. I cannot imagine that a McDonald's 20 years from now will be very much like a McDonald's today. Given a continuing shrinkage of youth markets for fast food, combined with a glut of fast-food restaurants, will the expanding population of older people, for whom time is not of the essence, make up the difference? Is it possible that today's fast-food chains will become more like the low-priced cafeterias seen in abundance now in Florida, such as Morrison's and Duff's restaurants, whose primary patrons are older people? Will Marriott's Roy Rogers come to be more like its Big Boy outlets or new Allie's chain?

In 1989, the $60 billion fast-food industry was already suffering from customer-traffic declines, as traditional fast-food consumers began moving up in their eating-out habits. Fast-food outlets have begun to address these conditions by making major changes in their traditionally rigid menu structure. But that might not be enough. While I don't expect ever to see candlelight in a McDonald's, I do wonder how long will it be before McDonald's brings out the stainless steel flatware and hard plates.

For restaurants in general to increase their attractiveness to older patrons, a great deal more than food and price factors must change. Furniture, lighting, decor, and even acoustical qualities of the dining environment, as discussed in Chapter 9, will need to be rethought.

## Many Industries Can Profit from the Aging of America

Try to think of an industry or profession that does not have older consumers. There are very few. Even the toy industry benefits greatly from older people, who are big givers of gifts to children. Gifts for children that are favored by older people tend to be financial gifts, for example, cash for bank accounts, stocks for college, etc.; clothes that improve or compliment physical appearance; and gifts that aid personal growth, for example, books, records, theater outings.

Another industry that could do well in older markets is the home improvement industry. Adult children of elderly are increasingly being urged by conscience, economics, and changes in zoning codes to add apartments to their homes for their parents. In many cases the children's homes will require structural changes to make them suitable for their elderly parents or relatives.

An comprehensive list of all the industries that have considerable obvious potential in older markets could be the subject of an entire book. Perhaps that statement will inspire someone to do it. But there is another entire dimension of business opportunities.

## Selling to Businesses Which Cater to Maturity Markets

A great number of industries and professions have tremendous business opportunities not in directly serving older consumers, but in serving those who do. Marketing services, ranging from product design and market research to advertising and promotional activities, are examples. Today none of those areas is distinguished by the presence of a great many major players. A few examples of support services industries serving those who sell directly to older markets are discussed next.

## Product Design Services

Product design is still a major untapped area. Until recently, product design activities for older people have largely focused on prosthetics. Recently, however, manufacturers of conventional consumer products have been coming up with designs to facilitate product usage by older people and, unwittingly, by everyone else as well. Maytag's recently designed washer-dryer line with large, backlighted numerals is a case in point. It has been a hit, because many washers and dryers are located in dimly lit basements or closets.

Chapter 9, which dealt with physiological changes in the older body, provided a number of clues for product designers to consider. Changes in finger dexterity, visual and hearing acuity, and other areas of the aging body will force major product design changes over the next several decades as product manufacturers seek to build sales among older consumers. Perhaps it won't be long before Sprint comes out with a telephone credit card that we can all read.

No doubt the design firm that came up with the idea of the shiny silver Sprint credit card was quite pleased with the symbolic connection between the glistening card and Sprint's highly promoted fiber-optic long-distance network. It's good symbolism but poor design in terms of the human eye. Older eyes, usually beginning when people are in their fifties, suffer from glare problems (a good reason not to use varnished paper stock for marketing materials). The Sprint credit card is difficult even for young eyes to see. And therein lies an important lesson. In developing and marketing products and services for older people, creative cleverness should always be weighed against the realities of the typical consumer's physiological and psychological characteristics. What may seem perfect to an enthusiastic and creative young designer may not be so perfect for the older user whose senses and other physical attributes have undergone changes.

Some organizations are specifically addressing design considerations for older markets. One such organization is the Institute of Technology Development, Living Systems Division, in Oxford, Mississippi. Under the direction of Dr. Margaret Wylde, the Living Systems Division has undertaken a variety of *ergonomic* design tasks. *Ergonomic* is the name given to the field of design in which design consciously follows the human form and motion patterns.

The Living Systems Division has designed a complete kitchen in which a person can prepare a meal, eat it, and clean up the pots and pans, all within a 3-foot radius of mobility. The division has embarked upon design tasks as diverse as bathtubs for the frail and a robot for studying human motions in various tasks as a guide to further living space and appurtenance designs.

Because of a greater physiological tolerance for ergonomically poor design, younger people have not noticed the "anti-human-form" designs that are more noticeable to older bones and muscles. Yet, what is more comfortable to old bodies is generally more comfortable to young bodies.

There is considerable opportunity for the ergonomic design business. But also those manufacturers buying the services of product design firms will have created a whole new set of reasons for consumers to trade in their current products which otherwise they would have had little excuse to replace.

## Market Research

For the market research industry the future holds trouble and opportunity. During the 40-plus years of boom times fueled by the explosive birthrate in post World War II United States, the field of market research had it easy. As cited in Chapter 1, real estate market research has never been particularly distinguished for its investigation of consumer behavior. While the market research conducted in a number of other industries has been of better quality, much has not been of the quality that will be required from this time forward.

For the first time, to my knowledge, research companies are being sued for alleged incompetence. I do not believe this can all be attributed to the litigious proclivities of our society. I think it results from growing feelings among users of market research that indifference to the pursuit of excellence has been all too common in the field, with more attention spent on the research business than on the business of research. I think we will see even more litigation as companies look for excuses for marketing failures in the 1990s.

Without births fueling the economy as they once did, company growth in many industries is increasingly tied to viable new products which need research and consumer testing, to old products designed in new forms, and to attracting market share from companies in the same line. Moreover, with the vast increase in both discretionary-spending dollars available to older people and the number of older people in the marketplace, there is increasing competition across product lines. Thus, researchers and others involved in marketing need to know more about how consumers choose a product in one line over a product in another line.

In short, because competition is becoming more fierce in a wide range of consumer product and services categories and lines, both within categories and between disparate categories, more is going to be expected of market researchers.

There are already firms established and operating with a specialty in maturity markets. Some have been founded by professionals with little experience in older consumer behavior, while others are coming out of the gerontology field. For a firm to be competent, its professionals must know what research tools and techniques can yield the desired information. It is not all that easy. One gerontopsychologist says:

> I would like to caution clinicians once again that most of what we know about intelligence and problem solving in the elderly has been learned using instruments and techniques developed for children and young adults. We are only at the beginning of charting adult functioning with techniques which are truly indigenous to the elderly.[11]

---

[11]K. W. Schaie, *Handbook of Mental Health and Aging*, Prentice-Hall, Englewood Cliffs, N.J., 1980, p. 280.

## Advertising and Marketing Support Industries

Free-lance author and journalist Bob Diddlebock researched what advertising agencies were doing in maturity market work and concluded, "While researchers are getting high marks for their work, many creative departments are not taking action."[12]

Advertising agencies are being dragged kicking and screaming into aging markets. Diddlebock quotes Ogilvy and Mather's Jane Fitzgibbon: "There's no long-term planning and thinking in advertising, and so this effort [to reach the over-50 market] will be a mad scramble." In other words, the forces are building among advertising clients to take their products into older markets, but because creative departments are still thinking in the youth-dominated mode of the past, they haven't been doing the homework required to take their clients *safely* into those markets.

Some firms, however, are already taking the big step of identifying themselves with maturity markets, something that hardly any agency in the United States would have done 10 years ago. One of those firms, New York-based Cadwell Davis Partners, has begun to establish itself as a skillful interpreter of older consumer buying behavior. Cadwell Davis developed a series of ads for *Modern Maturity*, the flagship publication of AARP, aimed at educating the marketing world about how to speak to seniors. Several of those ads are reprinted elsewhere in this book. Each ad is worthy of a one-day seminar. They reflect not only the interpretive and creative skills of Cadwell Davis, but also the years of hands-on experience of AARP with older consumers. Those ads can be trusted to be on target.

### Dumb Like a Fox, These Older People; So Use Them

In Oakbrook, Illinois, Ted Marzec, president of Marzec Communications, has formed the Silver Foxes program to provide seasoned direction to creative advertising people and others in developing advertising and media for marketing messages directed to maturity markets. Silver Foxes are women and men who were members of the marketing profession before retirement. As Marzec sees it, "The surest way of knowing that what you are saying to older consumers is right, is to ask them." His Silver Foxes program allows marketers to test messages on older people who understand the communications business before releasing them into the marketplace.

One of the most effective ways of taking messages into the maturity

---

[12]Bob Diddlebock, "Creative Departments Slow to Act," *Advertising Age*, May 17, 1989, p. S-6.

marketplace is direct mail, which is good news for agencies specializing in that field. That may change, given the ever-increasing volume of junk mail; however, for now, according to Donnelley Marketing, direct mail can be highly effective in reaching older markets. In a 1986 survey conducted by Donnelley, 85.5 percent of respondents in the 50-plus age category were responsive to direct mail offers, with an average dollar amount of those purchases at $29. Top items purchased by mail order include women's clothing, small household appliances, and furniture.[13]


## Modeling Age Is
## Becoming Profitable

The modeling agency of Rogers and Lerman has created a new *Senior Class division*, featuring 200 models aged 50 and older who are billed out at $250 per hour. Agent Peter Lerman says, "What people look for in turkeys and ham is not what they look for in cruise ships and cars. A Norman Rockwell granny is good for products that want to project time-honored trust and long-lasting relationships. [On the other hand] a modern granny is good for products like travel and automobiles."[14] Lerman's Senior Class division could hardly have been conceivable even 10 years ago. Today it stands as yet another example of the vast spread of business opportunities in the graying of America.

The oldest actor in commercials in the United States, perhaps in the world, is 103-year-old Jane Stoval, a perky woman who took her first flying lessons at age 89 and is still flying. Not long ago, she was filmed at the controls of her plane in a commercial for U.S. Healthcare, a health maintenance organization.

Ultraseniors like Stoval would seem to be perfect models for promoting a variety of products. When they meet an ultrasenior, people always ask, "To what do you attribute your long life?" Answers to that question could be associated with any number of products and lifestyle attributes, without any age stigma attaching to the product because of the human interest and humor that easily associate with people of great age. If Lerman's models are members of the senior class, then Stoval and her kind are members of the graduate class whom everybody loves and enjoys.[15]


[13]Elaine Sherman, "The Senior Market: Opportunities Abound," *Direct Marketing*, June 1987, p. 83.

[14]"Salt and Pepper Shakers," *American Demographics*, February 1989, p. 14.

[15]"Spry Seniors Put Spring into HMO's Spot," *Adweek's Marketing Week*, Nov. 16, 1987, p. 30.

## Public Relations Business Will Profit in Maturity Markets

Because so many older people approach ads with some degree of cynicism—and, in fact, ads and television commercials have become increasingly less effective in younger markets—the future holds many changes for the advertising industry. For one thing, we should see a much stronger role for public relations in product marketing activities, with advertising suffering some attrition in marketing budgets.

Robert Dilenschneider, president and CEO of Hill & Knowlton in New York, believes that will be the case:

> I actually believe that PR offers more dependable measurement than advertising today. Marketing executives will increasingly have to draw upon a far broader array of tools and inputs. The shift also means that the top marketing executives in major corporations of the future are as likely to come from the PR disciplines as from advertising. We see it already, and I expect the trend to accelerate.[16]

My experience in senior housing markets has convinced me of a considerably more limited value to advertising in older housing markets than in the younger markets in which I have also worked for a number of years. Generally speaking, the most successful programs around the country have used a high level of public relations activities in conjunction with advertising efforts. Like Dilenschneider, I believe the need for larger PR budgets will increasingly become recognized, especially in marketing programs directed at older people.

## Ethical Qualifications for Doing Business in Maturity Markets

The greed factor can be seen creeping, even rushing, into maturity market businesses. Aside from ethical considerations, the call to exercise high levels of good purpose and integrity is a prescriptive for those who would prosper in older markets.

Dr. Daniel Thursz, president of the National Council on Aging, has a particularly poignant way of illustrating this concern. He recalls the time, in March 1977, when a handful of Hanafi Muslims, an extremist sect, took over the B'nai B'rith headquarters in Washington, D.C., with 135 hostages in its control:

> I remember my shock and consternation at what I called then "professional voyeurism." [All kinds of people] arrived on the

---

[16]R. Dilenschneider, "PR on the Offensive," *Advertising Age*, Mar. 13, 1989.

scene to get on camera. They saw in the crisis an opportunity to advance their cause, their organization, their ego needs. And they were followed by a horde of social scientists, journalists, movie makers, novelists, etc....They wanted exclusive contracts to interview, test, [and] counsel the hostages and their families. Others wanted to write mini-series for television, or publish sensational pocket books which they promised would make millions for our organization. Those were the professional voyeurs who were ready to exploit the hostages and their families for their own prestige and/or income.

There is a thin line that separates two groups of professionals ... those who, while concerned with their advancement ... nevertheless understand the client group is primary ... the second group who has hitched their wagon to a clientele with which they identify in order to glean profits.[17]

Thursz tells that story to symbolize his perception of the extent to which greed and self-serving factors are beginning to permeate the aging environment. He would probably agree that it is an inevitable consequence of all the ballyhoo about the great riches that lie in senior adult markets. But there is a practical side to these comments, regardless of their moralistic tones.

## Maturity Markets Are Not for Opportunists

The riches that lie in maturity markets are there mainly for those who do it right in both technical and moral terms. I have observed that in the senior housing industry, the vast majority of those who do well are people with an emotional investment in their work who are motivated by a strong desire to do well by the older adults they serve. Moreover, the communications network that operates among older people is extremely efficient. From informal social groups, through the many special advocacy groups organized for the benefit of older people, to the growing body of special publications for and about older people, word travels quickly. Do it wrong, and murder will out. Let your motives be less than the best, and the world will be so advised. No other market operates quite like this!

## High Moral Position of a Company Is Essential in Maturity Markets

No one in business today should underestimate the power of consumer attitudes and activism to impose higher standards of moral behavior on

[17]This commentary appeared in the NCA newsletter to its members, September 1988.

businesses. It was consumers, through their boycotts at grocery stores, who gave full-bodied life to the California agricultural labor movement. It was the same type of forces at work to pressure U.S. businesses out of South Africa.

Activists from the boomer generation were behind these and other consumer-driven ethical campaigns. Today there appears to be a growing resurgence of activist ideals among older boomers. It is showing up in demands for less violence and sexual orientation on television. It is reflected in increased demands for a cleaner and safer environment.

Unlike older people of the past, boomers do not issue blank checks of respect and confidence in business and public institutions. They will continue to be skeptical and cynical, to scrutinize businesses regarding their integrity and, indeed, the moral justification for their existence. Given the experience and wisdom of maturity, boomers will be—if anything—more demanding of honest intentions and actions than in the past. Thus, a high level of ethics will be more a requirement than an option for companies seeking to do well in maturity markets, especially among those that form the Ageless Market, the most insightful of all older consumers.

I have discussed this phenomenon with a number of people. Some have observed that it is a reflection of the straightforward manner of many older people. "It's simple," said one. "Older people, like small children and dogs, have a sixth sense about your motives. If they sense them to be honorable, then they will reward you with their affection and loyalty."

Tom Peters, of *In Search of Excellence* fame, has been stressing for years that as the top echelon in a company thinks, the bottom echelon will act. If a company's top echelon is not sincerely devoted to the welfare of older consumers, but instead looks at older consumers as merely another source of income, then those in the lower echelon, who deal directly with the older consumer, will communicate those values to the consumer. When that happens, a company will face a tougher go of it in maturity markets.

Older consumers, as a class, are not as difficult to satisfy as many believe. But they are demanding, especially in terms of ethical behavior. What they demand most is honesty, a little bit of altruism in company demeanor, and empathetic understanding of consumers.

# 11
# Looking Ahead

## When Boomers Join the Maturity Markets

In my judgment, no serious discussion of the aging of America can be complete without some discussion of the baby boomers, that large group of World War II progeny born between 1946 and 1964. Like "the elderly," boomers have long suffered from being lumped together under a single label, as though all 76 million are moving through life in synchronized motion.

Baby boomers have dominated household-based markets since shortly after the first reports in 1946 of a birth explosion. No consumer industry—no sector of U.S. society—has escaped dramatic changes as a result of the sheer force of numbers of this remarkable 18-year-span cohort.

## Most Boomers Will Move Out of the "I-Am-Me" Stage

Today, 44 years after the birthing boom began, speculations abound about the boomers' impact on markets as they approach their middle age and later years. Many observers of the aging scene are painting a picture showing older boomers as frozen in a kind of early postadolescent stage of self-absorption, continuing the lifestyle patterns of self-indulgence widely attributed to boomers as they entered late adolescence and early adulthood. Widely quoted gerontologist Ken Dychtwald, age 39, was reported in *Advertising Age* to hold this opinion: "There is every indication that most generations grow up and out of the 'me generation.' Boomers don't."[1]

VALS' Arnold Mitchell estimated that in 1987 only about 5 percent of the population, mostly young people, were I-Am-Me's, and only about 9 percent were their close cousins, the Emulators. In light of earlier discussions about how immature egos can impede objective judgments, when I read predictions about boomers never getting out of the "me generation" phase, I seriously wonder whether those making such predictions may not be to some degree reflecting self-perceptions.

Like a reformed scarlet lady, the boomers are having a hard time living down their I-Am-Me reputation. The problem is that current perceptions are largely fashioned out of past perceptions, with no allowance made for the personal growth that accompanies maturity. If a Gallup poll were conducted, it would probably reveal that most boomers *currently* would like to stay young and continue self-indulgent lifestyles. But the widely promoted pejorative accusation that boomers don't like the idea of "old age" is not unique to boomers. Young and middle-aged people have always had anxieties about getting older. However, one of the untouted benefits of greater adult maturity, generally achievable only after the half-century mark, is the decline of such anxieties.

## Aging Boomers Will Be More Like Aging Pre-Boomers Than Not

Good news for boomers: The eternal youth that various behavior experts say boomers want *will* be theirs—not for the body (that will come to matter less) but for the person who resides in the body. Most boomers will march into the ranks of the Ageless Market or, more broadly speaking, the Ageless Society. What is remarkable is that many boomers will join the maturity markets (emphasis on maturity), and later the Ageless Society, sooner than most members of earlier generations did.

Boomers are not, as so widely predicted, destined for a later life of perpetual regrets over lost youth. Such predictions fly in the face of the findings of better than 50 years' research into adult psychological development. Such predictions deny the work of such giants in the field of human behavior as Erik Erikson and Abraham Maslow. Those predictions ignore the idea of passages through seasons of life that dramati-

[1]W. Walley and P. Reilly, "Media Giants Aim to Change 'Boomers' Image," *Advertising Age*, May 15, 1989, p. 1.

cally alter behavior, as reported by Daniel Levinson in *The Seasons of a Man's Life*.[2] They contravene the researched opinions of dozens of human development scholars who propose most people move away from self-indulgence in the later stages of adulthood.

## Boomers Have Never Been as Different from Others as Presumed

In their youth, boomers were *essentially* no different from the youth of other generations. They expressed themselves much the same as the youth of previous generations, driven by a genetically encoded imperative to challenge older generations, their institutions, and their values. Of course their styles were different, but that is true of every generation in relation to the previous one. And the idealism and rebelliousness of the boomers may have had a greater impact on the culture because there were so many of them. But no sound reasons have been given to support the idea that boomers have an inherently different psychological structure from their counterparts in earlier generations. Accordingly, in their later years, boomers will be more like previous generations of older people than not, insofar as their fundamental needs and general behavior are concerned.

Of course, boomers will have their own styles for living out the autumn years. Each generation in a progressive society has its own individual personality and modes and means of lifestyle expression.

## Basic Values Don't Change with Age; Lifestyle Values Do

A great deal of research indicates that basic values do not change for most people as they age. There is substantial evidence that *moral values* remain relatively constant throughout life; however, *lifestyle values* can and often do undergo great change. The narcissism and hedonism of youth are fundamentally a question of lifestyle, not morality. They are among those values that undergo the greatest amount of change. According to commonly accepted ideas on human adult development, boomers may be expected to experience changes in lifestyle values similar to those that earlier generations of older people have experienced (see the discussion in Chapter 5 of the three experiential stages of adulthood).

The leading-edge boomers, those born between 1946 and 1954, have

[2]Daniel J. Levinson, *The Seasons of a Man's Life*, Ballantine Books, New York, 1978.

been through their Possession Experience years and have moved into their Catered Experience years. The hedonistic and narcissistic tendencies that are so prominent in the Possession Experience years have presumably abated for many of the older boomers simply because they are more mature in an Eriksonian/Maslovian sense. Narcissism is most potent during the Possession Experience years, because being physically fit and attractive is believed by most people to enhance one's ability to succeed in the pursuit of money, fame, and romance.

## All Young Are Biologically Programmed to Be Self-Centered

Hedonism, usually closely allied with narcissism, is also most active during the Possession Experience years. Hedonistic tendencies are prompted by the more intense urgings for stimulation that are universal among the young of all creatures with a limbic system. The source of the quest for novelty has been identified as the hippocampus,[3] located in the brain's limbic system, which is sometimes referred to as the brain's "reward center" because of its ability to trigger the flow of natural opiates that make us feel good.

High appetites for stimulation motivate people to experiment and explore, activities important to species survival. The young, knowing less about what is needed for coping and surviving than the old, have more need, hence a stronger imperative, to learn life's lessons through novel pursuits than do the old.

Species survival is, in part, secured by nature's encoding into its limbic system–bearing creatures such high-potency appetites for stimulation during the youthful years. It is their responses to these strong appetites that give rise to the appearance of self-centeredness among youth. It's like the difference between a well-fed dog and a ravenously hungry dog. The well-fed dog will nuzzle up to you and please you with its affections; the hungry dog will think about nothing but self, until the appetite for food has been satisfied.

During the Catered Experience years and into the Being Experience years, under Maslovian theory, the potency of the drives for narcissism and hedonism declines in the maturing adult as a function of changes in ego-based behavior motivations. Highly matured adults are not less self-centered out of conviction; they are less self-centered as a result of biologically diminished urgings and satisfied appetites.

---

[3]Richard Restak, *The Brain: The Last Frontier*, Warner Books, New York, 1979, p. 29.

## Boomers Are Becoming Individuals

Those people who are making such absurd predictions that old-age boomers will turn nursing homes and retirement communities into geriatric 1960s-style communes are committing the cardinal sin of denying the true individualistic nature of mature adults—or that boomers will ever become mature.

It could be said that while adolescents *profess* their individualism (even as their behavior seems strongly determined by the dictates of a peer group), those in their Being Experience stage of life *are* individualistic. They do not behave with continual reference to peer group dictates and values. Remember: Maslow defined those who have achieved the highest reaches of maturity as simply "idiosyncratic" and "quite immune to enculturation." They are their own people, many finding much of their life satisfaction in solitary or cultural activities such as reading, listening to music, attending a college class, or walking through the woods.

When boomers walked in the woods during their younger years, they did so in groups. Music appreciation was a group experience. Reading habits were heavily oriented to group values and group-imposed agendas. The term *groupie* was applied to female boomers who tagged along with rock music groups in their late adolescent and early adult years, thus reflecting the lack of individuality of a group whose members claimed great individuality. Even the term *yuppie*, applied to affluent older boomers, better defines group behavior than individual behavior. But things are changing as boomers begin to age. Boomers will not be "gray groupies," as many have predicted. Group-defined behavior is antithetical to Being Experience-motivated personalities who, according to Maslow, become "god-like" in their detachment from others, though equally "god-like" in their concern for others.

## Many Leading-Edge Boomers Are "Aging" (Maturing) Ahead of Schedule

The oldest boomers are 44, as of this writing, which places them squarely in the middle of the Catered Experience years. The leading-edge boomers are indeed at the center of consumer services markets. But the precocious boomers, consistent with their patterns all their lives, are entering the Being Experience years ahead of schedule. In the process, they are forming the most extraordinary middle-aged generation of all time, one that presents the most complex sets of challenges to product and service providers and marketers in the history of modern marketing.

The amount of literature that is being devoted to the rising difficulties in marketing to the U.S. consumer has been on the increase. Even heads of major advertising agencies are saying that advertising cannot accomplish what it used to accomplish. Studies increasingly report about the growing difficulties that marketers are having with today's consumers. A 1988 article[4] in *Advertising Age*, entitled, "Research 'finds' fickle consumers," had this to report:

> A large but baffling bunch of consumers has been identified by food and beverage market researchers.
>
> They're called "moderates" and can be most easily described as a group whose attitudes toward food and beverages lack any consistency.
>
> Some 25% of consumers fall into this category....
>
> Its [the study's] findings highlight the difficulty of dividing consumers neatly into distinct segments.

Maslow would not have been surprised by the findings of the study, conducted by NPD Group, Port Washington, New York. He would have observed that with the mean age of the population rising from around 28 to nearly 34 in the last decade and a half, consumer attitudes and behavior naturally will begin to reflect those of more mature adults, whose behavior becomes more individuated as a result of greater maturity.

## Business Needs to Stay with the Boomers' "Horse"

U.S. business cannot afford to ignore older consumers, as it has in the past. In particular, business needs to begin thinking about boomers in their latest phase as middle-agers and budding members of the maturity markets—not as perpetual adolescents. As the boomers age, many businesses have no safe alternative but to continue to ride the boomers' "horse."

Consider this: Behind the "pig in the python," as demographers like to refer to the boomer cohort, lies a rather empty alimentary canal, with significantly fewer consumers in some important age cohorts to nourish business. For example, during the 1990s, the 18- to 34-year-olds will number 9 million less than in 1989. This group will also spend $41 billion less than the same age group did in the late 1980s.

Such awesome statistics of declining youth markets mean fewer cars, clothes, new homes, music videos, etc., to be sold in youth markets. In

---

[4]J. Graham, "Research 'Finds' Fickle Consumers," *Advertising Age*, June 26, 1989, p. 31.

addition, for those boomers who mature into a Being Experience-dominated lifestyle, the number of years a car is owned before replacement will lengthen, interest in buying another new home will abate, and lifestyles oriented to Being Experiences will dramatically diminish *per capita* expenditures on "things" as well as a wide array of services.

Those are less *predictions* than *projections* into the future of trends that are already observable. Market trends analyst Faith Popcorn, founder and CEO of New York–based Brain Reserve, talks of older boomers "cashing out" in their late thirties and early forties.

## Many Boomers Are "Cashing Out" and "Cocooning"

At a time in life when people traditionally are getting their second wind and moving into their peak career and earning years, many boomers, like yesterday's pre-retirees, are saying, "It's time to slow down and smell the roses" (a Being Experience). They are forgoing job promotions and even quitting good jobs to go out and find a saner lifestyle than the one they had in "the fast lane."

A recent issue of Eastern Airlines' in-flight magazine reported that "yuppies" are leaving the East Coast in droves for the Midwest, to rediscover a lifestyle they feel left the East Coast 25 to 30 years ago. Popcorn calls this retreat from career and commercially driven chaos the *cocooning effect.* I think there is more to it than the escapism that the term *cocoon* suggests.

## Boomers Are Returning to the Idealism of Their Youth

Fifteen to twenty years ago, the older of the boomers trimmed their hair, shaved their beards or put their bras back on, removed their outlandish jewelry, and joined the establishment to fulfill the urges of the first experiential lifestyle stage of adulthood, the Possession Experience years. Many succeeded beyond their expectations, transcending their earlier disdain for materialism.

Now, two decades or so after they radically redefined social decorum, with their caricatured behavior of youthful excess amid vows of global benevolence, many of these boomers are revisiting their ideals. They have begun asking themselves the perennial midlife question, Is this *all* there is? And many are saying, "The truest and best values of life are still those we marched for in our freshest and most vibrant youth."

With substantial gratification of their Possession Experience aspirations, many of the leading-edge boomers entered their Catered Experience years and found that passage also smooth. But the ease of passage through those two stages has disturbed many boomers who once sought to tear down the pillars of the materialistically oriented establishment. They are finding more than pleasant nostalgia in thinking back on the 1960s. They are seeing glimmers of great new possibilities in a new life, a new society, based on their "old values."

## Boomer Practitioners of "Romantic Capitalism" Are on the Scene

We are seeing the emergence of altruistic tendencies among middle-aged boomers that is not customarily seen until a generation is further into late adulthood. I see it in my own business operations. For the past 20 years, my research and consulting practice in residential real estate has covered most of the United States and involved hundreds of clients. In the recent past I have seen a remarkable change in the personalities of developers as more and more members of the boomer generation come on the scene.

Joseph Alfandre, president of Joseph Alfandre & Company of Rockville, Maryland, is an example. Joe, aged 38, is a grandson of a family who has been in real estate development for three generations. Years ago, Joe's father was a client of mine. Today Joe is also a client. The differences are considerable.

Joe, a leader in the neotraditional community movement,[5] says: "I have never really bought into the development industry." He means that his values and motives are quite different, for he is obviously a member of the development industry. Joe has determined that while the amount of money he makes is valuable as a marker, he is not trying to win some financial game. He says that if he cannot build communities that measurably enable a better life for people, he will stop developing. He calls his approach to business *romantic capitalism.*

This romantic capitalist is designing his communities for vertical socioeconomic integration on the principle that a true small town is a place where the bank president and the bank teller can live in the same neighborhood, if not on the same street. Most communities built since the end of World War II have been socially and economically—and blandly—homogeneous. Joe thinks the better living environment for all people, including older people, is not one that artificially segregates

[5] Neotraditional communities are communities planned in the style of small towns and villages of the preautomobile era.

people from each other. He espouses the development of living environments where the young can learn from the old and the old can find
new meanings in life from interaction with the young.

Joe also believes that a social and cultural infrastructure should be
planned into a community just as the physical infrastructure is planned
into it. So Joe is making provisions in his communities for funded cultural programs that will be designed and developed by residents. Even
before ground was broken on his first neotraditional town of Kentlands,
in Gaithersburg, Maryland, it had achieved such international recognition that England's Prince Charles asked for an audience with
Kentlands' town planner, Andres Duany, the nation's high priest of traditional town planning. Duany is also a boomer at age 39.

Joe typifies many affluent older boomers. Unlike wealthy benefactors
of social and cultural causes in the past, who were usually successful phi-
lanthropists in their fifties, sixties, and older, Joe and his counterparts
are not simply writing checks for buildings that will be named in their
honor. They are inclined *to build* the buildings.

## The Dawning of the Age of Aquarius II

My roster of clients includes an impressive array of Children of Aquarius who are revisiting their youthful ideals with as high a sense of mission as they portrayed in the tumultuous 1960s. This time, however,
they have greater wisdom and financial wherewithal to be *singularly*
more successful. I say singularly so, because these men and women are
no longer group-value-driven. Having moved far ahead in their maturity, they are acting with the detachment and idiosyncrasy of Maslow's
more highly matured adults. They are not working on defining their
identities, thus they no longer feel a need for group-based validation
and reinforcement of their values and motivations. Instead, they are
working on defining a new identity for the society in which they live.

As observed earlier, this same generation that created such upheaval
in traditions is the generation now leading the neotraditional movement. Boomers are taking us back to basics after having led society away
from them in the Age of Aquarius. We may now be in the beginning
stages of its sequel, the Age of Aquarius II. Much of what that means is
embodied in New Age thinking.

## Effects of New Age Thinking on Ageless Markets Will Be Considerable

The New Age movement is not a fad the boomers will grow out of, but an approach to life that they will grow deeper into as they become older. No marketer who underestimates the enormous influence of New Age thinking on millions of older consumers is going to enjoy more than incidental or accidental success in markets depending upon aging boomers.

Contrary to the thinking of many, New Age thinking is not a philosophic or mystical scheme that verges on being a religion. Catholics, Jews, Methodists, Episcopalians, Moslems, and people of other religions can be and are "New Agers." Above all else, New Age thinking is the embodiment of a creed that all things are of a piece, that no one thing is separate from any other thing. Accordingly, we each have an obligation to regard our place and time on earth as an office that we must fill with a sense of responsibility to all—a responsibility that extends beyond the time of our life on earth to all who come after us. That is the kind of thinking that Maslow attributed to B-cognizers, people at the higher levels of human maturity.

That kind of thinking is also an integral part of the creed system of most enduring religions on earth. The fact that such thinking is widely shared among the 76 million members of the boomer population necessarily portends a major impact from it on our society, including the business of marketing.

I asked Nancy Peppard, 39, about what boomers are going to be like in the future as members of the maturity market, since she, like Ken Dychtwald, is both a boomer and a gerontologist. Peppard sees boomers moving in a direction that presages major changes both in public policy and in the design, marketing, and rendering of products and services.

First, she talks about where the older boomers are today in their thinking: "I find a lot of people in my age range going through what I have been going through. We are beginning to look outside ourselves for meaning in life." Maslow would understand that; it's the direction taken by still maturing adults in middle age.

I think New Age thinking is something marketers interested in older markets need to take a long look at. I don't mean the Shirley MacLaine kind of thing. The so-called "New Age" movement of today began 20 years ago. Unlike other fads that youth

cultures embrace today and reject tomorrow, the New Age philosophy has become part of our culture and it has grown with
time. In both subtle and overt ways it now affects many facets of
our daily lives.

Within certain segments of the medical and financial communities, for example, the effect of New Age thinking is being felt.
Specialties such as homeopathy, a wholistic[6] preventative approach to health care, and psychoneuroimmunology, the study
of the direct relationship between the mind and the body, are
growing in respectability and visibility.

## Boomers Are the Real Force behind the "Kinder and Gentler Nation" Idea

Peppard cites restaurants that are now serving "nonstressed" beef and
chicken, animals that have grown in stress-free environments, as one
symbol of New Age boomers' sensitive concerns about all life. Socially
responsible investment funds and even credit cards that contribute a
percentage of their profits to charitable causes are other examples of
business's response to the greater sense of the cosmic connectedness of
all things that many leading-edge boomers have. Out of the boomer
masses has come the real power behind George Bush's call for a "kinder
and gentler nation."

From Peppard's point of view, boomers are projecting highly unique
behavior. In one sense I fully agree with her, but in terms of normal
human maturation potentials and processes, I believe boomers are not
unique. They have simply had unique opportunities and ways of expressing their maturity. Their altruistic behavior bears out Maslow's
thinking that if basic needs are met, people will naturally seek to satisfy
higher values. It is normative behavior for the highly mature!

Maslow, with his unique ability to synthesize the ideas of his contem-
poraries and predecessors, laid the groundwork for our ideas about human potential. Going beyond behavioristic and analytic explanations for
behavior, he focused on potential for growth, evident in the current national fervor for a "kinder and gentler nation."

## Are Madison Avenue and Its Clients Ready for the Age of Aquarius II?

Neither Madison Avenue, nor Detroit, nor Wall Street, nor many other
points on the compass are ready for the changes in consumer markets

---

[6]Many New Age adherents, like Buckminster Fuller who first spelled it that way, prefer
to write *wholistic* in lieu of *holistic* because of its use of the word *whole*.

just discussed. Few have taken note of the boomers' beginning passage, at long last, into the upper reaches of full adulthood, although signs abound. Stated another way, are U.S. businesses and the marketers of its products prepared for the Flower Child Reincarnate as a middle-ager—and ultimately as a member of the Ageless Society during the Age of Aquarius II? They had better get ready. Many businesses have "passed" on making a commitment to maturity markets because of assumptions that they are difficult markets to tap. But, to survive, they will have to learn how to do well in these markets.

In contrast to the 9 million decrease in 18- to 34-year-olds between 1989 and 2000, there will be an increase of nearly 13 million (47 percent) in the 45-to-54 age cohort. The handwriting is on the wall for U.S. business: With market size dramatically decreasing in the young adult markets, many businesses that are healthy today will be dead in 5 to 10 years if they don't understand that and start to take action now.

In numerous industries, much of the business that inevitably will be lost due to the demographic shift in the center of gravity of the total consumer market universe can be recovered only in the maturity markets.

Many businesses who become big players in the future consumer economy will likely be those who are already positioning themselves with members of maturity markets before they are forced to do so by dwindling younger adult markets. Notwithstanding the findings of recent studies showing that older consumers will readily change brands, those and other studies indicate that older consumers are extremely loyal to those who serve them well. For that reason, many later entrants into maturity markets will face fierce competition from those who planned and acted early and tied up the loyalties of older consumers. They also will face intense competition from other late entrants who, like themselves, will be fighting for their business lives because they belatedly learned the full economic impact of the great demographic shift in the last decade of the twentieth century.

## Toward a New *Humanistic* Gerontology

For a number of years, senior consumer advocacy organizations and the gerontological community have attempted to change public policy and societal views on older people. That older people are financially better off today than a generation ago is in part due to the efforts of such groups and people. But many people in everyday walks of life—and business—have not substantially changed their views in many regards.

The various academic, research, public policy, and services specialties undergoing development over the past half century have quite properly focused on basics, but now must move beyond. The field of gerontology has enjoyed the talents of many courageous and selflessly devoted people who, when it was a poorly funded discipline, struggled to give it respectability and greater substance. The older people of this country—indeed this world—owe a great deal to the pioneers in the field: to Jim Birren, founding director of the National Institute on Aging, who, more than any other person, focused public policy attention on aging people; to Robert Butler, who has become one of the nation's leading advocates on the mental health and well-being side of aging; to Bernice Neugarten, whose efforts have contributed much to the idea that older people cannot be lumped into a single class for health care, public servicing, marketing, or any other purposes. The pantheon of greats in America's pioneering work in the various fields of aging is filled with men and women sincerely devoted to the idea that we ignore the needs and desires of older people at great peril to our children and the future of society. But it is time to move on.

Remember Brian Hofland's characterization of the four models of senior communities? The first, the *social rejection model*, was designed to provide basic food, clothing, and shelter for people perceived by society to have become obsolete. We rejected their social value, but our conscience drove us to keep their bodies around. A little later, we adopted what Hofland calls the *social services model*, a model born out of an emerging welfare-state mentality. We introduced professionals to the senior living environment to deal with health issues of the aging. Still later, we began to develop the *participatory model*, one in which activity and social directors were hired to cure the problems of boredom and social withdrawal. Now, Hofland says, it is time to move on to the *self-actualization model*.

Hofland's four models, in terms of their humanistic implications, reflect the progression of society's advances toward a more enlightened view of the older person. It is not just in housing and health care that we need to promote *humanistic gerontology*, but in every field that involves product designs, marketing, and services intended for older people.

## A Call for Redefining the Meaning of Aging

In a sense, gerontology has been operating at the lower stages of Maslow's hierarchy. Its early focus was on basic physiological, safety, and security needs. More recently, gerontology has become more humanistic, with more attention to the psychological needs of older people. It has been reflecting on love and belonging. Less and less, older people are feeling like Paul Cummins, whose greatest fear upon retiring was "to become an alien in my own society." More and more, older people are gaining a sense of belonging, and beyond that, are able to maintain a sense of self-esteem, and a sense that they are esteemed by younger members of society. But these humanistic developments are in embryonic form.

There still is an overwhelming view that age is a handicap. Only slightly more enlightened are the views that older people are to be cared *for*, instead of being cared *about*. While many issues that involve the *caring-for* needs of older people continue to command attention at all levels of society, the greater need, in terms of the number of people involved, lies in Brian Hofland's call for self-actualizing living environments. Industry can lead the way in translating that call into realities.

There is much that the travel, health care, entertainment, publishing, consumer product, and other industries can do to promote a higher, natural order of existence for older people. They can make signal contributions through their products and services programs and by the images they convey in marketing communications. Educational institutions have a great deal to contribute, as well, toward the overall objective of a society in which one does not *get* old but one *grows* old, in Helen Luke's words.

The first goal of the National Association for Senior Living Industries (NASLI) is one of the most compelling facing an aging society. NASLI has pledged itself to work diligently toward redefining the meaning of aging. To accomplish that goal, we need to move away from *sympathetic* approaches, born out of paternalistic concerns, and engage in *empathetic* understanding of older fellow human beings who are generally more highly developed than the rest of us. We need to reacquaint ourselves with the idea that wisdom is found in richer abundance among older people than elsewhere. We need to put older people back into young people's lives, thus giving them a more solid footing in life than recent crops of youth have had.

We often hear, "Our children are our future." That is true. But they, alone, do not give the future meaning. Since the beginning of mankind, societies have consciously linked generations by so highly regarding the experience and wisdom of their elders that younger generations built upon, rather than rejected the histories of their elders. We have not done a very good job of that, it seems, in latter-day twentieth-century America. We can reverse that trend by things we can do in the workplace and marketplace.

In Japan, corporate goals include social objectives. Company personnel are deeply schooled in a company's social goals. Companies reflect
their social goals in their consumer advertising. Books advising foreign-
ers on how to deal with the Japanese strongly advise would-be Western
business partners to stress how their involvement will aid in achieving a
Japanese company's social goals: Delay detailed discussion of projected
financial benefits until after your prospective Japanese partner is satisfied that your company is genuinely committed to making a meaningful
contribution to society as a matter of major purpose.

Sociologists and psychologists, as well as many experts in business
management, have attributed much of Japan's storybook economic success to the motivational power of a company's social goals in inspiring
workers to perform. A corporate will to do good touches everyone in
positive ways—including customers. Japanese consumers are highly inclined to favor products and services of companies perceived as socially
responsible companies. The impact of this attitude in the marketplace is
to reduce the role of price in the consumer's determination of value of
a product or service. As previously noted, many older consumers in the
United States manifest such attitudes in their buying behavior. Thus,
instilling humanism into business practice can contribute to marketplace
success.

I challenge businesses everywhere—but especially businesses in the
United States—to share in NASLI's first goal: *to redefine the meaning of
aging*. Before we can enable the highest possible life quality for our
society's elders, we must eliminate age as a significant factor in taking
measure of a person's worth, a socially responsible goal that stands to
benefit all.

I call upon company leaders in every industry to draw clear mission
statements that incorporate into company goals the resolve to foster
higher life quality for all older people. Such a mission statement will enjoy the highest possible success if all personnel in the organization share
in its formulation, thereby empowering all with a sense of ownership of
the mission. With business making it *its business* to take on so important
a mission, the rest of society will surely follow. By serving better the elders of our society today, we not only improve the quality of their lives,
we establish a comforting precedent for those of us who have yet to become members of the Ageless Society.

# Index